S0-BZT-730

BEWARE
FAMILIAR
SPIRITS

BEWARE FAMILIAR SPIRITS

By
JOHN MULHOLLAND

CHARLES SCRIBNER'S SONS · NEW YORK

In appreciation to the late

JOHN WILLIAM SARGENT

and to

ELMER PENDLETON RANSOM

Introduction Copyright © 1979 Charles Scribner's Sons

Copyright 1938 Charles Scribner's Sons

This book published simultaneously in
the United States of America and Canada

Copyright under the Berne Convention

All rights reserved. No part of this book
may be reproduced in any form without the
permission of Charles Scribner's Sons

1 3 5 7 9 11 13 15 17 19   M/P   20 18 16 14 12 10 8 6 4 2

Printed in the United States of America

Library of Congress Catalog Card Number 78-66328
ISBN 0-684-16181-8

PREFACE

*T*HREE HUNDRED and fifty years ago, as a pious task, Reginald Scot, a man well versed in magic, wrote a book describing the chicanery by which rogues led superstitious folk to believe in ghosts, and witches, and devils. In the following two centuries others, who knew the artifices by which people could be fooled into accepting synthetic demons, wrote further books.

There was ample precedent then for magicians to bring to use their practical knowledge of the psychology and technic of deception when, in the last century, people became interested in mediums rather than witches, and rapping spirits rather than wailing ghosts. From the very start of spiritism magicians have felt it their duty to expose the methods of tricky mediums. I am a magician.

This account of spirits, their work and their masters, is written in the hope that the reader will use his faith to satisfy himself of an after life rather than to accept either the work, or word, of a medium without the most painstaking investigation.

J. M.

CONTENTS

INTRODUCTION

MAGIC, in the conjuring sense, is the art of deceiving people into thinking they are seeing miracles—violations of natural laws—and doing this for the sole purpose of entertainment. A magician is an honest charlatan. But just as the techniques of honest locksmithing can be used by thieves, so the methods of honest magic can be used by two broad species of scoundrels: the gamblers who cheat and the psychics who cheat.

Imagine that you belong to a club at which poker is sometimes played for high stakes. You suspect Mr. X of cheating. Would you hire a Ph.D. physicist to sit in on a game, as a secret observer, to check on Mr. X? You would not. You would hire an ex–card-hustler or a magician knowledgeable about the application of magic principles to poker. Suppose you are impressed by the psychokinetic demonstrations of a self-proclaimed psychic. Would you hire a physicist to observe the demonstrations and give you a report? You would be a fool to do so. A physicist, or any other kind of scientist, is no more capable of detecting this kind of deception, which is like no other kind, than a plumber or a car salesman.

There is an enormous literature on the history of

modern spiritualism, most of it written by sincere but gullible believers. But if you want the inside story, the real nitty gritty behind this sad, shabby history, you will find it only in those books that are written by persons thoroughly familiar with the curious methods of the crooked mediums and other psychic frauds.

There are not many such books. Some are written by former mediums whose consciences somehow failed to atrophy completely, who finally became so sickened by the damage they were inflicting on trusting souls that they abandoned their shameful careers and revealed their methods, or at least some of their methods. A recent example of such a book is M. Lamar Keene's *The Psychic Mafia*. Other books that cover similar ground have been written by magicians with a special interest in psychic fraud. One thinks of Harry Houdini's *A Magician Among the Spirits*, of James Randi's *The Magic of Uri Geller*, of Milbourne Christopher's *Mediums, Mystics and the Occult*, and *ESP, Seers and Psychics*. The volume you now hold is in this category. It is one of the best books ever written by a professional magician about the colorful charlatans of modern spiritualism.

I had the privilege of knowing John Mulholland. There are many top magicians who cannot write well, and many amateur magicians who write well but are poor performers. Mulholland was a rare individual who combined both talents. I can still remember as if it were yesterday the first time I saw him perform. It was at Lake Chautauqua, in upstate New York, where my parents had taken me for the summer. I was fifteen. Mulholland had been booked into the Chautauqua Institution's large amphitheater for what was advertised as a lecture on magic. It was a lecture interspersed with marvelous demonstrations. I recall Mulholland's fine routine with the Chinese linking rings, and his version of the classic "sympathetic silks" in which knots mysteriously transfer from one set of silks to another. Mulholland tore a deck of cards neatly in half—no mean feat in itself!—then, holding one half he counted the half cards to a number called out by someone in the audience. This was repeated with the other half of the deck and another called-out number. The two half cards found in this way proved to be the halves of a previously selected card.

Mulholland's closing trick was the vanishing of a birdcage. Even then I knew enough about magic to be impressed by the fact that he did not, as did Harry Blackstone, walk off the stage and return with the cage between his hands. Onstage he opened a box and took out the cage. It disappeared as he tossed it toward the ceiling. The audience sat spellbound while I watched with the intense interest of a boy who already had made magic his principal hobby.

At the time of this lecture Mulholland had just taken over the editorship of *The Sphinx*, then the country's leading magic periodical and one that Mulholland was destined to edit for twenty-three years. A few months earlier I had written up a trick of my own, and Mulholland had accepted it for publication. When the performance was over, I hurried to the amphitheater's stage entrance just in time to find Mulholland struggling to escape from a group of youngsters seeking his autograph. I mentioned the piece I had sent him.

"Follow me," he said, then broke into a sudden run. I trotted behind him to the house where he was staying, and we chatted while he changed from a tuxedo to street clothes. Before I left he taught me a routine with three paper balls that I still do to this day. Years later I renewed my acquaintance with him. My last memory is a lunch with him and other magicians at the Player's Club in Manhattan, shortly before he died. The luncheon was to honor his gift to the club of his priceless collection of books, bound magic periodicals, magic apparatus, and memorabilia of famous magicians. The collection is on display in the club's library, in beautifully finished shelves and cabinets that Mulholland, a skilled carpenter, built himself.

Mulholland wrote six other books about magic, but this is the only one in which he turned his attention from honest conjuring to the misuse of magic. It is a book about those twisted souls whose egos demand a public image of someone possessed of super-normal powers, about clever men and women who enjoy building careers by exploiting the naive and credulous.

Although the book is about charlatans of a period now past, it has never been more needed than today. Almost every month a new psychic scoundrel creeps out of the woodwork to pose as a clairvoyant, or a person who has the "gift" to predict the future or move objects and bend spoons with the power of his or her mind comes forward. I am ashamed to say that there are some magicians, happily a tiny minority, who regard these psychic frauds as brother and sister prestidigitators—fellow conjurors doing their best to earn an honest buck. It is not an honest buck. Change the word *spirits* in Mulholland's title to *psychics* and you have a new moral that makes his book as timely as if it had been written a week ago.

MARTIN GARDNER
January 1979

CHAPTER I

LOOK, MY LORD, IT COMES!

ALL THOSE who have seen ghosts are eager to talk about them. The unreality of the ghost would never mar the story; a visit with an imaginary ghost is just as thrilling an experience as it ever could be with a real one.

Not every one has seen, or even imagined he has seen, a ghost, and he who has can well realize his distinction. These apparitions were so terrifying that some people saw them, and dropped dead; others turned white haired in an instant. Ghosts have appeared in a great many forms, and sometimes they have made their presence known without themselves being seen. Rich and poor, young and old, East and West, land and sea have their tales of ghostly visitors.

Perhaps the most frequent ghostly apparitions are those which are unhappy, bound to some spot by guilt or an unfinished task or by the presence of their bones. It is these pitiable wraiths which cause most of the terror always associated with spirits.

A typical story comes from the naturalist Pliny the Younger (born 62 A.D.), who gives it as one of his reasons for believing in the reality of ghosts. There was a large and commodious house in Athens which, however, gradually became so notorious that no tenant would take it. The jangling of chains was heard, and those who were bold enough to venture inside saw an emaciated old man with matted hair and a long beard, shackles on his feet and chains on his hands. Those tenants who persisted in living in the house fell ill, and the terror preyed on their minds so that they died. Finally the house was for rent dirt cheap, and the philosopher Athenodorus, after finding out why, took it nevertheless.

On his first night in the house, Athenodorus sent all the servants and members of the family into the back of the house, and established himself in the front room, where the ghost was usually to be seen. He provided himself with light, tablet, and stylus, so that being occupied with writing his mind would not create imaginary terrors. He sat writing for some time. Then he heard the rattling of chains and dragging footsteps. He looked up and saw the bearded old figure in its shackles, beckoning to him. He waved his hand as if to say, "Wait a minute," and went on writing. The figure came and rattled its chains right over his head. He waved again, but soon rose and followed the figure, which walked slowly and painfully, weighed down by its chains. In the courtyard the figure suddenly vanished. Athenodorus piled up grass and leaves on the spot where he had last seen it, and went to bed.

The following morning he had the city authorities dig at the spot he had marked. Sure enough, they found a skeleton with chained hands and shackled feet. It was taken away and properly buried, and from then on the house was peaceful.

Not all the apparitions were ghosts, for the Devil and his demons also frequently made personal appearances. The tenth-century Briton, St. Dunstan, once seized what he said was the Devil by the nose with a pair of red-hot pincers, and made him howl for mercy. This was better work than that of Luther, who threw an inkpot at his Devil, but merely made a stain on the wall which can still be seen. There was one spirit which used to knock at the door of Luther's room before invisibly entering. During the present century a friend of Lord Halifax (a great collector of ghostly experiences), while at the Highland residence of the Campbells, repeatedly heard the slamming down of great piles of books beside him in the library. He could not see the figure which did it, but certain of the Campbells could.

By no means all of these stories are ancient or European. The unlikely town of Flushing, Long Island, used to contain an old mansion at the corner of Prince Street and Broadway. About the time of the Civil War a Southern family moved in. Before they had been there long the children were frightened by seeing a tall lady in a white dress, with a very red face, combing her long black hair. The terror grew until the family moved away to escape, and the mansion remained untenanted for thirty years.

Quite unconnected with this story was another, by a doctor in Flushing, who one winter night was awakened by a man, standing outside in the snow, asking him to come to his sick wife. The doctor dressed, and followed the man to the old mansion at Prince Street and Broadway. He was much surprised, since he knew the place had been empty for years; but the man managed to open the gate and the front door, and let him in. The doctor remarked that this damp, chill old pile was no place for a sick woman. The patient was in bed in a second-floor room— a woman in a nightgown, with long black hair, in the last stages of consumption, and having the accompanying very high color. The doctor wrote out a prescription, which he said must be filled at once, and left it on the mantel. Then he went home to bed.

The following morning he thought he would look in on his patient. He went to the old house, but could not get in. Then he called on the agent, who said of course he had not been able to get in—the house had been untenanted for thirty years. "I was there last night," the doctor said, "and I will prove it."

The two of them returned to the old mansion. It was then the doctor noticed that there were only his footprints leading up to the door. Opening the front door with some difficulty, they went in. Everything was as it had been for thirty years—dank, musty, untouched. On the second floor mantel was the doctor's prescription.

Ghosts not only make no footprints—they cast no shadows. In fact there are a wide variety of ways to discover whether a figure is that of a ghost or that of a living person.

Sometimes ghosts hardly make an impression on the eye. There was a Cape Cod cottage where sometimes at night the door of the living-room would open. Steps would be heard. Then the rocking-chair would tip forward, and slowly, slowly begin to rock.

In a certain southern colonial mansion, every night at midnight a coach drove up with four horses. A coachman jumped down, opened the door, and let down the steps. Two men would run out of the house, carrying the limp form of a girl; they would put her in the coach, fold up the steps, close the door, and the coach would drive away. This scene recurred every night as regularly as the stroke of twelve—but it could be seen only from the window of one second-story bedroom.

In an old house in Louisiana, a beautiful girl used to walk into the room, look at herself in the mirror for a time, suddenly scream—and vanish where she stood.

There was a haunted house in Pennsylvania where no one ever saw anything out of the way; but at the last stroke of midnight the front door would slam. Feet would pound up stairs. There would be a pistol shot. Then a scream. Then silence.

One room in a western New York inn had to be permanently locked because finally no guest could sleep there; for no sooner would one be in bed than a hand would appear, hover for a moment, and then snuff out the candle. The darkness was none the less terrible because nothing further ever happened.

In Rhode Island there was a home where the door from the hall into a bedroom used to open. A man with a frightful gash in his face would walk soundlessly in, looking neither to right nor to the left. He would cross the room, and go out another door, closing it behind him.

For these stories no one has produced explanations. Not all ghosts are so elusive; the Cock Lane Ghost of London, a world sensation in its time, was finally detected as the fraud of a little girl named Parsons, who produced rappings and scratchings from the ghost of a murdered woman until she was made to keep her hands above the bedclothes. Then the investigators waited in vain. Her father was put in the stocks, and later imprisoned, for his share in the fraud, which was the talk of all London, even of Paris and Madrid, in 1762.

Hysterical children and people with a grudge have often been caught impersonating ghosts. In countless instances mice in the walls, squirrels in the attic, or the settling of the house have produced noises which when coupled with a little imagination made convincing ghosts. Other visible ghosts turned out to be, when seen by more skeptical eyes, a rag fluttering in the wind.

Scotland, like all Celtic countries a home of the uncanny, has a number of unusual ghosts.

At Cadrain a man on horseback used often to ride up to a certain house, tie his horse to a rope hanging from the thatch, and then wander through the house.

At Auchabrick House, Kirkmaiden, once lived a privateer whose faithless brother intercepted his letters to his beloved. No matter how they bar the door, the scratch of his pen is still heard, rewriting the lost letters.

In a tudor room at Machermore Castle, Minnigaff, Galloway, is the print of a bloody hand on the floor. Part of the flooring was removed and renewed to get rid of this disfigurement; but the hand reappeared on the new flooring.

A lady once rented the mansion house near Castle-Douglas, Galloway. Two or three times she was disturbed at night by hearing a horse trotting around to the front door. When she looked out of the window, there was nothing. A few years later she returned to visit the house, and the owner showed off the improvements he had made. One was to tear out the partition between the bedroom and dressing-room; built into the wall was a horse's skull.

Mr. John Browne, of Durley, Ireland, had been made trustee for the minor children of a friend. In 1654 he himself lay dying. The trustee papers were in a great iron chest with three locks at the foot of his bed. Several friends were at his bedside. All at once the chest began to unlock itself, lock by lock; the lid slowly rose upright. John Browne, who had not spoken for twenty-four hours, sat up, and said, "You say true, you say true, you are in the right. I'll be with you by and by." He lay back, and never spoke again. The chest lid sank, slowly locked itself, and soon after John Browne died.

At Guilford, in England, a Mr. Bower was found murdered on the highway. There were three men in Guilford jail shortly thereafter, one a recent arrival. This one awoke about an hour after midnight to see an old man walk in with a great gash from ear to ear, a wound in his breast, stooping, holding his hand on his back. He tried to alarm the other two inmates, but they merely growled at him. In the morning he described the apparition, and found that it coincided exactly with the late Mr. Bower. A subsequent confession of a tinker showed that the tinker had knocked Bower from his horse with a blow on the back, while the two growling inmates of Guilford jail had cut his throat.

It seems advisable always to trust those who can see ghosts invisible to us. There was a Dutch lieutenant at Woodbridge, Suffolk, captured during the Dutch-English wars, who could see ghosts. He had a friend, a Mr. Broom, who couldn't. One evening as he was walking with Mr. Broom, he said, "Here comes a ghost down the street, looking up to one side, swinging one hand with a glove." Mr. Broom saw nothing. "We must make room for him to pass when he comes near," said the Dutch lieutenant, "now we must get out of his path." Mr. Broom, thinking this was nonsense, forcibly held the lieutenant in the road by the arm. Suddenly there came a shock which flung Broom in the middle of the street, painfully bruising one palm and one knee. The lieutenant lay like one dead. When he finally came to, they went to Mr. Broom's house. Just as they were going in the church bell began to toll. Mr. Broom asked whom it was for, and was told that it was for a Mr. Taylor, who had died suddenly, apparently at the precise moment of the collision. It was Mr. Taylor's habit to walk looking up to one side, and swinging a glove in one hand.

Even though no one saw the ghost who went through an uncanny performance with a stove-lid in an old house in Williamsburg, New York, it did its best to help. The people of the house were often disturbed, and not a little annoyed, by the dancing of one of the stove-lids. On several occasions it not merely bounced up and down on the stove, but jumped off, and jolted across the floor to one corner of the kitchen. The tenants not only never found anything to explain this but never did anything about it; which turned out to be silly, for five or six years later, the house was torn down, and in the foundation under that corner of the kitchen were two pots of gold.

Although the stories here set down are American and European, travellers have returned with substantially the same stories from the farthest corners of the globe. The main differences between foreign and domestic ghosts are that the foreign ones wear the costumes and have the manners of their countries. Ghosts do not seem to be very inventive for there are really but few different types of stories of ghostly appearances.

A common sort of visitation was the dire warning. Dreams are often believed to play a part in such warnings, sometimes with and sometimes without later waking events.

Josef Haydn records in his journal a concert given at a Mr. Bartholemon's in London on March 26, 1792. When the *Andante* was played, an English preacher got up in horror, and left the hall: he had dreamt that this very music would be the forerunner of his death. He went straight home, took to his bed, and was dead by April 25.

The warnings, on the other hand, are sometimes meant kindly. Cicero reports the case of the poet Simonides, who found an unknown corpse by the roadside. He had it given decent burial at his own expense. He was about to take ship when the dead man appeared to him in a dream, warning him that if he sailed by that vessel he would perish in a shipwreck. Simonides waited for another boat: the first ship set sail, and all on board were lost.

Seamen, travelling amid dangers known and unknown, of course sail constantly close to the wind of death. One of the most famous of stories is that of the Flying Dutchman, condemned forever to tack into a head wind, forever unable to make port. Princes Albert, George, and Victor, the grandsons of Queen Victoria, made a voyage around the world. The published account of their trip reports under date of July 11, 1881, that they sighted the Flying Dutchman off Sidney, Australia—a brig, perhaps two hundred yards away, sailing in an unearthly red light. The lookout cried "Ship ahoy!" The other two vessels making up the convoy signalled to inquire whether the flagship had seen the red light; the Dutchman was seen by a total of thirteen people. Some hours later the lookout who had sighted the ghost ship fell from the fore-top-gallantmast to the deck, and was shattered in every limb.

Lord Byron went to Lisbon by a packet-boat under one Captain Kidd (not, needless to say, the pirate captain). Kidd told Byron he had been awakened one night by heavy pressure across his body as he lay in his berth. He opened his eyes, and by the dim night-light recognized the form of his brother, who was then in India. Thinking it a hallucination or physical deception, Kidd closed his eyes, and tried to go to sleep again. But the pressure persisted, and when he looked again Kidd could even see that his brother's uniform was dripping wet. The brother lay there all night; only when Captain Kidd called the officers to observe and remove him did he disappear. Months later Captain Kidd learned that his brother had been drowned that night in Indian waters. Several officers were able to confirm the story and its dates.

Pliny the Younger had a young man in his house, the brother of a freedman, who one night felt that some one was sitting on his bed, cutting his hair with shears. The following morning his hair was indeed found cut, with bits of it lying around the bed. The same thing was repeated on a young slave by two figures in white garments, which came in through the window; again the hair was found cut. Pliny had no explanation for this except that it possibly indicated his good fortune in the dropping of a charge against him. This charge was in the Emperor Domitian's desk, but Domitian died in a few days, and the charge was never brought. It was the custom for people under accusation to let their hair grow, and Pliny thought possibly the apparitions had been a good omen.

Some apparitions have neither meaning nor purpose, and certainly no quality which could induce those who see them to invent the story.

A man of (we may gather) amateur scientific leanings was sitting at the window one evening in the pleasant old city of Würzburg, taking some observations of the stars. A female relative and her maid were walking in the garden. Suddenly the man saw a red ball, two or three feet in diameter, rise perpendicularly from the ground, revolving and shooting off sparks. It went straight up, and disappeared noiselessly at a considerable height, but the sparks fell on the clothes of the two women walking below, who had considerable difficulty in extinguishing them. The observer said he had no notion of what this phenomenon meant, but that he could admit no doubts that he had seen it.

In Slavata, Bohemian History, there is the report of a sudden fearful storm on July 20, 1571, after which many of the inhabitants saw a great troop of riders pass through Prague New Town, and then vanish in an instant. Many of the citizens who saw this fell ill, and some died.

A belief in the wandering spirits of the dead was all the more natural since it was believed from primitive times that every one had not only a physical body, but a separate, immaterial spirit. Many people believed that the spirit governed most, if not all, of the actions of the body. Many races believed too that a man's spirit can depart from his body almost at will, and is perfectly capable of carrying on an independent existence. Some people believed that the spirit could make itself visible or invisible at will, while others thought that the spirit was always visible to certain persons, and always invisible to the rest of mankind. The favored men who have seen such spirits say that they have the general appearance and accoutrement of the bodies to which they belong.

When the spirit leaves the body, the body is thereby put to sleep. This is represented as plainly true because when the spirit rejoins the body it brings with it memories of places and people which the body, immovable in bed, did not go near.

If the spirit leaves the body unattended for a considerable time, sickness of the body is the result; if the absence is further prolonged, it leaves the body in a coma. Death is caused by a permanent departure of the spirit to parts unknown.

The spirit's travels cause it to work up an appetite, just as the body would. For this reason primitive peoples leave out food and even wine for the propitiation of passing spirits. I like the idea of not having to wait until my death for my spirit to sow its psychic wild oats.

In Polynesia the shamans, called Kahunas or Tahungas, not only can see these roving spirits, but know how to catch them. There they believe that spirits are much smaller than men. If a kahuna catches a spirit, he can kill it by squeezing it together in his hands until the few drops of blood necessary to a spirit are squeezed out. I was actually shown such a flat and bloodless spirit. It looked like a tiny gingerbread man who had had an encounter with a steamroller. Once the spirit is killed, of course the body dies as well.

There are many special beliefs about the way spirits act. For instance, they can travel only in a straight line. The Chinese put a sort of screen in front of house-doors and gates, so that bodies have to walk around, and spirits simply cannot get in. They cannot cross water; the Swedes always crush half-eggshells lest the spirits use them as boats. The anthropologists have collected thousands of these beliefs.

It is quite possible for a spirit which has been away from the body to be unable to find its way back. For refuge it may then take possession of the first body it finds. This is the easier because it is also possible to have two spirits in one body. Perhaps this is what happens to one who wakes up of a Monday morning feeling not quite himself. Even today the Spaniards believe that they yawn because a spirit is trying to get in; they therefore make a cross before their mouths to keep it out.

This is closely related to the more modern belief in possession, witchcraft, werewolves and vampires. A man's spirit has only to take possession of a wolf, and you have lycanthropy. Some people believe that the spirit can actually physically transform the man's body into that of a wolf. A witch's spirit may wander about disembodied, visible only to its victims, and doing such mischief as it feels like. There is, however, the danger that an injury inflicted on the spirit will go home to the witch's body, as many witch stories show.

Werewolf stories have chilled the blood of countless generations the world over. One on the authority of the British traveller, Coffin, deals with a whole class of people in Abyssinia a hundred-odd years ago. The iron and pottery workers of Abyssinia were a class apart, a sort of outcast group, called "budas." If Christian they were not allowed to receive the sacrament; there were also Mohammedan and Jewish budas. They were distinguished by an odd sort of gold ring worn in one ear, and their peculiarity was that they could transform themselves into hyenas. Coffin had a buda among his train, who one evening asked for a night off, and, being given it, walked off toward the bush. In a suspiciously short time he was gone, but a large hyena was prowling around where he had been. The next morning the man returned to work. The other natives chaffed him about his night out as a hyena, and his answers rather strengthened than denied the charge.

This in itself was of no great significance; but Coffin

found the peculiar gold ring of the buda in the ear of several hyenas which he shot or speared.

No story of typical witchcraft could be more striking than the eyewitness account of Cotton Mather, the great Massachusetts theocrat and witch-burner. Mather and his father, President Increase Mather of Harvard College, were the religious monarchs and almost the political dictators of seventeenth-century Massachusetts.

"Four children of John Goodwin, in Boston, which had enjoy'd a religious education, and answer'd it with a towardly ingenuity—children, indeed, of an exemplary temper and carriage, and an example to all about them for piety, honesty, and industry—these were, in the year 1688, arrested by a very stupendous witchcraft. The eldest of the children, a daughter of about thirteen years old, saw cause to examine their laundress, the daughter of a scandalous Irish woman in the neighborhood, about some linen that was missing; and the woman bestowing very bad language on the child, in her daughter's defense, the child was immediately taken with odd fits, that carried in them something *diabolical*. It was not long before one of her sisters, with two of her brothers, were horribly taken with the like fits, which the most experienc'd physicians pronounced extraordinary and preternatural: and one thing that the more confirmed them in this opinion was, that all the children were tormented still just the same part of their bodies, at the *same time*, tho' their pains flew like swift lightning from one part unto another, and they were kept so far asunder, that they neither saw nor heard one another's complaints. At nine or ten o'clock at night, they still had a release from their miseries, and slept all night pretty comfortably. But when the day came, they were most miserably handled. Sometimes they were *deaf*, sometimes *dumb*, sometimes *blind*, and often all this at once. Their tongues would be drawn down their throats, and then pull'd out upon their chins, to prodigious lengths. Their mouths were forced open to such a wideness, that their jaws went out of joint; and anon clap together again, with a force like that of a spring lock; and the like would happen to their shoulder-blades and their elbows, and hand wrists, and several of their joints. They would lie in a benumb'd condition, and be drawn together like those that are ty'd neck and heels; and presently be stretch'd out—yea, *drawn back* enormously. They made piteous out-cries, that they were cut with *knives*, and struck with *blows*; and the plain prints of the *wounds* were seen upon them. Their necks would be broken, so that their neck-bone would seem dissolv'd unto them that felt after it; and yet on the sudden it would become stiff, that there was no stirring of their heads; yea, their heads would be twisted almost round; and if the main force of their friends at any time obstructed a dangerous motion which they seem'd upon, they would roar exceedingly: and when devotions were performed with them, their *hearing* was utterly taken from them. The ministers of Boston and Charlestown, keeping a day of prayer with fasting, on this occasion, at the troubled house, the youngest of the four children was immediately, happily, finally delivered from all its trouble. But the magistrates being awakened by the noise of these grievous and horried occurrences, examined the person who was under the suspicion of having employ'd these troublesome dæmons; and she gave such a wretched account of herself, that she was committed unto the gaoler's custody.

"It was not long before this woman (whose name was Glover) was brought upon her trial; but then the court could have no answers from her but in the Irish, which was her native language, although she understood English very well, and had accustom'd her whole family to none but English in her former conversation. When she pleaded to her indictment, it was with *owning*, and *bragging*, rather than *denial* of her guilt. And the interpreters, by whom the communication between the bench and the barr was managed. were made sensible that a *spell* had been laid by another witch on *this*, to prevent her telling tales, by confining her to a language which 'twas hoped nobody would understand. The woman's house being searched, several *images*, or *poppets*, or babies, made of raggs, and stuffed with goats' hair, were thence produced; and the vile woman confessed that her way to torment the objects of her malice, was by wetting of her finger with her spittle, and stroking of those little images. The abus'd children were then present in the court; the woman kept still stooping and shrinking, as one that was almost prest unto death with a mighty weight upon her. But one of the images being brought unto her, she oddly and swiftly started up, and snatch'd it into her hand; but she had no sooner snatch'd it, than one of the children fell into sad fits before the whole assembly. The judges had their just apprehension at this, and carefully causing a repetition of the experiment, they still found the same event of it, tho' the children saw not when the hand of the witch was laid upon the images. . . .

"However, to make all clear, the court appointed five or six physicians to examine her very strictly, whether she was no way craz'd in her intellectuals. Divers hours did they spend with her; and in all that while no discourse came from her but what was *agreeable*. . . . She profest herself a Roman Catholick, and could recite her *Paternoster* in Latin very readily; but there was one clause or two always too hard for her, whereof, she said, 'she could not repeat it, if she might have all the world.'

"In the upshot, the doctors return'd her *compos mentis*, and sentence of death was past upon her. . . .

"At her execution, she said the afflicted children should not be reliev'd by her death, for others beside she had a hand in their affliction. Accordingly the three children continu'd in their furnace as before; and it grew rather 'seven times hotter' than it was. . . .

"The ministers of Boston and Charlestown, afterwards accompany'd the printed narrative of these things with their attestations to the truth of it. And when it was reprinted at London, the famous Mr. Baxter prefixed a preface unto it, wherein he says: 'This great instance comes with such convincing evidence, that he must be a very obdurate Sadducee, that will not believe it.' "

Richard Baxter, the author of *Saints' Everlasting Rest*, was a great divine, and almost as prominent in England as the Mathers were in Massachusetts.

Ann Glover of Boston was only the first victim in an

absolute witch-madness that swept New England, center-
ing in Salem Town (now Danvers), and destroying a total
of nineteen human victims, as well as two dogs, accused
of witchcraft.

Cotton Mather was the instigator and chief moral support of the witch-hunt, although the Reverend Mr. Parris
of Salem Town was the more immediate instrument of
destruction. The royal governor, Sir William Phips, had
just arrived from England in May, 1692, when the prosecutions began. He had little doubt that they were justified, or at least that persons guilty of witchcraft should
be punished; furthermore he had a letter from Queen
Anne herself which raised no doubt of the fact of witchcraft, but accepted it as a problem to be dealt with.

Finally people began to accuse the accusers and other
personal enemies, threatening to bring on a regular French
Terror a century too soon. Only one of the judges at the
trials, however, Samuel Sewall, ever acknowledged his
guilt and his delusion after it was all over. Cotton Mather's stiff neck never relaxed, and his father burnt in
Harvard Yard a pamphlet by Robert Calef making sport
of the witchcraft idea.

The Salem witchcraft persecutions were by no means
peculiar to New England; in fact they were preceded by
similar epidemics in Great Britain, Germany, Ireland,
Spain, Portugal, France, Italy and Switzerland. Conservative historians number the victims at two or three
hundred thousand.

One of the most famous witches was Jane Brooks, of
Shepton Mallet. She came to the door and asked a twelve-

year-old boy named Richard Jones for a piece of bread. In turn she gave him an apple, and stroked his right side. Later in the day he felt great pain in his right side. He roasted the apple, and ate half of it (Snow White please note); he was deathly ill. At times Richard Jones could see Jane Brooks in the room. Once his cousin stabbed at the place where Richard said she was; the local policeman, going to Jane Brooks' cottage, found her hiding a stabbed hand.

Jane Brooks and her sister Alice Coward, a fellow-witch, came to see Richard Jones as he lay sick in bed. They said that what they had begun they could not perform, but if he would say no more they would give him money. With this they put a twopenny piece in his pocket. When this piece was put in the fire and heated, Richard Jones became very sick; when it cooled off again, he would recover. On one occasion the boy was seen to fly thirty yards through the air, crossing a garden wall in his progress; at other times he would be found hanging by his hands from a beam. An end was put to this by the execution of Jane Brooks on March 26, 1658.

A similar witch was Elizabeth Style, of Stoke Trister, Somerset. She bewitched a thirteen-year-old, Elizabeth Hill, causing thorns to be stuck into her. Elizabeth's father, Richard Hill, was riding along when his horse suddenly sat down on its breech. From then on it could not be ridden, but would sit down, and paw with its forefeet. A woman named Agnes Vining quarrelled with Elizabeth Style, and shortly after felt a pricking in her thigh. After various ups and downs she died, her hip rotted, and one eye swelled out.

Elizabeth Style confessed the full extent of her villainy, but died in prison before being executed.

Florence Newton of Youghal was probably Ireland's most famous witch. She bewitched an impudent serving-girl named Mary Longdon. Mary Longdon had fits in which she would rise three or four feet in the air, defying the efforts of several people to hold her. Then she would vomit up needles, pins, horse nails, stubs, wool and straw. Showers of pebbles would fall on her as she walked around. Pins would be found between her flesh and her skin, with the skin unbroken. Finally, Mary Longdon would be transported to various places such as between the bed and mattress of her master's bed, and even to a small board on top of the house between two sollar beams, whence she could be got down only with ladders.

The kind of witch which seems most familiar to us today —the vindictive old crone who lives in a lonely cottage and brings bad luck to those who cross her—seems to flourish particularly in Scotland. There was one such, named Old Jean, in Whinnieliggate, Kirkcudbrightshire. Her cottage was decorated within by cabalistic symbols, and she made her living by a sort of petty blackmail, cadging necessaries off people who were afraid to refuse her. On one occasion a farmer passed by her cottage with a cart-load of potatoes on his way to Kirkcudbright to ship them to Liverpool. She asked him for a couple for seed, and he refused. When he arrived at Kirkcudbright, the horse backed straight into the unprotected harbor, and was rescued with great difficulty.

People throughout the world have always believed in

the reality of spirits, and they have believed that these spirits had the power to do a wide variety of things. The Bible itself, though constant in its war on demons and familiar spirits, makes no doubt of their existence. Down through the centuries names of the most learned men can be listed who not only believed in ghosts, but were sure they had seen them. Ghosts, just like witchcraft, witches, and werewolves, were accepted as fact not merely by the people at large but by high officers of the Churches, professors, and college presidents, judges and men of science. Although these people believed in ghosts, they did all they could to keep away from them. Ghosts were messengers of doom. There is no more forceful description of absolute terror than "He looks as if he had seen a ghost."

CHAPTER II

TWO LITTLE GIRLS WITH AN APPLE

Not only in the beginning of the last century were the people of the world at large quite generally believers in supernatural occurrences but those living in a band of land running across upper New York State seemed particularly prepared to believe. There was a religious emotionalism in northern New York which made the people ready to accept a wide variety of home grown prophets with ideas which were brand new—at least in some respects. My friend, Carl Carmer, in his book, *Listen for a Lonesome Drum*, gives a delightful account of this land and many of its prophets.

It was to this statewide strip of prophet raising land that John and Margaret Fox brought their two younger daughters on December 11, 1847. The village to which they came is named Hydesville, which is in Arcadia township in Wayne County, some thirty miles away from the city of Rochester.

John Fox, a devout Methodist and said to be fond of hard liquors, was a man who had for a period of years lived away from his wife and children. I have never heard whether his absence from home was due to desire, circumstance, or liquor. At any rate he and his wife Margaret finished raising the family they had started before he had left home. All told there were, it is said, seven children though only four are characters in this account. These children are David S. Fox who lived but a few miles away from his parents' new home; Anna Leah Fox Fish who lived with her third husband in Rochester; Margaret and Katherine Fox who lived with their parents. David and Leah were both born before their father's sojourn away from home and Margaret, twenty-three years Leah's junior, and Katherine, eighteen months still younger, were born after the family was reunited. Mrs. Margaret Fox, the mother, was as devout as her husband though much more inclined to accept the superstitions of the times. Both were good, simple, country people.

The small frame farmhouse into which they moved was haunted according to the story interested neighbors were quick to tell the Foxes. The story it seemed was first started by Lucretia Pulver, the hired girl of the previous tenants who moved away. Those who had lived last in the house were the Michael Weekmans and their daughter. They couldn't stand the place either, for an unseen and icy hand was always hovering around the head of the little girl while she lay in bed and in the dark of night raps and pounding could be heard all over the house.

The story was the usual ghost story. A murder was said to have been committed in the house. The victim was an itinerant peddler and his body was supposed to be buried in the cellar. Naturally the spirit of a murdered man haunts the place where he was killed and does things calculated to stand the hair on end of any one with the temerity to stay in the house no matter how innocent of murder that person might be.

The pious John Fox was not in fear of the doings of the unhappy peddler and he and his wife had a happy Christmas with their little daughters Margaret and Katherine. (Margaret at that time was eight years old and Katherine six and a half—at least so they later said and I believe it to be correct. Some say Margaret was some six years older and that Katherine was three full years her junior. Not only do I prefer to accept a woman's statement as to her age but it makes the story better, for all the rest of the years given in the various accounts can then agree.)

The household led their peaceful lives into the new year without any ghostly visitations whatsoever. Toward the end of March, Elizabeth Fish, the granddaughter of John and Margaret Fox and, though seven years older than Margaret, the niece of Margaret and Katherine, came to Hydesville on a visit. She slept with her two young aunts in what was called the East Room. For several nights Elizabeth was frightened by being awakened out of a sound sleep. She didn't know what had startled her.

A few nights after Elizabeth arrived Mrs. Fox heard several distinct raps and they came, she believed, from the children's room. She rushed in but they were all asleep. The next morning, at the breakfast table there was considerable conversation about the "raps" of the night.

The next night more raps were heard and the rapping

occurred several times. It was decided the next day that the children's bed had better be moved to the parents' room. That night when the light was put out the raps came again.

After the raps had been heard intermittently for some time, according to a report of the event signed by Mrs. Margaret Fox, Katie exclaimed, "Mr. Splitfoot" (which was the children's name for the one who made the noises), "do as I do." She clapped her hands and instantly came the same number of raps. Then Margaret called out, "Now do just as I do; count one, two, three, four," striking one hand against the other as she counted. Again the raps one—two—three—four. "I then," said Mrs. Fox, "thought I could put a test that no one in the place could answer. I asked the noises to rap my children's ages successively. Instantly each one of my children's ages was given correctly, pausing between them sufficiently long to individualize them until the seventh, at which a longer pause was made, and then three more emphatic raps were given, corresponding to the age of the little one that died, which was my youngest child. I then asked: 'Is this a human being that answers my questions correctly?' There was no rap. I asked: 'Is it a spirit? If so, make two raps,' which were instantly given as soon as the request was made. I then said: 'If it is an injured spirit, make two raps,' which were instantly made, causing the house to tremble. I asked: 'Were you injured in this house?' The answer was given as before. 'Is the person living that injured you?' Answer by raps in the same manner. I ascertained by the same method that it was a man, aged thirty-one years; that he had been murdered in this house; and that his remains were buried in the cellar; that his family consisted of a wife and five children, two sons and three daughters, all living at the time of his death, but that his wife had since died."

This was on the night of March 31, 1848. That is a most important date for that conversation with the murdered peddler, in a dark room, late at night, in the tiny house in Hydesville was the beginning of spiritism. That homely simplicity of a farmer's wife inquiring about the family of a guest even when that guest was a ghost was something new. From that day on the fearsome family ghost became a household pet.

There seems to be a little confusion about who really asked the questions of Mr. Splitfoot. William Duesler, a neighbor of the Fox family, claimed that he had been the questioner and he wrote his account on April 12, 1848. Mrs. Fox's story appeared much later. The claims and counter claims and the conflicting testimony printed in books about spiritism make it a delightful subject to study. It is believed that Mrs. Fox had been the questioner and had described it all to Duesler.

The next night the lonesome ghost was asked if he minded if a few of the neighbors were asked in to hear him. He didn't mind at all and as the neighbors sat around in the dark he rapped and rapped. He would only come when Margaret and Katherine were present. Soon for miles around the chief topic of conversation was the Fox girls and their rapping spirit. The local excitement was so great that a pamphlet was written about the unseen intelligence which by the means of rapping talked during the dead of night.

Shortly the elder sister, Mrs. Leah Fish, came over from Rochester to visit her parents and her daughter who had by then left the haunted house to live with David. She became very much interested in the rappings and when she and her daughter returned home they took Katherine with them. A short while after that Margaret and her mother went to join them. The strangest thing of all was that even though the haunted house had been left behind the rapping spirit followed the children from place to place. It followed them to their elder brother's home and even to Rochester.

Even on the canal boat going to Rochester the rappings followed the girls. Sister Leah was most enthusiastic about the spirit and his raps but her husband Calvin disliked the ghost most thoroughly and expressed his opinion not only openly but vociferously. Friendly as he was to Leah, Margaret and Katherine the spirit disliked Calvin and began, still always during darkness, to throw slippers and other objects at him which still further annoyed him. Little by little the spirit became more bold and during supper would shake the table and once when Calvin rose from his chair to reach for the water pitcher the spirit slyly removed his chair so that when he sat down he fell on the floor and spilled the water all over himself. Calvin began really to hate that ghost.

Of course Leah had too many thrilling things happening in her home not to want the neighbors, whose curiosity was at the bursting point, to come in. Not only the neigh-

bors came but many of the city's most noted citizens also
visited the Fish home. The story was much too thrilling
to be kept within the city limits and shortly newspapers
all over the country began to carry articles about the
"Rochester Rappings." The foreign press took up the
story and while still children Margaret and Katherine and
their rappings became talked about all over the world.

Sister Leah, perhaps because she was more familiar
with the ways of the city, began, almost with the first people to visit her, to charge an admission fee to listen to the
raps. Leah collected as much as one hundred and fifty
dollars an evening from the rapt attendants to the rapping.

It was soon discovered by questioners that not only
could the children call upon old Splitfoot the peddler
who had been murdered but also upon the spirits of those
who after a blameless life had died quite naturally and
merely of old age in their own beds. It was also discovered
that most any other person in the spirit world could be
called upon to rap whether he had died but the week before or had been in his grave a thousand years. And so
the next big step in spiritism was reached. Those of the
spirit world did not need to be unhappy to come back
to earth, they did not need to have been murdered nor to
have left unrighted wrongs they had committed in their
worldly existence. It was just as easy to call back Grandmother or Aunt Hattie. Naturally when a person's own
dead could be brought back to him spiritism became of
interest to every one.

With the rappings of personal and general interest

Sister Leah looked for new and larger fields as she bundled up little Margaret and Katherine, raps and all, and took them to New York City. There she felt that an organized backing would be of great help so she started the first "Spiritualistic" society in the world. With the endorsement of the Society "Spiritualism" began to assume the form of a religion. Hymns were sung at the beginning and end of what they called a "séance"—foreign words are frequently found in the vocabulary of the believer—a pious frame of mind was requested, and every one naturally spoke in a hushed voice.

After having great success in New York City the girls were taken to cities large and small all over the country. Their séances attracted the attention of leading ministers and noted men of all the professions. Wealthy society people in large numbers came to listen to the raps and also many people attended who had to dig into the old china teapot to find the admission fee.

Among others who went to see the Fox girls and wonder at the doings of the spirits was Horace Greeley and after the nationwide tour was finished he showed his interest by sending little Katherine to school.

Five years had gone by since old Splitfoot had first been heard and, with Katherine in school, Margaret and her mother went to Philadelphia. There in their rooms at the Union Hotel they gave séances. One of those who came to see Margaret was the handsome young surgeon and explorer, Doctor Elisha Kent Kane, who was greatly attracted to the little girl. He arranged to have her give up her séances and be tutored. She lived in a suburb of

Philadelphia and Doctor Kane's aunt watched over her. At this time Margaret was thirteen years old, the aristocratic Doctor almost thirty-four. One of the trips of exploration made by Doctor Kane had been to the arctic to hunt for the ill-fated expedition of Sir John Franklin. Not only did he not discover Sir John but Doctor Kane's health was ruined by the trials of arctic travel. About two years after he had assumed charge of Margaret's education Doctor Kane, who had from the first been in love with the girl, decided his health might be aided by travel abroad. Before he left for Europe he married Margaret by simple declaration and without either a religious or civil ceremony. His travels finally brought him to Cuba, where on February 16, 1857, he died. Margaret and her mother were about to join Doctor Kane in Havana when the unhappy news was received. Margaret was ill for a long time after she had received the sad blow of the Doctor's death. Upon her recovery she discovered that her common-law marriage did not entitle her to any part of her husband's estate although his family did give her a little money.

Although it had been Doctor Kane's wish that she give up her connection with all séances Margaret found that to eat she would have to take them up again. Margaret travelled about this country and abroad for almost forty years rapping a bare living out of the ever increasing number of followers of Spiritualism. She had many difficulties, perhaps the principal one being competition, for literally thousands of those for whom the spirits would perform had called attention to themselves. These people had assumed the name of "mediums" and the ghostly work was entitled "manifestations." Comparatively few mediums were satisfied with mere rappings but had other manifestations for their patrons—"sitters" is the approved word. Further "Spiritualistic" organizations were formed not only in Europe and America but in Asia as well. The raps were a good introduction to spirit manifestations but were much too slow to give attention to more than a few sitters during the course of a séance. This very slowness had brought about the Fox girls' being urged by Mrs. Fish to attempt a séance during the day in a room with the shutters closed. It was quite as successful. Brother David was the one who added so greatly to the system for getting information from the spirits. At first it will be recalled the spirits would rap out a number or would answer questions by giving two raps for "Yes" and silence for "No." (Later this was changed to three raps for "yes" and two for "no.") David's idea was that if the spirit would knock as the alphabet was recited it would be possible to spell out words and sentences. This was a clever idea but as the sitters chanted the alphabet over and over while waiting for raps it became a very slow and tedious process. Other mediums with more exciting phenomena, which will be mentioned in another chapter, cut in on the number of sitters Margaret could get to a séance and her income was very small.

Another difficulty was that though in her early days there was a large proportion of the people who did not believe the raps came from those in the land of spirits these people had begun to organize and campaign with their disbelief. Ministers began quoting the Bible. Deuteronomy, XVIII, 10–12, "There shall not be found among you . . . a consulter with familiar spirits." Leviticus, XIX, 31, "Regard not them that have familiar spirits." In the next chapter of the same book is found in the sixth verse, "And the soul that turneth after such as have familiar spirits, and after wizards, to go a whoring after them, I will ever set my face against that soul and will cut him off from among his people." Many other references are to be found in the Bible and learned divines quoted them all in an attempt to rout the mediums. The Spiritualistic organizations explained that such references in the Bible merely proved that this talking with the spirits of the dead was fact.

Others who also cut in on Margaret's business were the serious men of science who acted as investigators. There were three such investigations of her work. The first was in Rochester where three members of the faculty of the University of Buffalo, Doctor Austin Flint, Charles A. Lee, and C. B. Coventry, studied the raps. They published a report in which they call the raps an imposition. They also "exclude spiritual causation" and state definitely that the raps "are produced by the action of the will, through voluntary action on the joints." They suggest that the knee joints are semi-dislocated and when moved will produce the phenomena of the rappings. They also state that they had observed a case where "noises precisely identical" were produced in the knee joint.

In 1857 under the direction of Mr. George Lunt, editor of the *Boston Courier*, another investigation was held.

Besides the editor the group consisted of three Harvard professors and four other men of the city. The committee was merely to decide whether or not to give a five-hundred-dollar award to Margaret Fox, which the paper was offering. All she had to do was to get the spirits to answer a single question of the editor which was unknown to herself. The committee declared that nothing had been done to entitle any one to the award and none was made.

The third investigation was made in November of 1884. Margaret gave two séances which five members of the Seybert Commission of the University of Pennsylvania attended. Two other members were at the first séance. The séances were quite unsatisfactory for when they did rap the spirits gave out mis-information and when Margaret's feet were put on tumblers no raps at all came. Margaret refused to have any more sittings and the commission's published report stated that the "so-called raps are confined wholly to her person, whether produced by her voluntarily or involuntarily," they had not attempted to decide.

Mrs. Fish dismissed the "Buffalo Doctors" and their report by calling Doctor Lee "a wily, deceitful man" and, although about thirty-four years old at the time, included herself with Margaret aged eleven as "two young creatures thus baited as it were by cruel enemies." The Boston committee merely didn't hand over the five hundred dollars and of course the editor was said to have influenced the committee in order to hold on to his money. The Seybert Committee was explained away by saying that had Margaret been well enough to have had another sitting she could have shown their "conclusion" to have been wrong.

By this time Sister Leah had married again; this fourth husband was David Underhill, a New Yorker and president of an insurance company. Katherine was Mrs. Katherine Fox Jencken, a poor widow with two sons to support, so she was practicing as a medium. Margaret still calling herself Mrs. Kane and, still a medium, was earning but a poor living. She had her father's weakness for drink and was lonely and unhappy though she derived considerable solace from joining the Catholic Church. Mrs. Jencken became involved over charges brought about by the Society for the Prevention of Cruelty to Children and both she and Mrs. Kane felt that they were being persecuted and believed it to have been started by other mediums.

Mrs. Kane was in London when she heard of Mrs. Jencken's trouble and wrote a letter to the Editor of the *New York Herald* which was published on May 27, 1888. In the letter she said, "My sister's two beautiful boys referred to are her idols." She also wrote "Spiritualism is a curse" and she connected the word "fraud" with "mediums." The letter was signed Margaret F. Kane and comparatively few, even of that proportion of the paper's readers who notice the letters to the editor, recognized the name. However, it may be certain that the newspaper men knew that Mrs. Kane was the internationally-known Margaret Fox and were therefore quick to get an interview a few months later when she returned to the city. The interview was published on September 24, 1888, and was headed "God Has Not Ordered It."

In the article Margaret explained that the raps were made from childhood by "the manner in which the joints of the foot can be used." She promised to give a public exhibition "exposing Spiritualism from its very foundation."

In an interview published a few days after, Henry J. Newton, president of The First Spiritual Society of New York, was quoted as saying,

"The idea of claiming that unseen 'rappings' can be produced with joints of the feet! If she says this, even with regard to her own manifestations, she lies! I and many other men of truth and position have witnessed the manifestations of herself and her sisters many times under circumstances in which it was absolutely impossible for there to have been the least fraud."

Sixteen days after the interview with Margaret the papers carried one with Katherine Fox Jenken. She was quoted as saying that what Margaret had said was true and "Spiritualism is a humbug from beginning to end."

Two weeks later the Spiritualists' worst fears were realized, for Margaret did publicly expose and publicly demonstrate that the weird rappings which had fooled thousands for forty years were made by snapping the toes. The meeting was held in the Academy of Music in New York City. The hall was filled. There were many Spiritualists who attended and as *The Evening Post* printed the next day, "The Spiritualists who were present were highly indignant naturally, and gave vent to their disapproval by hisses and groans."

Besides demonstrating how she made the raps by putting her stockinged foot on a thin board, Margaret Kane also explained how she snapped her toes. A paper the next day said editorially, "Mrs. Kane now locates the origin of modern spiritualism in her great toe."

Mrs. Kane also said:

"I think that it is about time that the truth of this miserable subject 'Spiritualism' should be brought out. It is now widespread all over the world, and unless it is put down soon it will do great evil. I was the first in the field and I have the right to expose it.

"My sister Katie and myself were very young children when this horrible deception began. I was eight and just a year and a half older than she. We were very mischievous children and we wanted to terrify our dear mother, who was a very good woman and very easily frightened. At night when we were in bed, we used to tie an apple to a string and move it up and down, causing the apple to bump on the floor, or we would drop the apple on the floor, making a strange noise every time it would rebound. Mother listened to this for a time. She could not understand it and did not suspect us of being capable of a trick because we were so young.

"At last she could stand it no longer and she called the neighbors in and told them about it. It was this that set us to discover the means of making the raps."

Margaret went on to say that, "There were so many people coming to the house that we were not able to make use of the apple trick except when we were in bed and the room was dark. Even then we could hardly do it so that the only way was to rap on the bedstead with our hands."

It was after Mrs. Fish had taken the girls to Rochester that they discovered how to make other raps. "My sister Katie," said Mrs. Kane, "was the first one to discover that by swishing her fingers she could produce a certain noise with the knuckles and joints, and that the same effect could be made with the toes. Finding we could make raps with our feet—first with one foot and then with both— we practiced until we could do this easily when the room was dark."

Mrs. Kane told that what had so frightened her niece Elizabeth Fish just prior to the first rappings was to pinch or slap her after she had gone to sleep and then she would awake, startled, to find Margaret and Katherine pretending to be asleep. Merely the natural inclination to tease so many children have. The slippers which had hit brother-in-law Calvin were thrown by the girls who also tipped the table and by a piece of unexpected foot work pushed his chair out so that he sat on the floor. Margaret and her sister also used to carry small objects about the house and put them in unexpectedly wrong places—vegetables stored in the cellar would be found under the covers in the bed, a spool of thread would be found in the kitchen sugar bowl, an embrace would give Margaret a chance to take secretly her mother's comb which would later be found on the lamp chimney. Merely two mischievously naughty little girls and a simple country mother unsuspecting and superstitious.

Mrs. Kane also explained that Sister Leah knew full well that the raps were bogus, that she also learned how to make the raps, and that as long as she travelled with the girls she would signal what answer to give to each question asked. Mrs. Fish was with the girls until after their first nation-wide tour. Even when Margaret and Katherine first began with the toe rappings in Rochester they were made to wear long dresses to hide their feet from any one with too inquisitive a mind.

Mrs. Katherine Fox Jencken sat in a box at the Academy of Music exposé and nodded her agreement to everything Mrs. Kane said.

Beside Margaret's rapping exposé at the Academy Doctor C. M. Richmond, who was an amateur conjurer and a student of mediumistic fraud when he wasn't practicing dentistry, and Frank W. Stechan, a western theater manager, demonstrated and exposed tricks of other mediums.

For some time thereafter Mrs. Kane continued in cities near to New York to repeat her exposure in the local halls. It was expected that this would give her sufficient income to live but she shortly discovered that while many people will pay to be humbugged few will pay to be educated.

A magician who, though still quite young, had made a name for himself and had great skill and adroitness was engaged to appear with Mrs. Kane as "lecturer," for her speaking voice was not adequate for large halls. He also gave exposés of the feats of other mediums as Doctor Richmond had done. His name is Elmer P. Ransom. He is a close friend of mine and we have had many talks about the Fox Sisters during the past twenty-five years.

He is in a position to clear up three points which the Spiritualists have "doubted" to be fact ever since the Academy of Music exposure.

First: Could Margaret actually make the raps with her toes or was it some trick of Doctor Richmond? Not only is Mr. Ransom certain that Margaret could make raps with her toes, but she taught the skill to Mrs. Ransom. Mrs. Ransom, may it quickly be said, agrees to that statement and explains that it is a matter of snapping the tendon of the toe as many people can do with their fingers. The bone of the toe must strike upon some article of furniture or the bare floor which acts as a sounding board before the rap is loud enough to be heard more than a few feet away. Mr. Ransom also explained: "Not every one can learn to do this toe snapping and even for one who could it would take years of practice to perform with the ease with which Mrs. Kane worked."

Second: Did Margaret Fox make her confession more than the one time when she was under compulsion at the Academy? Mr. Ransom travelled with Margaret to a number of cities where she said it all over again and again and of her own volition.

Third: Was it not true that Margaret never made her exposure except when she was so drunk she did not know what she was saying? Mr. Ransom has told me that they were well aware of Margaret's fondness for liquor and that those in her party never left her out of their sight on tour except when she retired to her room, and even then precautions were taken that there was no liquor in the room. Mr. Ransom also makes the flat statement that

Margaret was never under the influence of liquor during any of their appearances together.

The exposés losing their novelty for the public no more could be booked, so Margaret was once more without a source of income.

Now comes the strangest part of this whole weird story. Margaret Fox with her childish raps had never brought a message to a sitter which wasn't something she could guess, which she knew already, or which was just plain fiction. She didn't always know as much as she thought she did, her guesses were often poor as was her fiction. She was publicly exposed twice and discredited once and finally she confessed fraud and exposed her skilled trickery, as did her sister Katherine. Both she and Katherine in writing approved a book written by Reuben B. Davenport called *The Death-Blow to Spiritualism* and furnished him data regarding their lifetime of trickery. Lastly Margaret Fox Kane's card always carried the following sentence: "Mrs. Kane does not claim any Spirit power; but people must judge for themselves." Still when she needed money again, she sought her old supporters and went back to being a medium. For six years she lived in Brooklyn, New York, with her raps. She continued her séances until her death on March 8, 1895.

Thousands of believers in Spiritualism attended her funeral and followed the hearse to her grave in the Greenwood Cemetery in Brooklyn.

CHAPTER III

STARTLING WONDERS—MYSTERIOUS DISPLAYS

(3)

Six years after Mr. Splitfoot began to rap out messages to the Fox girls in their little house in Hydesville the spirits performed for two boys in near-by Buffalo. They were the Davenport Brothers, Ira Erastus, fifteen years old, and William Henry Harrison, thirteen.

As Buffalo newsboys they were undoubtedly familiar with all the stories of the Rochester Rappings and even in the unlikely possibility that they had not heard of the Fox girls' spirit their father must, of course, have read the stories. The father, Ira D. Davenport, was a member of the Buffalo Police Department and one would therefore suppose suspicious, at least, by training. The father however was the first to tell about the unusual occurrences which happened around the house. Knives, forks, spoons, and dishes jumped about the table and the table itself danced a jig. Young Ira was whisked through the air from a back room in the house and landed out in the street seventy feet away. Another time when Ira Erastus was delivering papers he suddenly felt "queer" and then lost consciousness. When he came to he was standing on

[49]

the bank of the Niagara River at a most solitary spot. Furthermore he was standing in the snow with no tracks anywhere around to show how he had got there.

At the family's next séance, for a family with things like that happening, particularly in 1854, would hold séances, George Brown told more about Ira Erastus' exciting experience. George Brown, by the way, was the name of the spirit who first attracted the attention of the Davenports. George Brown used to talk, not by the signal system of raps although he would rap now and again, but by putting young Ira Erastus to sleep and then talking by using the boy's vocal equipment. This going to sleep is talked about as "being in the trance state." Well, George Brown, talking with Ira Erastus' voice, explained that not only had he carried the lad to the river's edge but, just as an experiment, he had carried him across the river and back. Having safely completed his experiment of carrying the unconscious boy a mile and a half over and a mile and a half back George merely and quite unceremoniously dumped him in the snow. George, one night, gave a most gruesome account of how he met his death. It seems, according to the story, that one night when he was near the town of Waterloo he had been set upon by a number of robbers who had been quite ruthless in the way they murdered him. He knew who the men were, however. They were all members of the Townsend gang.

That not only Ira Erastus but also his brother William Henry could fly was amply attested to by friends and neighbors who attended séances at the Davenports'. At first only the neighbors were invited to witness the spirits

at work but they told about Ira Erastus flying from one
side of the room to another, chair and all. That is, at the
beginning of the séance Ira Erastus would be sitting on
a chair at one side of the room, and when the lights were
turned up after it was over, the chair and boy would be
on the other side of the room. It is in all likelihood unnecessary to mention that these séances were invariably
held in the dark. As the chair and boy went across the
room in the dark it was argued they must have flown.

Shortly the thrilling feats of George Brown and the
Davenport Brothers were being witnessed, or probably
the word should be "attended," by interested and curious
people who were neither friends nor neighbors. This was
the idea of George Brown who also thought it to be a
good plan to charge those who attended the séances. The
policeman father, at first, so it is said, didn't think so well
of attaching a fee to the work of the spirits but after all
he was a man with only a small salary and he and his wife
had, besides their two boys, their ten-year-old daughter
Elizabeth Louise to support. After the séances were
opened, at a fee, to the public but a short time, father
Ira D. was completely won over to the idea. So complete
was his conversion that he resigned from the police
department to devote his whole time to running the
meetings.

Beside George Brown's attendance at the séances the
spirit of John Hicks also made his presence known. I do
not know if any one of the Davenports had known Brown
when he was alive but Hicks was Davenport's deceased
brother-in-law. His spirit declared that his death had

been caused by poisoning administered by his wife. The authorities acting upon this advice exhumed John Hicks' body and no evidence of poisoning was discovered. Another spirit announced that he had formerly been Governor of Jamaica and that his name had been Henry Morgan and that he preferred to be called John King. His information, unlike John Hicks', proved to be worthwhile. John King said that it would be a good idea to travel and, what is more, ordered them to do so. It was an excellent idea for the townspeople had begun to be a little tired of the whole business from the unnecessary opening of graves to the amount of money the family was taking in from the people who had come, many from great distances, to investigate.

At the beginning the Davenport Brothers had merely sat with the sitters at the séance; then later they sat apart. Then, with lengths of rope, they were tied to show that they took no physical part in the manifestations. Then still later they hung a curtain across one corner of the room and many of the things which occurred took place behind the curtain where the brothers sat tied to their chairs. The séances were at this stage when acting upon John King's advice the Davenport boys and their father set out upon their tour. They hired large halls and in many places, where there were no stages, built a platform and hung their curtain there. The curtain did not seem to meet the requirements as they travelled and they devised a large box to work in which would be placed upon the stage. This box gave them the idea of a cabinet, a rather large affair, with three doors. It looked quite like an old-fashioned "clothes press" except that there were small diamond-shaped windows in the doors.

Only a year after the Davenport Brothers had begun their séances they had arrived at Union Hall on the Bowery in New York City. It will be recalled that in those days the Bowery was a fashionable street of shops and theaters and restaurants. Their performance, it would seem odd to call their theater séance by another name, was divided into two parts: One where they were roped and tied in their cabinet, guitars, tambourines, and concertinas put on the floor inside and the doors shut and the hall's lights turned down. Soon the instruments could be heard to strum, or rattle, or blow and eerie hands would stick out of the little diamond-shaped windows in the doors and slowly wave, then be withdrawn. The gas would be turned up, the doors opened and there would sit the Davenports still tied. The other part was done outside the cabinet. A spectator would be invited to the stage and would sit at a table facing the audience. The brothers would sit at each end of the table. The spectator would place one hand on the head of each and each of the brothers would grasp his arms with both of theirs. The musical instruments would be left on the table. Again the gas would be turned down and the spectator would be lightly rapped on the head with a guitar and all the instruments could be heard to play. Many people said that they could see or at least hear the instruments fly all about the stage and even about the hall over the heads of the audiences.

As with all other séances there were those who were prepared to accept everything which happened or was supposed to have happened as a demonstration of spirit agency and others were just as certain that however the things were done it was unquestionably trickery. Both these groups always come with their minds made up beforehand and no matter what occurs take it as proof backing their opinions.

The newspapers were divided also and we again find believers, scoffers and fence walkers. One account carried the sentence, "The entertainment was really of a most remarkable character, and said to be calculated to confirm the opinions of believers in things supernatural." Another paper said, "Whether they are spiritual or otherwise, they are certainly very mysterious, and if the result of legerdemain, sleight-of-hand, or some new law or physical force, they are equally extraordinary and inexplicable." The *New York Sun* reporter not only gave no opinion but did a good piece of reporting in discovering whether or not the Davenport Brothers claimed spirit aid. He said in his report, "Their audience always take a lively interest in the performance, and are rather inclined to make a personal matter of it. About one-half of them are believers, and attribute everything to the spirits; the other half are skeptics, and either laugh at the affair or grow indignant and growl, according as they are good or bad tempered. The Davenports make no pretence of sacred intervention. They neither offer any explanation nor give one, on request, but like sensible men, do what they say they do, and leave the audience to make for themselves what explanation of it they please."

The Davenport Brothers continued to travel about the

United States for ten years. In those days most of their trips were made by stage coach and carriages although they used canal boats and river steamers whenever possible. It was amazing how profitable they found their performances to be in even the very small towns. They travelled to the far South and to the newly-opened West with their cabinet and tambourines, guitars, and concertinas. A story of their travels which is often told was their visit to Phœnix, Arizona, which was only a little town at that time. There they were imprisoned for giving a performance without a license. The next day they were missing from the prison and according to the stories of the Spiritualists, during the night their chains fell from them and the jail door opened and they were likened to St. Peter. Another story had it that they went into a trance and when they awoke found themselves outside the prison walls. There seems to be a little confusion about the whole story and some accounts say that it all happened in Oswego, New York.

The conditions of the times made travelling very difficult and arduous and though Ira Erastus seemed to thrive through it all William Henry, who never really had been strong, was in poor health. The father had long since ceased travelling with the boys and they had several different "lecturers" appear with them at various times. They also had William Fay in their company as manager and as understudy for the ailing William Henry. Fay was also a Buffalo boy who had started with the Davenport company as ticket taker.

Professor Loomis, of the Georgetown Medical College,

wrote a long account of the Davenport Brothers' work and stated his conviction that what was done was due to a power with which he was unacquainted. On the other hand members of various audiences had carried dark lanterns into the meetings and had flashed them on the stage during the period of darkness at the performance. These lantern carriers invariably claimed that they had caught the Brothers in doing things which they were supposed not to do nor, because of the ropes with which they were tied, supposed to be in a position to do. These bursts of light did not lessen the general public interest in the Davenports' work nor in any way lessen the strong conviction among the Spiritualists that spirits alone could account for all that happened.

On August 26 (or 27), 1864, the Davenport Brothers, William Fay, by then in the rôle of chief assistant as well as understudy, the Reverend J. B. Ferguson, and Palmer the business manager sailed for England. Ferguson, a Virginian, had at thirteen taught a country school for the Presbyterian Missionary Society. Later while studying at the Woodstock Academy he earned his living on the side first as a printer and then as a writer in a newspaper office. Once having been made a minister he became famed for his religious editing and his eloquence. He received two honorary degrees and his large congregation in Nashville, Tennessee, was devoted to him. Quite early in his life he became convinced of the genuineness of spirit manifestations and with his ability as a public speaker, his erudition, and his missionary-like zeal in advocating the Spiritualistic propaganda, he was the ideal person, from the

Davenports' view, to introduce them to the British public.

An English account of the Davenports at the time of their arrival follows: "The Brothers were remarkably alike, aged respectively twenty-five and twenty-three years. They had long black curly hair, broad but not high foreheads, dark eyes, heavy eyebrows and moustaches, firm-set lips, and a bright keen Yankee look."

Certainly the Davenport Brothers created great interest in spiritism in England and undoubtedly convinced, with their demonstrations and the Reverend Ferguson's eloquent talks, a large number of people that spirits do return. This conviction came even though every program and show-bill ever put out by the Davenports carried wording similar to that which follows which was taken from a bill of 1873: "Mysterious and unaccountable phenomena take place, all of which are produced by invisible agencies which, through ignorance and superstition, have been attributed to Demonology and Witchcraft."

Very early in their career the Davenports had discovered it necessary also to print a note on their advertising matter which would give them a reason for refusing any members of the audience volunteering to assist in the performance. The wording follows: "N.B.—The Brothers reserve the right to reject the Committee at any time they discover a disposition to deal unfairly or refuse to comply with the conditions governing the Manifestations." It was comparatively rare, before the Brothers went to England, that they had to reject a committee man but with the British they encountered more difficulties. In the first place it will be recalled that this was at the time of America's Civil War and the English, being sympathetic with the South, freely showed their dislike for their Northern visitors. They seemed to class Ferguson, a Southerner, with the Davenports.

Then, too, the Brothers ran into skeptics who were able to do more than merely doubt. Because the Davenports' performance was more complicated than the simple rapping of the Fox Sisters, it was not so easy to expose in print. Therefore several magicians, who realized that at no time were the Davenports so securely tied as to be unable to escape, practiced the trickery until they could duplicate the entire performance.

Naturally John Henry Anderson, the noted British magician, was one of the first to attack the Davenport Brothers for he had been publicly condemning spirit rapping both during his performances and in his writings for years before the Davenports went to England. On his program was printed as early as 1854: "Although the Wizard is not a great orator or lecturer, he will deliver a few remarks on what is called Spiritualism, or humbug of the first water, proving that there are still greater humbugs in England than himself, for which he is very sorry, he thinking that he was the Ne Plus Ultra in that particular line of business." The opening sentences of the part of his book called *The Magic of Spirit Rapping, Table Turning, &c., &c.,* give his opinions of the subject and are very much the language he used from the stage: "There could be no fitter appendix to a work on Modern Magic than one which should fully expose the greatest trick of the age as practiced by the most unprincipled of all jugglers. In no country, and at no time has a more absurd and remarkable delusion gained possession of the public mind than that which has been recently obtained under the names of 'Spirit Rapping,' 'Spiritualism,' or 'Spirit Manifestations'." Both the stage lecture and the book were completed by a very thorough exposure of mediumistic methods. John Henry Anderson, while on tour, had first studied spiritism in America and with his interest in the subject he naturally started after the American Davenports upon their arrival in England. He did reproduce their entire performance but without the smoothness which was shown by the Davenport Brothers. Furthermore at that time he did not expose the methods by which he accomplished the effects. Other magicians, among them Professor Redmond and Tolmaque, also duplicated the mysterious "Spirit Cabinet."

Before the exposure which really attracted public attention, however, the Davenport Brothers had a series of meetings with two Liverpool men named Hulley and Cummins. These gentlemen were of the opinion that in some manner the Davenports were able to release themselves after being tied with the ropes. When the Brothers came to Liverpool they therefore used a special knot to tie them. According to the *London Telegraph*, soon after the tying "commenced, one of the Brothers complained he was being hurt. Doctor Ferguson cut the rope, and soon after, the other brother made a similar complaint and Doctor Ferguson cut that rope, too; and he and the brothers disappeared from the platform." A riot was then started by the audience, the cabinet was smashed to bits and taken as souvenirs, the police were called and the evening ended by the theater returning every one's money. ·

Hulley and Cummins followed the Davenports to Huddersfield and taught what they called their "Tom Fool's Knot" to other men. Again no performance, again a riot and the returning of admission fees. The same thing happened when the Brothers went to Leeds. The tom fool's knot received considerable publicity as did the disorders in the theaters. The Davenport Brothers decided it was time to tour the Continent.

The Davenports and Fay, or as the bills of that time read "The Davenport Brothers and Mr. Fay," went first to France. The opening performance in the Salle Herz of Paris was similar to those at Liverpool and Leeds for the cabinet was smashed, a riot took place, and the theater refunded the money. The Davenports and Fay followed this fiasco by a special, private, and very successful séance for the Parisian press and the newspaper accounts helped to restore confidence in the two Americans. From then on their Continental tour was a success. It was quite fashionable to visit the Davenport séances to see the "startling wonders and mysterious displays." The Brothers claimed to have appeared before the Emperor of the French, the Czar of Russia, and the Kings of Belgium, Holland, and Prussia, in their respective palaces before they returned to England in the spring of 1868. It seems quite well established that they had appeared for these command performances and that later they also appeared before Queen Victoria.

It is not to be imagined that the Davenports and Fay

had completely easy sailing during their Continental triumphs for Robert-Houdin, the leading magician of France, made a detailed study and just as detailed an exposé in his posthumously published book *Magie et Physique Amusante*, pages 203–264. When the Davenports arrived in France Robert-Houdin was in retirement but his dislike of sham and his keen interest in trickery made him study the tricks of the Americans. He had put his brother-in-law in his Theatre Robert-Houdin after having done as well as he could to make a magician out of the man. Hamilton was the man's name and though he had been taught to do Robert-Houdin's performance he had none of the technical skill, background, or comprehension, of the master. Hamilton wrote a letter to the Davenports in which he said: "The phenomena surpassed my expectations, and the experiments are full of interest for me. I consider it my duty to add that they are inexplicable." I realize that it will be hard for the reader to accept that even today Spiritualists are using that letter as proof of the Davenports' mediumistic abilities. One believer quotes the letter and follows it with the remark, "There are some honest, truthful magicians in the world, after all."

The great value of Robert-Houdin's treatise of the Davenport Brothers' mysteries lay first in recording and exposing in the correct order the most minute details of the performance and second in describing clearly the methods and the psychology by which it was possible to do the tricks while seemingly permitting the audience to control the conditions. The whole account is so complete and so clear that any skilled magician, by studying the book and after the requisite practice, could perform every one of the mysteries of the Davenports.

The "perfectly serious" and perhaps completely confused Doctor T. L. Nichols wrote: "A biography of the Brothers Davenport," which contains an account of the early part of their European tour. Doctor Nichols, by the way, succeeded the Reverend Ferguson as lecturer with the Davenports. It has been said that Nichols did not have the minister's simple faith and, as a matter of fact, was fully cognizant of the Brothers' trickery. If the spiritualists will read that book only they can still claim the Davenports to be true mediums. If any one is really interested, however, I suggest that he read Robert-Houdin's writings. Those who do not read French will find that Louis Hoffmann made an excellent translation which was published under the title, "Robert-Houdin's Secrets of Stage Magic and Conjuring."

Back in England the Davenports and Fay ran into two pairs of antagonists who really influenced public opinion to a great extent. As a matter of fact every one accepted the Davenports merely as clever tricksters with the exception of a few who with complete disregard of facts continued to prefer to believe in spirits.

One of these exposures to attract the interest of the public was made by Sir Henry Irving and Edward A. Sothern and several members of their company. Sir Henry termed the Davenports' performance a "shameful imposture" and determined to discredit them by the ridicule of a burlesque of their work. The first time the actors gave their mock exhibition was in a club in Manchester.

At popular request the performance was repeated for the public in the Library Hall of the Athenæum of the same city. With his great skill at make-up Sir Henry became the double of the Reverend Ferguson. He assumed the minister's deportment and manner of speaking. His opening speech follows:

"Ladies and Gentlemen—In introducing to your notice the remarkable phenomena which have attended the gentlemen, who are not brothers, who are about to appear before you, I do not deem it necessary to offer my observations upon their extraordinary manifestations. I shall therefore at once commence a long rigmarole for the purpose of distracting your attention, and filling your intelligent heads with perplexity. I need not tell this enlightened audience that the manifestations they are about to witness are produced by occult power, the meaning of which I don't clearly understand, but, we simply bring before your notice facts, and from these you must form your own conclusions. Concerning the early life of these gentlemen, columns of the most uninteresting descriptions could be written; I will mention one or two interesting facts connected with these remarkable men, and for the truth of which I personally vouch. In early life, one of them, to the perfect unconcern of everybody else, was constantly and most unconsciously floating about his peaceful dwelling in the arms of his amiable nurse, while, on other occasions, he was frequently tied with invisible hands to his mother's apron strings. Peculiarities of a like nature were exhibited by his companion, whose acquaintance with various Spirits commenced many years ago, and has increased to the present moment with pleasure to himself and profit to others. These gentlemen have not been celebrated throughout the vast continent of America, they have not astonished the civilized world, but they have travelled in various parts of this glorious land—the land of Bacon—and are about to appear in a phase in your glorious city of Manchester. Many really sensible and intelligent individuals seem to think that the requirement of darkness seems to infer trickery. So it does. But I will strive to convince you that it does not. Is not a dark chamber essential to the process of photography? And what would we reply to him who would say 'I believe photography is a humbug, do it all in the light and we will believe otherwise'? It is true we know why darkness is essential to the production of a sun picture; and if scientific men will subject these phenomena to analysis, they will find why darkness is essential to our manifestations. But we don't want them to find out, we want them to avoid a common-sense view of the mystery. We want them to be blinded by our puzzle, and to believe with implicit faith in the greatest humbug in the nineteenth century."

E. A. Sothern and two other actors, with great fidelity of make-up, appeared as the Davenport Brothers and Fay and reproduced accurately the entire performance. I have never seen an account of this performance by England's leading actors mentioned in the writings of the Spiritualists but probably they dismiss this reproduction of the tricks as they do so many others by saying that the manifestations did not take place with the rapidity of the true phenomena.

Another explanation was given for the excellent performance of Maskelyne and Cooke who carried on their reproduction of the Davenports' trickery for many years not only in the provinces but in London. Benjamin Coleman, noted among Spiritualists, wrote that Maskelyne and Cooke were "very powerful mediums, who find it much more profitable to pander to the prejudices of the multitude by pretending to expose Spiritualism than by honestly taking their proper place in our ranks as spiritual media." Mr. Coleman goes even further, "All inquirers who desire to study the psychological character of spirit manifestations should be recommended to visit Messrs. Maskelyne and Cooke, who have gone on practicing them with a perseverance worthy of a better aim, and who are now, in my opinion, the best of the living mediums for the production of strong physical manifestations. This statement, often repeated by me, has been met with the remark, 'But they themselves say they are not mediums'; as if what they say should influence the minds of any intelligent Spiritualist who sees what they do."

John Nevil Maskelyne was trained in mechanics and delicate work as a watchmaker and as an amateur magician was skilled in sleight-of-hand. He first saw the Davenports in the Town Hall in Cheltenham and discovered their methods. He attempted to denounce the Brothers at that time but no one else in the audience came with his training in trickery so as to know what to look for nor happened to see what he saw. Many people in the audience doubted Mr. Maskelyne's statement and therefore to demonstrate that he had spoken the truth he made a cabinet and with his friend Mr. Cooke practiced until they were in a position to duplicate everything which they had seen. Their demonstration excited the greatest interest and people in nearby towns asked that Maskelyne and Cooke put on a performance for them. They were so busy that they had to give up all other work. This, by the way, was the start of Maskelyne's Mysteries which ran in London for more than fifty years. The great grandson of John Nevil Maskelyne is one of England's most successful magicians now. His father was also most successful and each member of the family continues the family interest in exposing fraudulent mediums.

It will be quite understandable that with all they had gone through in England the Davenports' posters advertising their appearances in London the spring of 1868 carried the following sentence: "The Brothers Davenport and Mr. Fay have returned once more, and probably for the last time, to this Metropolis, where they will give a few Séances previous to their departure for the United States."

While the Davenports were abroad their sister Elizabeth Louise is said to have carried on the rope tying business in America.

On their return voyage the Davenports must have derived a great deal of satisfaction from reading and rereading Sir Richard Francis Burton's opinion of their demonstrations. "I have spent a great part of my life in Oriental lands, and have seen there many magicians," said Sir Richard. He also said he had witnessed the demonstrations of several magicians claiming to duplicate the mysteries and gave as his belief that they did not even attempt what the Messrs. Davenport and Fay succeeded in doing. He finished by saying, "Finally I have read and listened to every explanation of the Davenport 'tricks' hitherto placed before the English public, and, believe me, if anything would make me take that tremendous jump 'from matter to spirit,' it is the utter and complete unreason of the reasons by which the 'manifestations' are explained."

Back in America business was more profitable than when they had left in spite of the number of those who had learned that the mysteries of the Davenports' program were mainly due to the knowledge which they had of getting the committee to tie them in a manner whereby they not only could release themselves but could get back into their restraints in a twinkling of an eye. The darkness made no more difficulty to their manipulations than darkness would hinder a violinist in playing the instrument. However it made it seem harder and kept the audience from seeing what went on and darkness makes everything eerie.

Three years after the Davenports had begun their second tour of the United States they arrived in La Crosse, Wisconsin. There, needing an advance manager for their performances, they engaged an alert twenty-two-year old magician named Harry Kellar who needed money to be able to get enough equipment together for a bigger show.

With Kellar's knowledge of magic it was but a short time before he was perfectly aware of the details of the Davenports' work. Furthermore Kellar and Fay became close friends, and through him Kellar learned about those points in the work which came up only occasionally when there were antagonistic committees.

Soon Kellar became not only advance man but also manager and assistant. He related shortly before his death an incident which happened at that time. "We were giving a dark séance," said Mr. Kellar; "the Brothers were sitting on chairs at the front of the hall. The front row of spectators joined hands, not so much to prevent assistance from reaching the mediums, which was the ostensible reason for this arrangement, as to keep inquisitive strangers from causing trouble. The boys were tied to their chairs, a committee from the audience having attended to that detail. Ira Davenport had slipped his hands out of the knots and was manipulating the tambourines when he ventured too near the front row and one young chap caught him by the shoulder. 'I've got him!' the excited captor shouted, 'I've got him! Fetch a light!' Quick as lightning Ira slipped off his coat and leaving it in the young man's hands, darted back to his chair and slipped his hands in the knots again. 'Light the gas,' called Ira. It was lighted, and he was found securely tied. His coat was in the young man's hands. 'My friend here,' continued Davenport coolly, 'thought he had me. You see he was mistaken; he simply had my coat. If he had me, why didn't he keep me? You may notice, I have not left the chair. How could I? The truth of the matter is, the spirits took off my coat and carried it over to him.' The audience went wild, and the young fellow hunted a hole in the floor to crawl into. The accident suggested one of the best tricks the Davenports ever did. After that Ira would take off his coat, put it on his

[68]

boot, slip his hands into the knots and call for a light. As it flashed through the hall he would kick his coat into the air, and there it would be discovered. The effect of coming from darkness into light and beholding a coat in mid-air several yards above the floor was simply marvellous to the uninitiated."

William Davenport was very fond of a dog and a monkey he took about with him as pets. One day he told Kellar to take the animals into the Pullman car. "It can't be done, Bill," said Kellar, "the conductor will make you put them into the baggage car." Davenport answered, "You do as I tell you, Harry. You might as well understand right now that you're my servant." Kellar in describing the incident said, "I quit the concern there and then and, what is more, Bill Fay went with me."

"Fay and Kellar" toured Cuba, Mexico, and down through South America. The second half of their program was a duplication of the Davenports' séance which, however, was offered as trickery. The tour was most successful and the partners made forty thousand dollars clear within eight months. Upon their return to this country Kellar had more than enough money to start with a big show to tour the country and later the world. I knew Kellar well and though he regretted while he was with the Davenports having to live under the fake pretense of spiritism he never regretted the opportunity to study the mediums from behind the scenes and to learn the complete humbuggery of their work. I saw Kellar's presentation of the Davenport cabinet.

After his return from his Latin-American tour William

Fay rejoined the Davenports and made another foreign tour with them. This trip took them around a great part of the Eastern Hemisphere. In Melbourne, Australia, William Henry Harrison Davenport died on July 1, 1877. William Fay settled in Australia a wealthy man and Ira Erastus returned to the United States where he lived quietly in the country for eighteen years.

In 1895 William Fay left Australia and rejoined Ira Erastus Davenport and in the spring they started out on tour again. The revival was not successful and after appearing in only a few cities they gave up. Fay returned to Melbourne and Davenport to his retirement.

My close friend the late Harry Houdini in his book *A Magician Among the Spirits* told about visiting Ira Erastus Davenport and about their talks. Ira Erastus made no pretense to Houdini whatsoever. They talked merely as two men in the same line of business would talk. Each related experiences to the other and Davenport explained his method of getting out of ropes and in again. Davenport also told Houdini that there was not an iota of truth in the levitation and similar stories. Ira Erastus in his old age lived in retirement at Maysville, Chautauqua County, New York, with his daughter Zellie. He died on July 8, 1911.

CHAPTER IV

SLATES, LIGHTS, AND GUSTS OF WIND

*I*F ONE reads the really enormous volume of material published about mediumistic efforts he will find a vast amount of data to substantiate whatever opinion he holds when he begins. But, when a person with no preconceived opinion studies the subject, he finds a bewildering mass of disjointed and confusing statements. As these statements do not agree even, quite frequently, in two accounts published at different times by one writer, the unprejudiced reader finds he cannot accept them all as facts. When a man states that he is an honest person writing no more and no less than everything which occurred, and then does not even agree with another individual's written account on such a detail as the date of the recorded incident, what is the reader to believe? His task is made even more difficult when he discovers that the second person also has a record for being honest and diligent in his recording. The only possible conclusion is that those who write on psychic subjects do not have sufficient knowledge of the matter to write a factual account; that they permit prejudice and wishful thinking to color their reports, or that they write with a total disregard for truth. One studying the subject soon reaches the point where he believes there has been a great deal of ignorance, of unreasonable predilection, and of premeditated deception by those who have written on the realm of the spirits. He also believes that the conscious and unconscious misrepresentation has been done by both the believers and the scoffers. He is then in the quandary of deciding what he can do to get at the facts for it is quite obvious that taking a middle course between two inaccurate records is an unlikely way to discover truth.

It seems to me that there should be a few rules regarding the acceptance of mediumistic phenomena. For instance when a medium is detected in fraud it may be the correct attitude to attribute such deception to an over-zealous inclination to have something happen. But to ask that a medium be trusted who has been found time and again to practice trickery depending on a skillful technic resulting from lengthy practice is to ask a blind faith few can give. It seems to me that it would be fair to assume that once a medium is detected in cheating, safeguards may with justice be made to discourage that particular kind of sham, and that upon being detected several times in trickery it may be assumed that at such times as the medium was not caught it was because the investigators were not adept enough at discovering the methods used. It would also appear just, after a medium has been detected several times in practiced deception, to accept as fact a confession by that medium that all phenomena had

been brought about by trickery, even when none was detected. It is hard to accept the viewpoint that a medium
lies in confessing trickery at times when it has not been
discovered, but is almost always a person of veracity during the dark of a séance.

Margaret and Katherine Fox were detected in physical
trickery more than once. They both publicly admitted
that everything was accomplished by practice and skill,
and taught their methods to others. People alive today,
of unquestionable integrity, attended both the confessions
and the lessons. This has been brought out above quite
fully. Likewise it has been shown that the Davenport
Brothers were merely stage mystifiers to whom the public,
after a little urging by the hired lecturers, were quick to
attribute spirit aid. It would seem, at first glance, that
those who witnessed the work of either the sisters or the
brothers must have been simple-minded as well as fantastically credulous to have accepted the work of either
pair as proof of the return of souls from the spirit world.
As a matter of fact it has been said time and again by the
disbelievers that such believers are fools. Name-calling is
frequent on both sides, it is found in reading about the
subject; and the believer's vocabulary contains not only
the words *fraud* and *fool* but all their synonyms. It would
be a simple matter to come to a decision upon the subject
were all the followers upon either side simple-minded.
Such, however, is not the case, for brilliant minds are
found on both sides. It may be said merely that the simple-
minded disbeliever who in his disbelief stays away from
mediums is less apt to be noticed than the simple-minded

believer who, sitting in the front row at a séance, gasps, "Isn't it too wonderful," to the most flagrant deceit.

If bright people accept the work of the Foxes and the Davenports as genuine demonstrations of the visitation of spirits, even though their tricky methods are well known, what is the reason? That question brings up a point which must be understood before anything else in the subject becomes understandable. It is one of the basic principles in the practice of deception, whether that deception be used to fleece the unwary at cards or in the séance room, or legitimately, by a magician, to entertain in a theater. The principle is that, to avoid detection, more than one method must be used. These different methods need not be followed in systematic rotation, and indeed it is better that one method be used now, another then. In this manner a person who visits several séances by one medium will see some particular demonstration given under circumstances which the particulars of some later exposure will not satisfy.

For instance the Fox Sisters made raps not only with their toes but also by tapping with their fingers, as well as bouncing an apple on a string. Those three ways are not all by any means, for remember that for part of their lives not only were the sisters together, but Leah also travelled in their company. If one were watched too closely another made the raps. Again it will be discovered in the records that Margaret and Katherine both held séances in company with other mediums, and it is testified that these mediums would on occasion also rap to confuse the investigators. It is also well known that certain spectators, probably through an eagerness for a good demonstration, will now and again make raps in their own corners of the room.

Again with the work of the Davenports it was a matter of a variety of methods. Under usual conditions these men could get the committeeman who was tying them to their chairs to use a system from which release was practically instantaneous. Other less agreeable individuals would have ideas of their own in tying. The Brothers would then depend upon the fact that it is practically impossible to tie a person to a chair with one long rope, for enough slack can be obtained to get one hand, at least, free. William Fay, rather than strain too hard when he was tied too securely, would reach in his hip pocket (the hands were always tied behind), and get a knife and cut his bonds. That is not easy, but, when it is remembered that the wrists, not the hands, were tied, and that the wrist bends in all directions, it is much more simple than it would seem. Once having freed his arms, Fay would continue to slash the rope. When released completely from his bonds he would pocket the knife and the short bits of rope, and bring forth a duplicate of the original rope which he always carried with him for emergencies. When the lights were turned on, the rope, without a knot, would be seen flying through the air. It was believed the spirits untied him.

The Davenports also had several ways of getting an arm free when sitting outside of the cabinet and being held by a spectator. In the first place the spectator, with but two hands, could not hold the men in their chairs and at the same time hold their hands. It therefore seemed quite sensible that he put his hands upon their heads to see that they did not rise from their seats or move their bodies. The Davenports then, to show that they did not use their hands, would each clasp one of his arms near his shoulder with both their hands. Through the heavy cloth of a man's coat one hand can be made to feel like two. Each brother would therefore be able to free one hand. With one hand each they could do a variety of quite perplexing things. But that method was only used when they had no choice of a committeeman. Usually they did have a choice and at such times he would be a confederate. A number of things immediately become less miraculous when it is known that at times the Davenports employed as many as ten confederates. It was a night when a confederate was used that Alexander Herrmann (the stage magician known as Herrmann the Great) described in an article in the *Cosmopolitan Magazine*. The performance was being given in Ithaca, New York, and many Cornell College students were in the audience. They had brought "pyrotechnic balls so made as to ignite suddenly with a bright light." When the lights were struck the Davenports were found to be on opposite sides of the stage waving musical instruments around in the air. Most of their performance depended upon the belief by the audience that the committeemen were of good faith. Frequently they were, and the Davenports had ways to circumvent their scrutiny; but when confederates were used miracles happened.

When the stories about the Fox Sisters and their rappings had been generally published around the world, others came forward to announce that they too could call upon spirits to rap out answers to questions. Others too found spirits willing to ring bells and do all the other things which the press had reported occurred with the Davenports. At one time, so it is estimated, there was a medium who could get signs of spirit presence in every town in this country, in many villages, and a hundred or more in each of several cities. There were more mediums in America, the birthplace of spiritism, than anywhere else, but it is surprising how fast they sprang up and multiplied in the rest of the world. To go into detail as to the mechanical, electrical, and physical methods used by those mediums who were exposed would in itself fill a large volume. Furthermore by the time the book was published there could be one or more new methods to make the material incomplete. I have no thought of giving a detailed description of technic, but a brief list of some ways by which fraudulent mediums have produced their effects will show the possibilities of imposture.

One of the methods used generally to produce raps was with a confederate either in the room as one of the sitters or in an adjoining room. If the confederate was in the room he might himself make the raps with his knuckles on a chair, table or the wall, or he might, as one of those supposedly holding the hands of the medium, merely be an inactive confederate.

If the medium worked alone and was a woman (which was generally the case in this type of work), she could carry a light stick sewed into the material of her skirt.

The stick would be at the side of the skirt, and would run from the hem to the hips. With this stick—skirt and all—a medium could rap on a table a couple of feet away from where she sat.

One of the methods frequently used required but a slight alteration in an ordinary electric bell. What is called "the make-and-break" was detached. This change made the bell knocker hit but once for each time the button was pressed. The bell, of course, was removed, and the bell mechanism screwed about the room so that the knocker would hit upon wood. Usually the electric wire ran under the carpet, and a special switch was used to enable the medium to operate it with her foot. Often, however, confederates were used to press the switch. Obviously some of these methods could be used only where the medium had the run of the house.

There was also designed a much smaller mechanism than the regular home bell although it operated on the same magnetic principle. This would be put in the leg of a table which had been especially hollowed out for the purpose. At times this was operated by a gravity switch. This meant that tipping the table slightly would make the connection. There were still other designs of electrically operated rapping mechanisms, and a variety of switches. One for instance was so constructed that raps would occur, at the proper intervals to be impressive, for as long as the electric contact button was held down. This eliminated the necessity for movement with each rap.

Another means for getting raps at a distance from the medium was with a weight on the end of a string. The string would be hung over the rung of a chair or the brace connecting table legs. Jerking and releasing the string, which of course could not be seen in the dark, would make the weight rap on the floor.

One of the most interesting of the mechanical means used to produce raps is but very little larger than a box for safety matches. It had to be constructed by a skilled chronometer-maker, and was similar to the striking mechanism of a clock; and as a clock repeats the twelve hours again and again until it runs down, so this mechanism repeats the raps. It is made to give a set series of varying numbers of raps, and once the series has been run through it gives them all over again. It is amazing how easy it is to memorize the sequence and to ask questions to which the raps will be fitting answers. In the dark this automatic rapper is put on some flat wooden surface about the room, and retrieved and pocketed just before the light is turned on at the end of the séance. I own one of these mechanisms, but have never been able to obtain one of the still smaller models enclosed in a tiny wooden box upon which the raps are made. The advantage of this rapper, according to the medium who showed it to me, is that it can be left in the pocket. He had his hidden in a package of cigarettes, which, in case he was searched before the séance, he would take from his pocket and, with his change and his wallet, place in full view on a table as if to aid the committee. He, of course, refilled his pockets after the search.

No matter where the rapping sounds actually are made the sitters will believe that they come from the table-top, the mantel, or whatever place, or direction, their attention is directed to. In the dark it is impossible to determine the spot from which a sound comes.

A variety of other methods for producing raps might be mentioned, but the above several, I believe, will suffice to show how difficult it would be to know definitely that raps heard in the dark were not produced by human agency.

One of the earliest of those to produce spirit raps was Daniel Dunglas Hume. His manifestations were not limited to raps, but with a few exceptions they were quite similar to those of other mediums of the time. He had the greatest of success, but in all probability he was distinguished more for his social adroitness than for his manifestations. He did everything he could to dissociate himself from other mediums; as a matter of fact he had little but denunciation for any of them except Katherine Fox. He wrote a book expressing great hatred for fraudulent phenomena, and explaining at some length the methods by which they could be produced. He divided fraudulent mediums into three types: charlatans who "find it profitable to impose themselves . . . upon credulous spiritualists"; persons really possessing mediumistic power, but "who, being utterly unprincipled, rather prefer to cheat than not, and who will, therefore, lie and deceive, even when no encouragement exists to do so"; and another group of real mediums who "when much tempted, resort to fraud." The book raised a storm in the Spiritualist press; many mediums hated Hume; but none returned the accusation of fraud. There were those outside Spiritualism who declared that Hume too was a trickster, but no one ever offered proof during—or even after—one of his séances that he resorted to any subterfuge whatsoever.

Hume was an immigrant Scotch lad who heard raps and saw manifestations in the town of Norwich, Connecticut, not long after the Fox Sisters had begun. In his autobiography he tells of having seen at Troy, New York, the departed spirit of a playmate named Edwin, who had just died at Norwich. The rappings, table-tippings and moving chairs so annoyed Hume's aunt, with whom he lived, that she turned out the local ministry—Baptist, Congregationalist, and Methodist—to pray over the boy. They did their best to drive out the devil which they felt sure was in him, but were rudely interrupted by further raps. Before calling in the three ministers to pray over Daniel, his aunt had tried the experiment of throwing a chair at him when raps occurred in the kitchen. After the three ministers had failed, she threw Daniel's Sunday suit from the window, and pushed him out of the house. This was unkind on her part, but at the same time it was the real beginning of an almost fabulous career.

Hume was born at Currie, near Edinburgh, on March 20, 1833, the son of humble working people. His father took too much to drink, and Daniel was adopted by his aunt, Mrs. Mary McNeil Cook, who took him to Norwich, Connecticut, at the age of ten. His mother also came over, but settled in Troy, New York.

The boy was nervous and delicate, and according to his own story always more interested in religion, dreams and visions, than in birds'-nesting or mumbly-peg. After the death of his young friend Edwin he did not have another major vision until 1850, when he learned in this way that his mother had died.

Hume's first step into the great world was not the proper omen for a romantic career: he went to the little mill town of Willimantic, to stay with a friend. Here he met a Mr. and Mrs. Hayden, who had set up in business as regular mediums. They naturally took an interest in the young man, who was delicate-looking, attractive if not handsome, and of a likeable disposition, though inordinately vain.

It seems to me that this first professional step in the life of a medium is almost the most interesting stage of all; but unfortunately one can scarcely ever get at the real truth about it. Hume, for instance, was not an object of public interest beyond a small group of believers in eastern Connecticut, and there is little evidence concerning his life there outside his own writings, which, if not worthless, are at least hardly more dependable than the attacks of his enemies.

Two descriptions, both written later, are all we have to go on for the external appearance of Hume's youth—one from a neighbor: "He was in those days a local celebrity, and journeyed from town to town, giving séances. I remember him as a tall, heavy-faced, awkward, reddish-haired stripling, with the lost expression of countenance that physicians ordinarily associate with the epileptic malady." The other is from Calvin Stowe, Harriet Beecher Stowe's husband: "Hume spent his boyhood in my father's native town, among my relatives and acquaintances, and he was a disagreeable, nasty boy. But he certainly has qualities which science has not yet explained."

However we may imagine his apprenticeship to the Haydens, he was born with or somehow acquired a wisdom, a precaution which carried him far beyond them. It was Hume's distinction that he never directly took fees, and that he moved in the most aristocratic circles, beside the fact he was never publicly caught out in his sittings.

Hume always protected himself admirably in two ways. In the first place, he said that he had no part in the manifestations; he could neither cause nor stop them, nor influence them in any way. This meant that there might be séances with no results at all—as on various occasions there were. In the second place, since his sittings were all private gatherings, open by invitation only, and with no fee, he could choose his sitters. Any one who was obstreperous or hostile was quite truly abusing the hospitality of Hume and his hosts.

From his local Connecticut stage, Hume graduated into a circle in New York, where he was soon investigated by a committee consisting of William Cullen Bryant, Professor Robert Hare, of the University of Pennsylvania (the inventor of the blow-torch, and a noted scientist), and Judge J. W. Edmonds, who had been one of the mainstays of the Fox Sisters. These three celebrities declared themselves satisfied that everything was genuine— the raps, the table that tipped without spilling off what was on it, and the rest of the repertoire. Even before this time a Connecticut circle reported that they had seen (in total darkness) Hume "levitated," with his feet a foot off the floor; an elaboration of this was later Hume's most famous manifestation.

Hume had two separate offers to pay for his education for the Swedenborgian ministry, but both he declined because, as he afterward said, a wider and more useful sphere was his as a medium. About 1855, however, he began to show symptoms of tuberculosis, and his doctors agreed that he must go to Europe. Upon this his friends, headed by Professor George Bush, a Swedenborgian, subscribed the cost of sending him to England.

In March, 1855, the sickly young man landed in Liverpool. He changed his name from Hume to Home, emphasizing a relationship which he claimed to the Earl of Home. In London he went to a hotel in Jermyn Street, run by a Mr. William Cox, who had also been host to Mrs. Hayden. Cox was a believer, and he put up Home free of charge.

As a sign of gratitude Home held a séance the evening of his arrival. There were raps, the table turned, and a picture fell off the wall. Apparently no one thought to notice whether it broke. Cox was convinced especially by seeing two decanters where there was but one before.

He was so much impressed, in fact, that he arranged a séance for Lord Brougham, the moving spirit of the Society for the Promotion of Useful Knowledge and other popular-education movements. Lord Brougham asked if he might bring along Sir David Brewster, the well-known Scottish scientist, author of *Letters on Natural Magic*.

Brewster's description of the séance is a good one to quote, since he was by no means prejudiced in Home's favor:

"Mr. Cox, who knows Lord Brougham, wished him to have a séance, and his Lordship invited me to accompany him, in order to assist him in finding out the trick.

"We four sat down at a moderately sized table, the structure of which we were invited to examine. In a short time the table shuddered, and a tremulous motion ran up all our arms; at our bidding these motions ceased and returned.

"The most unaccountable rappings were produced in various parts of the table, and the table actually rose when no hand was upon it. An accordion was held in Lord Brougham's hand and gave out a single note. But the experiment was a failure; it would not play, either in his hand or mine.

"A small hand-bell was then laid down, with its mouth on the carpet, and, after lying there for some time, it actually rang when nothing could have touched it. The bell was then placed on the other side, still upon the carpet, and it came over to me and played by itself in my hand. It did the same to Lord Brougham.

"These were the principal experiments. We could give no explanation of them; and could not conjecture how they could be produced by any kind of mechanism. . . . The object of asking Lord Brougham and me seems to have been to get our favourable opinion of the exhibition, but, though neither of us can explain what we saw, we do not believe that it was the work of idle spirits."

Before this was published Home and his adherents rashly stated in print that Sir David was a convert. To this Brewster replied that he had seen a number of "mechanical conundrums" which he could not explain, but that he had no notion that they were of spirit origin, and he wound up by saying in a letter to *The Morning Advertiser* that Home "insults religion and common sense, and tampers with the most sacred feelings of his victims." There is certainly some justice in the Spiritualists's complaint of Brewster; if he thought the matter so important, he should have continued his investigations until he did find out the trick, or was convinced.

Several of the scientists who squabbled with Home did their cause an ill turn in similar fashion, declining to investigate because they thought their time worth more than even the discovery of possible genuine phenomena. Home's adversaries were prominent and rather numerous, including Robert Browning, Faraday, Anthony and Thomas Adolphus Trollope, Professor Tyndall, G. H. Lewes, and Thomas Huxley; but in general they were content to abuse without exposing him, which certainly was a poor service to mankind. It was Huxley who said: "Supposing the phenomena to be genuine, they do not interest me." On the one or two occasions when it is claimed that Home was detected in fraud, the investigators were persons of considerably less eminence.

Against his list of opponents, Home could show converts or sympathizers such as, among others, Mrs. Trollope, Elizabeth Barrett Browning, Sir Edward Bulwer-Lytton, Robert Chambers (the Edinburgh publisher and popular writer, author of *Vestiges of Natural Creation*), Charles Lever the novelist, Robert Dale Owen, Napoleon III and Empress Eugenie, Sir William Barrett, the scientist, the physicist William Crookes, and Alfred Russel Wallace, co-propounder with Darwin of the theory of evolution. Alexandre Dumas was best man at one of Home's weddings; John Bright, the great reformer, was at least half convinced; Victorien Sardou, the French dramatist, and John Ruskin supported the King of the Mediums.

The members of this distinguished troop, however, did little more for Home than the stiff-necked rationalists did against him; their investigations were conducted in such a way as to make the charge of gullibility an easy one. Crookes and Wallace, in particular, who were Home's mainstays, conducted test séances which were satisfactory to them as physicist and biologist, but which were a long way from satisfying his opponents that the possibilities of conjuring were cut off.

In short, Home's manifestations were explicable by elementary trickery, but it was never proven that he used the methods he could have used. This leaves him to the present day the football of writers on spiritism, who paint him now as a saint, now as a cheap crook.

It seems to me that he obviously was no saint, and that if he was a crook he certainly was not a cheap crook. He was an adventurer in the grand manner, the darling of kings, expelled by the police, successively Presbyterian, Methodist, Congregationalist, Roman and finally Greek Catholic, refusing fees, cherishing a fortune in jewelry— in short, the medium was more interesting than his spirits.

After his initial triumphs, paced by a stay as Bulwer-Lytton's guest at Knebworth (which resulted in his introduction to the Brownings, and in his gaining one bitter and noisy enemy and one devoted supporter), Home went to Italy as the guest of a Mr. Rymer. Rymer was a prosperous convert, and Home accompanied his son to Italy. In Florence, Home stayed a good deal of the time at Mrs. Trollope's villa, and Mrs. Trollope tried to entice Charles Dickens to a séance. Dickens refused haughtily, and afterward took pleasure in printing attacks on Home in his magazine, *Household Words*.

At one séance in Florence, Home caused a piano on which Countess Orsini was playing to rise suddenly in the air. Some of his other manifestations, escaping from rope-ties, making water puff out smoke, and the like, are testimony to his skill more at dissociating himself from conjurers and jugglers than at giving unimpeachable manifestations.

The row with Brewster occurred while Home was in Italy, and toward the end of his stay there an interruption occurred in his mediumship. He could get no manifestations at all. Home himself attributed it to some fault of his own for which the spirits wished to punish him; he sought solace, as more intellectual men have done, in the Roman Church. He was baptized by a Jesuit on Easter Monday, 1856, in Rome. Pope Pius IX granted him an interview, and gave him a special blessing. It is odd, since Spiritualism and Catholicism have always been deadly enemies, that not only Home but Doctor and Mrs. Thomas Low Nichols, leading Spiritualists, should have maintained simultaneously their Spiritualism and their Roman conversion.

Soon after his conversion Home went to Paris, where his mediumistic power suddenly returned full force. Incidentally, it has not often been remarked that if Home was nothing whatever but a cheap swindler, it was strange that he should deliberately abstain from his only means of livelihood for close to a year. There are stories that just before being received into the Church he entertained the idea of entering a monastic order; and possibly the disappearance of his mediumship and his temporary religious change of heart were related as effect and cause.

When his mediumship returned, Home began to use it at once, despite a vigorous wrangle with his confessor and with the Church. There are vague stories that he had some connection with Madame Blavatsky* at this period; but there is nothing vague about his success at the court of Napoleon III.

He made his début at a command performance where he got messages from Napoleon, Marie Antoinette, Queen Hortense, Rousseau, Pascal, and St. Louis of France. After this flying start he gave a long series of séances for the Imperial family, with such guests as the King of Bavaria, the Grand Duchess of Baden, and the Duchess of Hamilton.

He followed the court to Saint Cloud and Fontainebleau, and then to Biarritz. All this time he was building up a complete ascendancy over the Empress, which made

*The records show that at least at one time Mme. Blavatsky was a bitter enemy of Home. I have heard, but cannot verify, a story that Mme. Blavatsky had been a medium professionally in Brooklyn, New York, before founding the Theosophical Society. She definitely had lived in Brooklyn, and her writings contain many references to mediums and their phenomena. She, however, attributed many of the manifestations of the séance to elementals rather than to spirits.

him an object of detestation to every one else at court.
The newspapers lampooned him. Count Walewski, the
Foreign Minister, thought he was a Prussian spy, and
finally the Emperor himself put his foot down. France
buzzed with gossip as to why he suddenly decided to leave
for America.

It was while he was at Biarritz that he came closest to
out-and-out exposure, though even this was reported at
second hand. Doctor Barthez, the Emperor's private physician, took an immediate dislike to Home, whom he
thought a dissembler, and in a letter to his wife he reported
that Home was detected. Baron Morio, one of the guests,
he said, saw that Home had removed one foot from his
shoe (he wore elastic-sided, or Congress, boots), and that
the toe of his sock was cut off so that he could manipulate
things with his toes. After this, Barthez says, Home
claimed he was ill, but when Barthez examined him there
was nothing really the matter at all. Without examining
the originals of Barthez's letters it would be hard to come
to any solid conclusion—except that the method of trickery which he mentions is thoroughly practicable, and was
used by Harry Houdini in his stage exposures of spiritist
frauds.

Home let it be thought that he was going to America
to fetch over his young sister to be educated at the Empress's expense, but he ended up by staying in Europe. In
the course of a tour he gave séances for the Kings of
Württemberg and Prussia and for the Queen of Holland,
who gave him a splendid diamond ring. From Belgium he
was ordered to Italy for his health.

In Rome he met an aristocratic Russian lady, Alexandrine de Kroll, who was both wealthy and a god-daughter of the Czar. She was a Spiritualist, and believed herself a medium. The combination was electric: the commoner, Home, received all the proper sanctions, and his engagement to the aristocrat was officially announced. She went to Russia to prepare for the wedding, while Home ventured back to Paris. Here he made the acquaintance of Alexandre Dumas. Dumas was always interested in Home, and this fact, combined with his desire to get material for a travel book, made him accompany Home to Russia for the wedding, as best man.

In St. Petersburg the two were of course entertained in Russian splendor by the bride's family, and Home gave a "command séance" at the Winter Palace before Czar Alexander II. The Czar was so much astonished at the performance that he gave Home a diamond ring as a wedding present.

The marriage was celebrated twice, once according to the Greek Catholic ceremonial, once according to the Roman.

Afterward Home gave a number of command séances for the Czar at Tsarskoe-Seloe, supposedly very successfully. A story was circulated by one of Home's enemies to the effect that the medium dematerialized a valuable chain of emeralds, which a policeman then found rematerialized in Home's tail-pocket. I must say that I do not believe this tale, first because no one so shrewd as Home, however dishonest, would take such a risk at such a time and in such company, second because on the birth of

Home's son the Czar sent the mother a ring, and acted as godfather at the child's christening.

With wife and child, Home went to England in the summer of 1859. Here he opposed a prominent new American medium, the Reverend Thomas Lake Harris, and went into a sort of temporary partnership with another, John Rollin Squire. This broke up because Squire got such messages as one beginning, "I do not wish to intrude myself upon you, gentlemen, but on another occasion I trust I shall add to your knowledge," and ending, "Pray allow me to thank you for your strict attention."

In the summer of 1860 Home visited Currie, his birthplace—something he had long wanted to do. After this he re-established himself in London, and here, at a séance for the Duke of Sutherland, he was levitated for the first time in Europe. The room was, it is true, so dark that the sitters could not see one another; but they felt Home's boots above their heads, and he left a pencil mark on the ceiling. Other mediums were known to "float" by putting their shoes on their hands, which they then waved, and by marking the ceiling with a pencil on the end of a rod.

At Mrs. Milner Gibson's he did it again. This is the description given by a journalist guest, Robert Bell, in Thackeray's *Cornhill Magazine:*

The room was darkened until "We could see, but scarcely distinguish, our hands upon the table." Then the blinds were pulled down, darkening everything still more. Then, Bell says, "I clutched a spirit hand, which went out like air in my grasp. It was palpable as any soft substance, velvet or pulp, but pressure reduced it to air." Other more common manifestations then followed. But then Home suddenly said that he was moving. "His voice was heard above our heads. He had risen from his chair to a height of four or five feet. . . . We watched in profound stillness, and saw his figure pass from one side of the window to the other. He hovered round the circle for several minutes and passed, this time perpendicularly, over our heads. I heard his voice behind me in the air. He now passed to the farthest extremity of the room, and we could judge by his voice of the altitude and distance he had attained. He had reached the ceiling, upon which he made a slight mark; and soon afterwards he descended and resumed his place at the table. An incident which occurred during this aerial passage, and imparted a strange solemnity to it, was that the accordion, which we supposed to be on the ground under the window close to us, played a strain of wild pathos in the air from the most distant corner of the room."

It is hardly necessary to suggest inflated gloves and the notorious fallibility of the ear in judging direction as possible explanations; but no one ever reported searching Home for the gloves.

Home's life for some time thereafter was eventful, but not important to the story of Spiritualism: his wife died, and he sued her relatives for some property which they claimed reverted to them; he wrote the first volume of his *Incidents in My Life*; he took up sculpture, and as a result found himself in Rome.

Within a month Home was expelled from Rome by the

police, with the approval of the Church, for mediumistic practices. Cardinal Matteuci told Home his book was on the *Index Expurgatorius,* and that a priest had been unfrocked for reading it. Home tried to get satisfaction through diplomatic and political channels, but failed at every turn; England did not care what had happened to her leading spirit medium.

England's poet, Browning, however, cared a good deal, and he wrote a poem of 2000 lines, *Mr. Sludge, the Medium,* devoted to abusing a thinly disguised Home and his dupes with every resource at his command.

Home then went on a quick trip to America; then back to Russia, where he appeared again before the Czar and the Grand Duke and Duchess Constantine (which casts further doubt on the emerald-stealing story); then he returned to London. Here he found a regular epidemic of other mediums, American and native. Evidently his own business was quiet, for he turned to giving dramatic readings and to the legitimate stage, at both of which he proved to be very good.

He returned to active work in Spiritualism by accepting the resident secretaryship of the newly founded Spiritual Athenæum, in Sloane Street (where the arch-charlatan Cagliostro had once lived). Home's friends had little difficulty in getting a hundred members of aristocracy, clergy, and rich bourgeoisie to chip in five guineas each per annum.

At the formal opening, in January, 1867, there was an exhibition of drawings by a Miss Georgina Houghton, who had done them under the guidance of the Archangel

Gabriel. One might sooner have expected a trumpet solo from a pupil of this teacher.

The Spiritual Athenæum was by no means a net gain to Home, for one of the early subscribers entangled him in an affair which brought him more bad publicity than anything else he ever did. This subscriber was a seventy-five-year-old widow, Mrs. Jane Lyon, who had an income of six thousand pounds a year, but took pleasure in rooming in a grubby neighborhood for thirty shillings a week. She was a Spiritualist, wanted to recall her dead husband, and so was sent to the Athenæum.

Home got a message from the late Mr. Lyon at the very first meeting, and Mrs. Lyon was overjoyed. She subscribed for six years' membership in the Athenæum in advance.

Soon Mr. Lyon reported that he wanted Mrs. Lyon to adopt Home as her son. Five days after the initial meeting, Mr. Lyon told Mrs. Lyon to settle £24,000 on Daniel. Home dumped Mrs. L. straight into a cab, and rushed off to the Bank of England to nail the matter down.

Mr. Lyon's next request was that his widow bequeath all her property to Home, and that Home should legally adopt the name of Home-Lyon. The will was drawn up in full form, signed and witnessed. The following morning, however, Mr. Lyon changed his mind, and sent Home a rapped message that the will was to be destroyed. He added that Mrs. Lyon was to give Home a birthday present of £6000, which she did forthwith. To make all shipshape, he specifically notified Mrs. Lyon that he did not want her to sit with any medium except "Daniel; he is the best medium on earth."

Then came a message that Mrs. Lyon was to execute a mortgage giving herself a life interest in another £30,000, the principal reverting to Home.

Mrs. Lyon, having decided to adopt Home, wrote him letters addressed to "My dearest Son," and signed, "Your affectionate Mother." Home replied in kind. He also took the legal steps necessary to change his name to Home-Lyon.

Then came the catastrophe that was bound to come. Home went to Malvern for the medical attention of a friend, Doctor Gully. He did not consult Mrs. Lyon, and she was much annoyed. Apparently he was really very sick, and she soon forgave him. In fact she gave him a latch-key to her rooms. But then Home made the mistake of going to Malvern again, and this time Mrs. Lyon consulted another medium, who got a message saying that Daniel was mercenary and untrustworthy.

In an instant Mrs. Lyon swung round. She demanded the return of everything she had given him. Home tried to pacify her, finally offering to relinquish the deed making him her heir on condition that she would leave him with the £30,000 she had given him, and allow him to resume his own name.

Even this she refused to do. She had him arrested to prevent his leaving England, and he was released only on giving up the deed; she also sued to recover the sums she had given him.

The suit was an enormous sensation—almost a "trial of

the century." The real center of the action was the question whether Spiritualism and its works could be accepted in a court of law. Practically, in other words, did spirits produce the messages to Mrs. Lyon, or did Home produce them?

That Mrs. Lyon acted freely under the instructions from the spirits Home could show: he had letters from her proving that the various gifts were made of her own free will, and all sorts of testimony that he had behaved with regularity. Mrs. Lyon also contradicted herself, committed bald perjury, and behaved in a way both vindictive and stupid.

But the question then obviously came to mind, if Home had not produced the messages, why should he refuse to return the money? Home claimed that Mrs. Lyon had turned against him because he would not let her go further than the relationship between mother and son. But if this was so, why had he accepted the money in the first place—unless he was willing to acquiesce? His standing in the public eye sank toward the bottom. His counsel produced forty affidavits of character, from persons ranging in rank from Robert Chambers to a housemaid, but the damage was done.

Furthermore the impression Home's statements produced on the judge, Vice-Chancellor Sir George Markham Giffard, was most damaging. Home said in court that he had been "bodily lifted up from the ground, in defiance of the law of gravity."

"Do you mean that you were carried into the air by supernatural agency?" Sir George asked. Home assented, and, as Horace Wyndham says in his biography of Home, "His Lordship nearly collapsed. It was as much as he could do to record the answer in his notes."

All in all, it was a pot-and-kettle situation; but if the pot was plainly a superstitious liar, the kettle was a spiritist, and had by admission received the money owing to messages produced by his own mediumship. While Vice-Chancellor Giffard began by saying that Mrs. Lyon's "innumerable misstatements had embarrassed the court and discredited much of her testimony," he characterized Spiritualism as "mischievous nonsense, well calculated, on the one hand, to delude the vain, the weak, the foolish, and the superstitious; and, on the other hand, to assist the prospects of the needy adventurer." On this basis he found that Home's gifts from Mrs. Lyon were "fraudulent and void and must accordingly be returned."

The uproar, the battle between most of the newspapers on the one side and the Spiritualist press and prominent believers on the other can be imagined. Home did not come out with his reputation in much better shape than did Mrs. Lyon, but one thing flatly established was the attitude of the British courts toward spiritism.

Home's greatest defeat was followed soon by his greatest triumph. Various sitters had previously reported his "levitation" to the extent of a foot or two. At his own home, Sir William Crookes, the physicist, whom Home used to call "William," asking to be treated just like a conjurer under suspicion, saw Home levitated eighteen inches, and passed his hands over, under, and around the floating medium. On other occasions he saw (presumably in full darkness) Home and his chair rise up at the table. Home would tuck up his feet, and hold his hands in the air. Mrs. Crookes too once believed she was raised. But the classic example of Home's levitation came in the presence of two noblemen, Lord Adare and the Master of Lindsay, and an officer, Captain Wynne.

There has been almost as much argument about this levitation as about the Lyon trial. It began among the witnesses themselves.

Lord Adare said the séance occurred at 5 Buckingham Gate on December 16, 1868. Lord Lindsay said it occurred at a house in Victoria Street on December 13. Lord Adare said "the light from the window was sufficient to enable us to distinguish each other, and to see the different articles of furniture." But he later remarked that the room, on the third floor, was 75 feet from the ground and away from the street light. Lord Lindsay says "the moon was shining full into the room."

The witnesses agreed that after an ordinary rapping séance Home went into the next room and opened the window. Lord Lindsay said there was no support of any kind outside the window, while Lord Adare wrote, "Outside each window is a small balcony or ledge nineteen inches deep, bounded by stone balustrades eighteen inches high." There was a sort of agreement that Home next floated in at the window of the room where the witnesses sat. They had their backs to the window, but Lindsay in the light of the moon saw Home's shadow on the wall as he stood upright outside the window. Lord Adare then went into the next room to shut the window from which Home had floated. "I remarked," he writes, "that the window was not raised a foot, and that I could not think how he had managed to squeeze through. He arose and said, 'Come and see.' I went with him; he told me to open the window as it was before; I did so, he told me to stand a little distance off; he went through the open space, head first, quite rapidly, his body being nearly horizontal and apparently rigid. He came in again feet foremost, and we returned to the other room. It was so dark I could not see clearly how he was supported outside. He did not appear to grasp, or rest upon the balustrade, but rather to be swung out and in."

It seemed to me advisable to check each statement, in so far as possible, of the gentlemen who were there. I therefore checked on the brilliance of that night's moon; and according to *The Nautical Almanac and Astronomical Ephemeris* for the year 1868, which was published by order of The Lords Commissioners of the Admiralty, the moon was brand new on December thirteenth. That meant that there could be but little moonlight that night; but there was also a note in the Almanac that the moon set at the same time as the sun set on that date, which, of course, meant that there would be absolutely no moonlight. It seems quite reasonable to suppose that gentlemen who did not know where they were, and the date upon which they went, and who saw things by the light of a new moon which had set may have erred in other details.

The interest aroused by this manifestation continues to the present day, and has thus outlasted the noise of the

Lyon case. None of the uproar around Home has shaken the faith of the believers in his powers and honesty.

Home continued his travels and séances throughout Europe, and while in Russia in 1871 married another aristocratic lady, Julie Gloumeline. Once more the Czar sent a jewel as a wedding present. Home was now a member of the Greek Catholic Church, which took the same attitude toward Spiritualism as did the Roman; but of course as special purveyor to the Czar, Home was above its reach.

In 1872 Home returned from a trip to Switzerland for his lungs, and in 1874 was sent abroad again by the doctors. He gave some good séances at Florence, but on the whole his powers seemed to be waning with his health. In 1877 he wrote a book called *Lights and Shadows of Spiritualism.* Here he maintained his policy of attacking rival mediums, and went so far as to explain a large number of fraudulent methods. Almost the only manifestations he did not denounce were rappings and levitation. But it was nearly his last show of fight. His health grew constantly worse, and for the last years of his life he could hardly muster the strength to give seances at all. He conducted a large correspondence and some journalistic squabbles, but his great days were over.

Finally in 1886 his wife took him to Auteuil to consult a specialist, but too late. On June 21 Daniel Dunglas Home died.

There is a story that Home once was caught putting a bottle of phosphorized olive oil on a mantel before a séance. There is no proof of this so far as I can discover.

However, few know the possibilities of such a bottle when uncorked in a dark room, and still fewer would notice either the bottle itself or the medium's action. This bottled phosphorus has been used by many mediums during the dark of a séance to produce "spirit" lights. As long as the bottle remains stoppered the phosphorus gives off no light, but as soon as the cork is removed, and air is permitted to reach the phosphorus, a faint unearthly glow results.

It is said that some mediums for their light bringer used almond oil to cover the bottled phosphorus. It does not make any difference in which fatty oil phosphorus is dissolved; the effect is the same. In order to put out the light it is necessary merely to stopper the bottle. The light then gradually fades away as the air in the bottle is used up.

The usual method of getting the phosphorus to use in the bottle was to break the heads off parlor matches instead of purchasing the white phosphorus itself. Because white phosphorus is so poisonous it is no longer used in the manufacture of matches sold in America. Match-heads were also used to get tiny flickering lights about the room. For this the medium held a match-head between the moistened forefinger and thumb of each hand, and as he waved his hands about he would wiggle his forefinger enough to expose the match-head. Each time the finger moved there would be a tiny firefly-like glow in the darkness.

Luminous paint frequently has been used for spirit lights. The most frequent use was to paint some design on a small piece of cloth such as a handkerchief, which could be hidden easily. Such paint requires, to produce its most brilliant light, that it be exposed to the sun the day it is used.

Home was one of the many mediums who attracted attention by having a table tip, and turn, and float. "Table turning" probably convinced more people that the mediumistic phenomena were genuine than any other one manifestation, because so many had seen an ordinary table turn in the privacy of their own families.

Table turning can be said to have been the chief evening diversion of countless families, many of whom had no interest in spiritism. Several people would draw up their chairs around a small table, and each person would put the tips of the fingers of both hands on the top of the table. It was usual to have the fingers spread out with the thumbs touching, and then in order to complete the "circuit" to have each one touch the little fingers of the persons on either side. Every one held his hands as still as possible. Frequently the members of the group would sing together. All at once, and at times only after a long wait, the table would begin to twist and turn. Sometimes it would wriggle all the way across the room, and the sitters, in order to follow it, would have to leave their chairs. It was reasoned that if an ordinary parlor table would act so with the members of one's own family, it was quite reasonable to expect a table to act even more strangely in the presence of a medium.

People of unquestioned integrity exerted every effort to make certain that they did nothing which would cause the table to turn or twist. They all declared that it felt as if, suddenly, the table began to exert power. It was found, too, that tables would do more cavorting when surrounded by certain people than they would with others. It was also discovered that for some people a table would maintain its inanimate calm.

Some of the more skeptical doubted that the table was moved by spirits or by "animal magnetism," and believed that consciously or unconsciously the tables were turned by the sitters. Professor Michael Faraday, chemist and physicist, among others, devised experiments to discover what made the tables move. When a small piece of paper was put under the hands of each sitter the paper would slide about but the table would not tip. He also had each person at the table put his hands on top of a small board which was bound, by rubber bands, to another board, resting on the table top. Between these two boards was a glass roller. Each sitter had his own boards and rollers. A way was devised to record any movement of the upper boards. It was discovered that, quite unconsciously, pressure was exerted by the sitters. Observers also noticed that when some sitters thought the table would turn one way and some the other there would be no movement at all. They also learned that some people were more heavy-handed than others. With a light table or one with a top larger than the spread of the legs it is surprising to note how little pressure is needed on one side to make a table tip.

Even after it was demonstrated scientifically that table turning was accounted for by leverage and unconscious muscular action many people still accredited it all to supernatural agency. It is most difficult to convince some people that concertedly they have exerted pressure enough to move a table when they felt that they were doing no such thing. The singing in unison helped put the pressure in concert. Then when these same people went to a séance and saw tables do things which were not to be accounted for by the theories of Professor Faraday and the other scientists they scorned the scholars completely.

The multiplicity of methods used to tip and raise tables in a séance is almost as great as the number of mediums performing the feat. One of the simplest was to slide the hands back until one or both of the medium's thumbs could catch hold of the table top. Another way was to exert no pressure on the table at all, and in the event that the sitter opposite the medium did press on the table, to permit the table to tip far enough away from him so that he could get the toe of one foot under the table leg. He would then immediately put pressure on his side, and, holding the table between his hands and his toe, move it about at will. By this method a small table can be made to float two feet off the floor.

Please remember that I am noting methods which are known to have been used by mediums in their séances and under the guise of spiritism.

Another method was to catch the under side of the table top with the knee; and still another was merely to kick the table into the air. At times a very light and small table would be used, and the medium alone would put his finger-tips on the top. Even so the table would rock, tip, turn, and float in air. This was accomplished by having a small removable projection on the table top which could be caught between the fingers or in the ring of the medium.

When the medium was in his own quarters he could have the table rise by using a wooden stick thrust through a hole in the floor and rug by an assistant in a lower room.

With heavier tables metal hooks were worn by the medium and by a confederate who would take his place at the opposite side of the table. The hooks were concealed in the sleeves or at the waist and would go under the table top. Two men could by this means raise from the floor a table on which a man could jump without bringing it down.

In the exposure part of his book, Daniel Home, in a chapter called "Absurdities," described a medium whom he had visited. The medium had been tipping a table to answer questions in the same manner as with raps. Home wrote:

" 'But,' said I, 'the table always tips towards you. Will not the spirits tip it in an opposite direction?' "

" 'Oh, certainly they will!' He commenced trying to tip as desired. As his hands were laid flat on the table, and had no purchase, they naturally slid along the top without effecting anything. He looked towards me.

" 'If you will put your foot against the leg of the table nearest you (and, of course, farthest from the medium), the spirits, my dear brother, will tip as you wish.'

"The coolness of the request amused me. I did as desired. My foot afforded the requisite fulcrum, and the table began to tip towards me in the liveliest manner possible."

Home also wrote of the inanity of the answers to questions of sitters which were written in many séances. These answers were written on common school slates in many instances. Doctor Henry Slade was the first medium to popularize slate-writing.

Slade evidently did not have a particularly colorful early life and nothing seems to have been recorded until he began as a medium. Doubts have been cast on the title of "Doctor," and his slate writing was completely exposed a number of times, but he too had his host of followers and believers. One of my friends still insists that the writing which appeared on the slate when he visited Slade could have been written only by spirits.

Slade made his headquarters in New York, although he travelled widely. Whether at home or on tour he received substantial fees for his séances. The first note I have about Henry Slade is that Ira Davenport knew him in Michigan in 1860.

Slade's performances were, in a magician's sense, distinguished by their "cleanness" and "neatness." He used no paraphernalia except an ordinary table with leaves and some common slates. He would sit down at the table, with his one sitter at his right. Usually some of the chairs around the table would move, sliding or tipping; the sitter would feel pinches and slaps of "spirit hands"; and finally the slate-writing would begin. Slade would carefully clean both sides of a slate, and then hold it against the under side of the table-leaf, his thumb on top of the table, his fingers holding the slate. Usually he would have the sitter hold the other end of the slate in the same way. A message of some sort would then appear on the upper side of the slate. At other times he would put the slate on the table, with a bit of slate-pencil under it, and the message would appear on the under side of the slate. This was all he usually did—his spirits were writers.

On occasion, however, he proved a clever conjurer in other lines. In 1877–88 he was investigated by Johann Friedrich Zoellner, Professor of Physical Astronomy at the University of Leipzig. Zoellner was interested in four-dimensional space, and believed that spiritistic phenomena might prove his theory.

One of the tests was to produce knots in a ring of cord without separating the ends. For this purpose Zoellner and one of his colleagues sealed the free ends of some hempen cords on to pieces of cardboard. At the end of the séance one of the cords had four simple overhand knots in it.

Zoellner was overjoyed, but it has since been pointed out, in the first place, that the experiment had been tried without success some months before, so that Slade knew what was wanted, and, in the second place, that no real precautions were taken against the substitution of a knotted cord for the original.

Again, Zoellner put some coins in small cardboard boxes, which he sealed by gluing paper strips around them. According to the fourth-dimension theory, it should be possible to remove the coins without opening the boxes. This experiment failed once; six months later Slade returned to it, and when he put the boxes on the table, and held a slate under the table, a five-mark piece and two smaller coins appeared successively on the slate. The boxes when opened contained nothing but two small pieces of slate pencil. This last was a touch a magician would love. The effect of the "experiment" is practically destroyed by the fact that the boxes remained unopened for six months, and that Zoellner had kept no record of the value or date of the coins. Zoellner thought up a few really tough ones, such as linking two turned wooden rings of different woods, and passing paraffin into a hollow blown-glass bulb; but these manifestations Slade never produced. He passed the two rings on to a console table leg instead, and old Zoellner was just as pleased.

In a previous test with scientists Slade had not come off so well. This was just after his arrival in England in 1876. He baffled spiritists and investigators alike—for fees totalling hundreds of pounds—from mid-July until September 15, when he gave a sitting for Professor E. Ray Lankester and Doctor Horatio Donkin. These two became convinced that Slade did the writing with a piece of slate-pencil held under his forefinger-nail, and they grabbed one of the slates before it was supposed to be written on, and found a message there. They thereupon swore out a warrant against him for fraud.

The trial caused a furor and particularly sensational was the performance in the witness box by the magician, John Nevil Maskelyne, of slate-writing feats. After several days' hearing, Slade was condemned to three months' imprisonment at hard labor. With the help of Spiritualist adherents he appealed the sentence, and escaped because the conviction did not contain the words "by palmistry or otherwise," which appeared in the statute. Professor Lankester got out a new summons the following day, but

Slade had left the country, and the new summons was use-less except to prevent his ever returning.

Slade's conviction was another example of the dislike of British justice for spirit mediums. As a matter of fact, Lankester's exposure was far less conclusive than several that were made in America: Slade claimed that he had heard the spirits begin to write, and had said so, but that his words had been drowned in the uproar. He also pointed out that he kept his fingernails trimmed too close to hold a piece of pencil as claimed by Lankester and Donkin. Thus it happened, as so often before and since, that in-vestigators were on the right track, but did not take the best means to prove it. The fact seems to have been that Slade did write with his forefinger; but the pencil was at-tached to a thimble-like device, not caught under his fin-gernail. And the simple snatching of the slate (instead of more carefully planned exposure) still gave him at least the excuse which he used.

Much more to the point were two sittings which Slade, early in his career, gave to John Truesdell, of Syracuse, a man who for years made a hobby of investigating medi-ums, and who gave sittings which many people insisted were genuine, though he later wrote a book exposing himself along with other experts.

At Truesdell's first sitting he told Slade's servant his name and business, and was soon admitted to see the medi-um. The first part of the sitting consisted of chair-tip-ping, spirit slaps and pinches, etc. During the latter, Truesdell managed to pull back from the table in pre-tended alarm, just in time to see Slade's foot withdrawn

from the sitter's lap and replaced in the slipper. The
slate-writing involved two messages, one written on the
slate held under the table, the other while the slate lay on
the table top. Truesdell was very certain he detected the
tricks used to produce both of these messages, but not
having interfered in the process he could have sworn only
that it *could* have been done so. The second message, incidentally, was signed *Henry Truesdell*, a person unknown
to his namesake John. Slade said he believed John Truesdell had been so alarmed by the manifestations that his
spirit-friends could not get through to him, so that
strangers had been substituted to pave the way.

Some months later, being again in New York, Truesdell called once more on Slade. This time he told the servant his business, but said he would prefer to have the
spirits divulge his name. The servant obviously did not
recognize him. Truesdell had removed his name from his
hat-lining, but had left in his overcoat pocket "an un-
sealed letter which would convey to the physical eye the
erroneous impression that my name was Samuel Johnson,
of Rome, N. Y."

The attendant showed Truesdell into the séance room
to wait for Slade. Truesdell occupied his leisure by scru-
tinizing the room. Under a sideboard he found a slate, on
the under side of which was written the following:

"We are happy to meet you in this atmosphere of
spiritual research. You are now surrounded by many
anxious friends in spirit-life who desire to communicate
with you, but cannot, until you learn more of the laws
which govern their actions. If you will come here often,

your spirit-friends will soon be able to identify themselves and to communicate with you as in earth-life. *Allie*."

Truesdell wrote under this message, in a flourishing hand, "Henry! Look out for this fellow—he is up to snuff! Alcinda," and replaced the slate under the sideboard. (Alcinda was, as Truesdell knew, the name of Slade's dead wife.)

The séance began as before, with physical manifestations. When the slate was held under the table, the name "Mary Johnson" appeared on it, which Slade explained as the name of the sitter's sister. This Truesdell felt forced to deny. Hoping for better luck, they moved the table over near the sideboard, and tried again. The spirits were so active that the slate slipped from Slade's and Truesdell's fingers, and fell to the floor. Slade quickly picked it up, and after a couple more ineffectual attempts to get a message under the table he put it on the table-top, with a bit of pencil underneath. The table trembled violently, and the sound of writing, with dotted *i*'s and crossed *t*'s, was plainly audible.

Finally the writing stopped, and Slade turned over the slate. It contained *two* messages.

After several minutes of stupor, Slade went livid. "What does this mean?" he cried. "Who has been meddling with this slate?"

"Spirits," said Truesdell.

"A moment later," he adds, "this great manipulator of unseen forces was as mellow as a ripe apple." Slade then talked to him for an hour, apparently discussing the tricks of the trade as with an equal. It was after this and a previous exposure of Charles H. Foster, the "ballot test" medium, who also discussed his methods afterward, that Truesdell set up as an amateur medium himself.

One of Slade's most thorough tests was before the Seybert Commission, who had also tested Margaret Fox. This group of investigators, by the way, was picked by the University of Pennsylvania in accordance with a bequest establishing a chair of philosophy, and requiring the investigation of Spiritualism as a condition. The essence of his performance was the same as usual, but there were a great many sittings, and various members of the commission actually saw him make substitutions of slates. They also found slates already written on before sittings. "Two compasses, which we placed on the table during one séance, remained unaffected by Doctor Slade's presence," says their Report.

Besides actually observing several fraudulent manipulations, the commissioners declared that they saw no manifestations which could not easily have been performed by the same or similar fraudulent means. On the other hand, they held a sitting with Harry Kellar, the celebrated magician, who had been with the Davenport Brothers, in which Kellar worked under more difficult conditions than Slade, and produced messages in French, Spanish, Dutch, Chinese, Japanese, Arabic, Gujerati, and German. The commissioners who saw this performance were completely unable to explain it until Kellar exposed his methods to the Acting Chairman, Mr. Furness. In connection with this performance, the following conversation with Slade took place:

Coleman Sellers (an amateur magician and an inventor of prominence): Do you know a man named Kellar, who is exhibiting in this city?

Slade: I do not. I never knew him.

Mr. Sellers: You may, however, be able to explain to me a very remarkable slate-writing experiment which Kellar has performed. (Description followed.) How did Mr. Kellar do that?

Slade: He is a Medium. He does that work precisely as I do it.

Sellers: But can he not do it by trickery?

Slade: No, it is impossible. He is a Medium, and a powerful Medium.

Mr. Furness gave a description of Slade which brings him vividly to the eye: "He is probably six feet in height, with a figure of unusual symmetry, his hands are large but shapely, the nail of the second finger of his right hand is rather longer than the others, and appeared in the center to be slightly split and worn. His face would, I think, attract notice anywhere for its uncommon beauty. He has a small, curling, dark moustache, and short, crisp, iron-gray hair, of a texture exceeding in fineness any that I have ever seen on a man's head. His eyes are dark, and the circles around them very dark, but their expression is painful. I could not divest myself of the feeling that it was that of a hunted animal or of a haunted man. The color on his cheeks is very bright, but it is said to be artificial. He complained bitterly of ill-health and of water around his heart, which he said at times he could hear and feel 'swashing about.' A noteworthy man in every respect."

My friend the late Frederick Eugene Powell and I talked many times about his séances with Slade. Powell, during the time I knew him, was an eminent professional magician, although at the time of the séances he had been an instructor in mathematics in the Pennsylvania Military College. Even at that period he was fully conversant with the methods of magic. Powell went to see Slade out of curiosity, and though he told his colleagues (one of whom accompanied him to the séances) in detail how all the slate-writing was accomplished he did nothing which might be called a public exposure. He explained to me that it all looked so obvious to him that he felt that it must be so to others. Of course what in his youth he failed to realize, he said, was that knowing mystification he knew where and when to look.

More damning than all the exposures, public and private, which were made of Slade's trickery, was the confession obtained by Remigius Weiss. Weiss was one of those called by the Seybert Commission regarding Slade's methods. Houdini told in his book *A Magician Among the Spirits* of looking up Weiss (who, by the way, was better known as Albus) and learning about the confession. There is no question of its authenticity, and it makes the evidence quite complete.

"The undersigned, Henry Slade, known professionally as Doctor Henry Slade—the powerful Spiritistic medium —by reason of force of unfavorable circumstances, years ago became a Spiritualistic slate-writing (etc., etc.) medium, and Spiritistic lecturer and he confesses that all his

pretended Spiritualistic manifestations were and are de-
ceptions, performed through tricks.

"(Signed)   H. Slade."

According to Rupert Hughes, in his article "Seeing
Things" in *Pearson's Magazine*, Slade "after repeated
exposures, sank to the dregs of his trade and died in a
Michigan sanatorium."

In the main slate writing depends upon two ideas: one
is to substitute a blank slate for one on which writing previously has been put, and the other is secretly to write
on a slate. As with the previously mentioned phenomena
there are a wide variety of methods both for substituting
one slate for another and for writing secretly.

The slate with the message on it can easily be changed if
it is anywhere within reach of the medium. Under a small
rug, on hooks under the seat of the chair, in a special large-
sized pocket inside the medium's coat, in a desk, table, or
bureau drawer, under a dictionary—but the idea is plain
that a duplicate slate could be hidden in any one of these
or similar places. Why does not the sitter see the change
made? Methods vary, and it would be much too long to
go into the technic of substitution and the psychology of
timing, but in the main it is enough to state that if the
medium gives the sitter not only something to think about
but something physical to do, his own actions will not be
noticed provided they are done in a natural manner. Do I
mean to say that an intelligent sitter will not notice the
medium leaning over, opening a bureau drawer, dropping
one slate in and taking out another? Yes, that is quite
what I do mean.

Again substitution of slates like so many other phenomena is best done with a confederate. A hole is made in the wall behind the sitter and at the height of his head when seated. As the medium asks the sitter to hold the slate on top of his head the confederate through the hole in the wall puts the new slate in the sitter's hands, and draws the old slate back through the hole. I had this done to me and refused point blank to believe it possible. Even when it was explained to me, I felt certain that there must be another method. I then watched it done on others who were as complacent as I had been. In the same manner a hole in the floor (with a trap door in the rug) allows a confederate to exchange slates while the medium is supposedly holding the slate under the table.

Of course both those methods, as well as their variations, require a house which can be torn up and money enough to make alterations. But the same substitution can be made through a curtained door, or, among other ways, a confederate can come into the room with a tray (holding the slate underneath) and by putting it down and picking it up "ring the change."

Under the same head as substitution comes covering a slate with a false and removable surface. Under this clean false surface is the face of the slate with the writing. This cover has at times been made of black silk and at times of a thin sheet of slate. All that is necessary to bring forth the message is secretely to remove the masking false surface.

Although Slade used to write with his forefinger many find that the pencil attached to a cap for the thumb makes for more legible writing. I can write much better with the thumb than with the forefinger, I find.

Writing also was made to appear on a blank slate by chemically treating the surface. It can be done, and I have a list of twenty-odd formulæ for such writing, but chemical formulæ and trifling divergencies in method are dull and confusing. Much more interesting are two methods of getting writing on the inside of double slates fastened together.

In one of these methods the medium gives to the sitter a hinged slate which has corresponding drilled holes on the edge of each side opposite the cloth hinge. A small padlock goes through these holes. The sitter washes the slates, drops a small piece of chalk, which the medium gives him, between the slates, and securely padlocks them together. He then holds them under the table so that the medium too can grasp them. Later upon taking the slates from under the table, and undoing the lock, a word is found written on one slate. The secret is that the piece of chalk is specially made of chalk dust, glue, and iron filings. The medium has a small magnet in his hand and when the slates are under the table uses the magnet to drag the chalk about the slate. The one difficulty is that the medium must needs learn to write upside down and backwards.

The other method is when two slates are brought to the medium securely tied together and left in his care. It is possible to wedge them open—no matter how securely corded—enough to get a thin wire tipped with slate pencil inside the slates. From then on it is no more difficult to produce writing inside the slate than it is to hold a new pencil by the eraser and write a word that way.

Spirit writing was not always produced on slates. It was brought out on paper (chemicals again), on cloth, and even on the arm of the medium.

One way of bringing writing out on cloth will suffice. The medium, with an indelible pencil, writes backwards on a blotter. He then moistens the sitter's handkerchief, perhaps with cologne, and presses it on the blotter. If it then is quickly rolled into a ball no one can see the moment the writing actually appears.

A simple description of the method by which a trick may be accomplished—and it makes no difference which trick is explained—gives no idea of the effect that trick can have upon those who witness its performance. The presentation, on the other hand, is something which cannot be set down in print. The score of Carmen, except to the trained musician, will give no idea of the thrill an audience can get from a well-sung and well-presented performance of the opera. There are so many details which can mar a performance of either opera or trickery, and many details which may add immeasurably to the success.

One of the incidental but effective details of many séances was the icy draughts which accompanied the other phenomena. A large number of the ghost stories also mention a chill wind striking the witness to the ghost. Whether or not there is a wind the chill to most people would be quite understandable. A great many people can be talked into feeling a draught which does not exist, and some often feel a non-existent draught which has not been even mentioned. It is probably true that many of the cool breezes which struck those at a séance were imaginary. There have been several tricks of swishing curtains, by foot or hand, until they bulged out in response to a supposed breeze. It is probably unnecessary to remind any one of the childhood stunt of blowing either hot or cold air between the lips.

There are several accounts of scientists proving with self-recording thermometers that cold breezes did occur in connection with the occurrence of certain physical phenomena. The records showed a temperature drop of several degrees in the séance room.

One medium, Eusapia Palladino, according to many of her sitters, was able to cause great gusts of wind to blow things about even across the room from herself and also to have a small cool breeze come out of the top of her skull. Both of these phenomena many people believed were never satisfactorily explained.

Palladino was an illiterate petty shopkeeper from Naples, with no pretensions to breeding or even to common honesty. A good biographical sketch of her is impossible because she seldom told the same story twice herself. According to one of her stories, Palladino was born in Apulia in 1854, and discovered her mediumistic power at the age of twelve or fourteen—just about the time that Home was creating a sensation again in Florence. One tale was that she discovered her power while a servant in a spiritist family; another that she found it out in the family circle where she was being prepared for a convent;

another that the first of her two husbands (who are both supposed to have taken her name) was a magician. This she denied, but said that he was connected with the stage, and knew some tricks which he used to show off.

She first came into European prominence in the late eighties, when she convinced Professor Chiaia, of Naples, that her phenomena were genuine. Chiaia undertook to interest Cesare Lombroso in her work, but did not succeed until 1891, when that eminent scientist too became convinced that Palladino's work was super-normal.

Then followed a long series of séances all over Europe —1892 in Milan, 1893 in Naples and St. Petersburg, 1893 and 1894 in Rome and Warsaw, 1894 in France under the eye of Professor Charles Richet, with the assistance of Sir Oliver Lodge, F. W. H. Myers, and Doctor Ochorowicz of Warsaw, 1895 in Naples and Cambridge, and many others. Richet and Lodge, in particular, were thoroughly convinced that Palladino had produced genuine manifestations, although they found that she also cheated when she could.

The sittings in Cambridge in 1895, however, followed on the publication of a report on the French sittings, which report had been severely criticized by Doctor Hodgson of the Society for Psychical Research. Doctor Hodgson claimed that the report gave no evidence of effective precautions against trickery. The Cambridge experiments, however, were so conducted as to satisfy even Doctor Hodgson, who took part.

There was only one difficulty: no convincing phenomena appeared. F. W. H. Myers, Hodgson, and the other sitters were certain that the great bulk of the manifestations at Cambridge resulted from trickery, accomplished in ways which they described.

Palladino continued her career on the Continent and was caught time and time again in fraud. Nevertheless she had a host of believers in her powers, even among those who had found her cheating.

During November and December of 1908 a committee of three appointed by the Society of Psychical Research went to Naples to investigate Palladino and held a series of ten sittings in their hotel rooms. The committee was made up of two Englishmen, the Honorable Everard Feilding and W. W. Baggally, and Hereward Carrington from America. It was expected, because of his knowledge of the methods of magic as well as having been successful in exposing a number of fraudulent mediums, that my friend Carrington would not be impressed with Palladino's séances. However, during those ten séances and in others he later attended he believes that phenomena occurred which could not be accounted for by her agency whether or not she used trickery.

Later in the same year McClure, the publisher, financed a trip to New York for Palladino. In New York she gave several séances in a science laboratory for a group composed largely of University professors. One of these was the eminent scientist Professor Robert William Wood who secretly conducted several tests. At one séance he arranged a light in the cabinet which was hidden from the medium but by which, from a vantage point on top the cabinet, he clearly could see. When articles were moved inside the cabinet they were picked up by an arm pushing in the curtain of the front. Professor Wood could not state definitely that the covered arm was one of Palladino's so he arranged to have, for the next séance, an x-ray machine in another room to watch her movements. There was no next séance, for Palladino became wary and failed to appear.

Sewell Haggard, editor for McClure, and Professor Walter B. Pitkin, the two gentlemen who organized the investigation for Mr. McClure and who handled the funds set aside by him, felt that while it seemed clear to the entire committee that Palladino resorted to tricks, the evidence collected was not conclusive enough for publication and the whole matter was dropped.

Professor Pitkin said to me, "Palladino was the cagiest human being I have ever had to deal with and as a newspaper man I have had quite a little to do with slick people."

Shortly after Palladino walked out on this series of coldly scientific investigations she was lured to give two other séances under conditions she felt to be more favorable.

These séances were given under what seemed to be most cordial conditions. Ladies were invited to keep Palladino from being suspicious and besides a number of professors the group also included several magicians. My close friend and teacher in magic, the late John William Sargent, was at both of the séances as a professional magician who knew the methods used in producing trickery and as an outstanding authority on the psychology of deception.

W. S. Davis, J. L. Kellogg, and Professor Joseph Jastrow likewise knew magic's methods and went to both séances. My friend Joseph L. Rinn, also magically informed, attended one.

Rinn and Warner C. Pyne, a college boy and at that time a neighbor of mine, came to the one séance without notification to Palladino—and on their hands and knees. Before the séance was actually under way it was suggested casually that one of the professors had a mechanism which would register the medium's power. This casualness was all part of a plan carefully worked out. The apparatus was sent for and brought into the room carefully wrapped in paper. While the package was being undone all the members of the group crowded around the table—and around Palladino—in order to mask the snake-like entrance along the floor of the black-clothed Rinn and Pyne. They crawled under the chairs of the sitters; one at each side of the table. The séance began and Rinn and Pyne were both in a position to see that Palladino was able to free one hand and one foot from those who were supposedly holding her. With this one free hand and one free leg she caused all the things to happen which she claimed were due to spirits. Not all of the phenomena which she was said to be able to cause occurred that evening but most of them did and every one was produced by her manipulations.

Allowing the medium to free her hand and foot was also part of the committee's plan. In other words without her knowledge that it was done she was permitted to cheat. This part of the committee's work was severely criticized by those who believed in Palladino's mediumistic powers. If not watched carefully she would cheat but when closely guarded would produce genuine phenomena, they said. However, the critics are unjust to the committee for at one séance both the medium's hands and both her feet were held steadfastly and for so long as this continued absolutely nothing happened.

Palladino was caught cheating times without number even by those who believed in her, and she made no bones about admitting it. Where Home relied on his gentlemanliness and on never having been caught, Palladino used her very charlatanism as a protection. The theory was that she would cheat whenever she could, because it was easier and surer than the genuine manifestations, and brought the money in just the same. Therefore the investigator knew from the start that he could believe nothing she said, and that if he gave her the slightest chance for fraud she would seize it. This put the burden of the phenomena on the investigators' opinion of their own precautions. Many of the scientists of Europe appear to have been unable to resist this test of self-confidence.

When Palladino died in 1918, there were thousands who saw in her the final and convincing evidence for spirit communication.

CHAPTER V

FACES, FLOWERS, AND THUMB–PRINTS

B Y POPULAR demand the medium's phenomena rode in the wake of progress. Gone were the unadorned rappings of the past; the spirits favored their followers with the operation of elaborate mechanical contrivances. For instance the spirits found it easy to work a telegraph key enclosed in a small wooden box. Certain mediums were able to produce the effect by fraud, thanks to the fact that the telegraph key could be adjusted to touch the lid, which was squeezed by the medium in the dark to give the signals.

One of the most effective phenomena requiring apparatus is performed with a series of balls suspended by strings of varying lengths from a frame fastened to a table. The table and all the apparatus used are unprepared. The medium sitting motionless at the table causes any desired ball to swing back and forth while all the others remain motionless. The medium's control will then stop the swinging, and will start any other ball instead. This time the control is not spiritual but actual—people who have taken college physics courses remember these pendulums as a favorite classroom demonstration. My physicist friend Doctor Shirley L. Quimby says of this classical illustration of forced vibration, "A vibrating system responds most vigorously to a succession of impulses which are timed to the period of oscillation of the body if set in motion and left alone. A common example of this is the occurrence of vibrations in various parts of an automobile at certain speeds. Again, one or more strings of a piano can be excited to sustain audible vibration by humming or singing in its neighborhood. This phenomenon is advanced by some as an explanation of the collapse of the walls of Jericho in response to a blast of the enemy trumpets. In the pendulum experiment the classroom method is to agitate the mounting by a variable-speed electric motor." It takes prolonged practice to vibrate the mounting by hand accurately enough to make any desired ball start swinging, which explains why the pendulums were never more popular with the spirits.

Even the more advanced work of invisible spirits did not content some sitters; many wanted to see as well as hear from their departed loved ones.

When the spirits actually appeared, it was the eldest of the Fox sisters, Mrs. Anna Leah Fox Fish Underhill, who was first or one of the first to produce them. In 1860 she showed to Robert Dale Owen (the son of the celebrated reformer and Spiritualist convert, Robert Owen) a veiled and luminous female figure which walked around the room. Katherine Fox acquired the new power within a few months, and in January of 1861 she began a long series of sittings with the financier Livermore, usually producing a figure in shining garments which Livermore positively recognized as his dead wife.

The spirit forms are all much the same in appearance, though they vary as to headdress, moustache, beard, and size. The usual procedure is to tie the medium to a chair in the cabinet, and then the spirits become embodied and walk around the circle. Despite the preliminary precaution, physical similarities have very often been noticed between the medium and the spirit, and after the first awe wore off (in the course of a couple of years) Spiritualists as well as skeptics began grabbing the ghosts, only to find time and again that they were hugging the medium in shining raiment of muslin. D. D. Home and his faithful adherent Sergeant Cox were particularly severe on the whole notion of materialization séances. Sergeant Cox wrote:

"The great field for fraud has been offered by the production and presentation of alleged spirit-forms. All the conditions imposed are as if carefully designed to favour fraud if contemplated, and even to tempt to imposture. The curtain is guarded at either end by some friend. The light is so dim that the features cannot be distinctly seen. A white veil thrown over the body from head to foot is put on and off in a moment, and gives the necessary aspect of spirituality. A white band around head and chin at once conceals the hair and disguises the face. A considerable interval precedes the appearance—just such as would be necessary for the preparations. A like interval succeeds the retirement of the form before the cabinet is permitted to be opened for inspection. This just enables the restoration of the ordinary dress. While the preparation is going on behind the curtain the company are always vehemently exhorted to sing. This would conveniently conceal any sounds of motion in the act of preparation. The spectators are made to promise not to peep behind the curtain, and not to grasp the form. They are solemnly told that if they were to seize the spirit they would kill the medium. This is an obvious contrivance to deter the onlookers from doing anything that might cause detection. It is not true. Several spirits have been grasped and no medium has died of it; although in each case the supposed spirit was found to be the medium. That the detected medium was somewhat disturbed in health after such a public detection and exposure is not at all surprising. Every one of the five* mediums who have been actually seized in the act of personating a spirit is now alive and well. There need be no fear for the consequences in putting them to the proof."

Almost the whole history of materialization séances is one of blind faith and lack of precautionary measures, followed by ignominious exposure. The Eddys of Chittenden, Vermont, were important mediums in this field. Though not a medium himself Zephaniah Eddy's children—Miranda, James, Francis, Mary, Delia, Webster, William and Horatio—all were mediumistic. C. C. Massey, a convinced Spiritualist, Henry Slade's Attorney and translator of Zoellner's *Transcendental Physics*, which supported Slade's genuineness with more heat than caution,

*Since this was written by Sergeant Cox the numbers have greatly increased. I doubt if there remain now five "materializing mediums" who have not been seized in the act of personating a spirit-form.—D. D. Home.

wrote as follows about one séance given by the Eddys:

"A dusky young man would look out, and we had to say in turn, all round the circle, 'Is it for me?' When the right person was reached, three taps would be given, and the fortunate possessor of the ghost would gaze doubtfully, upon which the ghost would look grieved, and that generally softened the heart of the observer, and brought about a recognition in the remark, 'Lor, so you be ———.' And that sort of thing went on night after night at the Eddys'."

The productions of Mrs. Mary Andrews, of Moravia, New York, are described by John Truesdell:

"After waiting anxiously for a quarter of an hour or so, the black curtain (of the cabinet) was quickly drawn aside by some invisible hand, and a face appeared at the aperture for an instant and vanished. Several similar faces were presented without being recognized, when a female figure, with long gray hair and an old-fashioned cap on the head, which was fully recognized by one of the party as his grandmother, who had been dead for over twenty years, was seen for a second. When questioned by some one of the company as to her identity, this individual gravely informed us that he was positive—he knew his grandmother by the number of ruffles she had on her cap. This evidence seemed to be entirely satisfactory to all present! The next face that presented itself appeared to be that of a young man with black hair and a long dark mustache. At first, no one seemed to recognize this face, when finally a skeptical individual from Syracuse remarked that it might be the spirit of Mr. B. (B. was a man over seventy years of age when he left this world, whose hair was as white as snow). I replied, "If this is the spirit of B., he must have shaved off his long black whiskers.' Immediately the figure reappeared, fully answering the latter description of B.; but our Syracuse friend, not being as yet fully satisfied, inquired, in a tone just loud enough to be heard by the medium, if Mr. B. had not lost two fingers from his left hand. To our surprise, in a few seconds, the required right hand, with two fingers bent down out of sight, was seen slowly passing by the aperture."

Perhaps the foremost English medium was Miss Florence Cook, of Hackney. She began at the age of about sixteen by attending séances of Herne and Williams, who were considered the leading professional mediums of the time (1872). Herne and Williams, keeping up with the fashions, had introduced ghostly forms at dark séances. Soon Miss Cook was giving séances with Herne; and she had an important innovation—her ghosts were produced in full light. She kept up her work into the twentieth century, but had some unhappy experiences when sitters grabbed the ghost, and found the medium's chair empty. On one occasion when a ghost was seized by one of Miss Cook's sitters, two other guests helped the spirit to escape the interferer before the cabinet could be searched. Sir William Crookes came to her defense in print, and afterward conducted some experiments which included photographing both Miss Cook and "Katie," the spirit form, at the same time. He did show quite clearly that at least on this occasion medium and spirit were definitely separate;

but as Miss Cook's own bedroom was used for a cabinet, there was no telling who the ghost might or might not have been.

Although the theatrical effect of the performance is good, materialization has peculiar drawbacks for fraudulent mediums. Detection is easier, and the victims' indignation greater. The Reverend S. J. Barrows, grandfather of my friend Barrows Mussey, attended such a séance in Boston, accompanied by a believer, a General who had lost his wife, and by a student from the Massachusetts Institute of Technology. At the séance, the General's wife (who had been tall and slender, with a pronounced Southern accent) returned to earth in a short, dumpy figure, with a breath smelling of garlic. The M. I. T. man then asked to see his sister Caroline. He talked with her at some length, finally saying that he was doubly glad to know her since this was the first he had learned of her existence. Doctor Barrows then seized Caroline's wrist, and began counting her pulse. He did so, despite her struggles, until the medium, discreetly showing a blackjack, said, "Let go her hand, or I'll hurt you." This was an actionable threat, so Doctor Barrows said "Normal; thank you," and left the séance.

The next séance was attended by the General (still a believer) and by a number of detectives. These turned up the lights in the middle of the séance, and started bundling ghosts into the police station wagon. One of the detectives, a small man, became involved in a struggle with the medium, who was large and burly, with a heavy black beard. The officer was getting much the worst of it, when his wife, with great presence of mind, lit a match under the medium's beard, thus producing a final triumph for law and order.

This seems a fairly regular pattern for the career of materializing mediums. One pair, the Reverend William Reilly Thompson and Mrs. Eva Thompson, were made associate ministers of the First Spiritualist Church of New York on the strength of their materializations, and Sir Arthur Conan Doyle asked my friend Samri Frikell, a successful amateur psychic investigator, to have a look at their séances. Samri Frikell, by the way, is the pen name of Fulton Oursler when writing on the subject. He made it by combining the names of two magicians, Samri Baldwin and Wiljalba Frikell.

Frikell and the late Robert Thomas Hardy, a literary agent, attended a séance on West 70th Street in New York early in 1922. It began, as many sittings do, with prayer and hymn-singing in a darkened room. After a number of hymns, a small, moving luminous circle appeared at the back of the cabinet. It expanded, rose, and rather suddenly became the luminous figure of a woman, with an iridescent star on her head. She announced herself in a clear whisper as the "cabinet control," and was greeted warmly by several of the habitués of the Thompson séances. She vanished in the cabinet, and was replaced by another figure, according to Frikell exactly like the first one, but minus the iridescent star. There were several of these similar forms in succession. One professed to be Frikell's dead sweetheart, Mary; she gave him some information on "little Marie" and "Uncle John," and gave him a spirit caress when he put his head into the cabinet by her direction. Later, Frikell's father materialized, and talked about his black sheep son, George. All of these characters except Frikell's father were imaginary.

Frikell and Hardy both were convinced that something should be done and from the séance they went straight to the police, who assigned three detectives to the job of prosecuting the Thompsons.

In the meantime Sir Arthur Conan Doyle himself attended a sitting, and on him, too, he wrote, "it left a bad impression."

Then Frikell attended a séance in company with Detective Andrew McLaughlin, Detective Genevieve McLaughlin, and Detective Haik of the New York Police. It went on as usual until the spirit of Miss McLaughlin's Aunt Emma appeared. Miss McLaughlin asked Aunt Emma about the future, and the moment Aunt Emma replied, thus violating the ordinance forbidding fortune-telling, the detectives turned the séance into a free-for-all.

Eventually the Thompsons were convicted and fined. Conan Doyle congratulated Frikell on his work in clearing fraudulent mediums out of the way; but H. Clay Brownell, the head of the First Spiritualist Church, was indignant at Frikell's intrusion, saw to it that the Thompsons got the best possible defense in court, and declared that his chief interest was to get a law passed preventing such interference as Frikell's with the sacred rites of the Church.

The ring of the ghost-baiters closed ever tighter around the regular, old-fashioned materializing medium, and no man of Sir William Crookes's eminence today would think of attending a séance like Florrie Cook's. But a new form of materialization provides the most effective present theory of physical manifestation.

The hypothesis now held by leading scientific adherents of Spiritualism is that the physical phenomena are caused through a substance called ectoplasm. This, they say, is a tangible substance, but of uncertain composition, which is produced or given off by the medium's body. It may shape itself into a materialized object; or, creating an extra limb ("pseudopod") on the medium, it may move objects at a distance, work mechanical test contrivances, or simply be visible on a photographic plate.

Thompson had, as is usual, prefaced the séance with a brief lecture in which he said that the materializations were formed of ectoplasm taken from the medium's own body, and that therefore to touch the spirit forms except under careful direction might prove fatal to the medium.

Ectoplasm first gained prominence through the séances held by Baron von Schrenck-Notzing of Munich with the medium "Eva C." (Marthe Beraud, *alias* Rose Dupont) in Paris, and later with "Stanislawa P.," a Polish shop-cashier, in Munich. Baron von Schrenck-Notzing introduced new methods into the investigation of séances: he photographed the manifestations by flashlight, and some he even caught with a movie camera. He emerged from his series of experiments absolutely convinced, and he produced a monumental book on them, with a large selection of his photographs. Certain sitters later rose to complain of his methods—they demanded to know why he carefully suppressed all personal information on the mediums, while going into the tiniest details of their physical, physiological and psychological make-up; they claimed he omitted from his records such facts as the discovery in the cabinet on one occasion of six black pins; they said his book ignored the very presence of certain qualified sitters who had claimed the phenomena were a fraud. A former collaborator of Schrenck-Notzing's was even moved to write a scientific study of the psychology and personality of psychic investigators.

Schrenck-Notzing himself divided Eva C.'s phenomena into three classes: the genuine, the "unconsciously fraudulent" (produced by the medium while in trance, but with physical means), and the "mixed" (such as the materialization of a cloth by psychic means, and then using it to disguise the medium as a spirit). He certainly takes a long step ahead of previous investigators in giving the photographs so that his readers may judge for themselves, apart from the printed reports of the séances. The use of a red light instead of total darkness was another improvement.

I must confess that to my eye the photographs rather let the Baron down. Mostly they show either fully formed materializations of faces and figures, or the ectoplasm itself in various states. Eva C. also developed a third hand which sometimes took things that were handed into the cabinet. One of the photographs plainly shows the third hand fumbling for a cigarette—too plainly, for it is obvious to any observer (as in this case it was to Schrenck-Notzing) that the third hand is Eva's left foot. Another picture, taken

suddenly by an unfriendly sitter, shows a spirit face floating over Eva's head, and also shows Eva's right hand
holding it there in a rather cramped position. The faces
as a whole look (to one inclined to see them that way) like
paper cut-outs, and in some cases folds and crumpling
can be distinguished.

This leaves the question of the ectoplasm. The photographs show it sometimes exuding from the medium's
mouth, sometimes lying draped on other parts of her
body. In every case, naturally enough, it looks perfectly
tangible and material, though sometimes it looks like
gauze, and at other times like tangled string. Hostile
observers claimed that this was just what it was, and that
the medium had learned to swallow and regurgitate various textile products, probably first smearing them with
potato starch to make them smooth. My friend Harry
Price proved the use of the method of regurgitation in
the case of a medium called Mrs. Duncan.

In fact, at one of the sittings with Stanislawa P., Doctor Mathilde von Kemnitz (later famous as Frau von
Ludendorff) stated that she saw that the medium had attached the end of a gauzy ectoplasm to a thread pinned to
the front of the cabinet, and that in causing the ectoplasm
to disappear the medium forgot it was pinned down, and
had to close the curtains of the cabinet to undo it. According to Doctor von Kemnitz, Eva C. was more adroit
than this, but no more genuine. It is certainly true that an
outsider would have been more inclined to trust Eva if the
fact had not come out (over Schrenck-Notzing's protest)
that she had previously been active as a medium under

various names, and that she was five or six years older than Schrenck-Notzing claimed. She had given séances for Cesare Lombroso in Algiers some years before. Photographs published by Lombroso and by Schrenck-Notzing showed materialized spirits almost identical in appearance and dress, though the one in Algiers was named Bel Boa, while the Parisian ghost was nameless.

Ectoplasm is not always gauze or string, for some mediums have used lung tissue and other sections of animal interiors.

Ectoplasm has been adopted as the orthodox explanation of materialization proper and of "telekinesis" (moving objects at a distance), but there is another class of phenomena which does not come under that head. These are "apports"—ordinary physical objects, brought to a séance despite locked doors and sealed windows. This type of phenomenon, by the way, was a favorite with pre-Fox ghosts.

An early though fraudulent example is reported by John Truesdell. At a séance in Syracuse, the heavy séance table was broken by a huge stone, dropped apparently from a great height on to the middle of the table. According to Truesdell's explanation, the phenomenon was produced by one Joseph Cafferty, a member of the medium's household. The stone weighing about 30 pounds came from the excavations in progress for the Syracuse water-works, and gained entrance to the séance in the seat of a rush bottomed chair the rushes of which were largely broken through. In this way the stone sank down almost level with the seat and Cafferty threw his coat over the chair to hide it entirely. When the séance lights went out, Cafferty passed the sitters to his right and left each the hand of the other, so that while they thought they were holding him they were holding only one another. At the appropriate moment he stood up, and got the stone from under him, and hurled it to the table as hard as he could.

Perhaps the most popular apports have been flowers. "Flower séances" are an old widespread form of séance. Sometimes but one or two flowers would be brought, sometimes whole table-loads. Miss Nichol, later famous as Mrs. Guppy, lived in the household of Doctor Alfred Russel Wallace's sister, and at a séance for him in 1867 she produced fifteen chrysanthemums, six variegated anemones, four tulips, five solanums, six ferns of two kinds, and one *Auricula sinensis* with nine flowers. On another occasion Mrs. Guppy's spirits placed a wreath of flowers and ferns on the head of a sitter. These spirits were versatile: not confining themselves to flowers, they handed around to the eager sitters fruit, bread, and live eels and lobsters.

Another medium who produced apports was the Reverend William Stainton Moses, long a pillar of the Spiritualist movement in England. He was perhaps most conspicuous for his automatic writing, and for a long time he was also editor of the Spiritualist paper, *Light;* but quite early in his mediumship (which he discovered in 1872) he found himself attracting from other rooms to himself the mysterious presence of books, opera-glasses, gloves, pincushions, shells, stones, snuff-boxes, candlesticks, and statuettes. Liquid perfumes also appeared, sometimes sprayed into the air, sometimes poured into the sitters' hands, sometimes oozing from Moses' own head and running down into his beard.

Moses was an excellent example of the "private medium"—the medium who gives séances only for friends, and who has no tangible gain from his Spiritualistic work. Not unnaturally, sensible Spiritualists value séances by such mediums far more highly than those given by professionals; there seems no incentive whatever for fraud. The Reverend Stainton Moses was above suspicion if any one ever was. Born in Lincolnshire in 1839, he took several prizes at Bedford Grammar School, and did well at Oxford, though his health prevented his distinguishing himself in his examinations. From 1863 to 1870 he was a curate, doing the hard work of a parish priest in the Isle of Man and in the west of England. His health was always bad, and in 1870 it forced him to quit his curacy; he became tutor to the son of some friends, Doctor and Mrs. Stanhope Speer, with whom from then on he lived in London. A year or two later he also took the job of English master at University College School; he continued this work until 1889, when his health once more got the better of him.

He did not become interested in Spiritualism at all until 1872, when Mrs. Speer asked him to read Robert Dale Owen's *The Debatable Land*. He then attended séances by Home, Williams, and others, and soon afterward found himself producing raps and table-tipping at the Speers' home. At subsequent séances he got the apports I have mentioned, then spirit lights, music, and finally volume after volume of automatic writing, dictated largely by his control, Imperator.

Stainton Moses' character is a puzzle. The very plenti-
ful records, by Moses himself and by his friends, describe
the manifestations in such a way that they practically
scream "fraud"! The exact and careful descriptions seem
to tell us even what methods were used. No precautions
were ever taken, and once or twice when some one suggested a test of some sort, Imperator was offended, and
refused to manifest for a couple of days. It is a natural
fact that private mediums are almost never exposed: even
to suggest precautions against trickery by a person such
as Stainton Moses is unthinkable to the medium's friends,
for it shows a suspicion which any decent person would
repudiate. But on the other hand the ordinary private
medium has no proof of his genuineness which can convince strangers, and Stainton Moses even less than most.
The whole thing, to an outside observer, seems to come
to the question of how completely Stainton Moses was
fooling himself. There was no fooling involved in the
automatic writing, which in content was straight liberal
theology, and came to the medium without conscious cere-
bration; but the raps, lights, and apports were observed
before the automatic writing. To sum it up: to suggest
that Stainton Moses was dishonest is preposterous; to
suggest that his phenomena were genuine is almost more
so.

The visitor to the ordinary "flower séance" is faced
with no such dilemma. Two members of the Seybert Commission visited such a séance in Philadelphia, where a large
group sat around a table in the dark, and after a time
found some rather wilted flowers, of kinds then in season,

lying on the table. In the Centennial year (1876), so the medium's sponsor insisted, the table had been heaped high with fresh and blooming garden beauties, but at this time the mediumistic power, he believed, was suffering a recession. The Seybert men, while they did not actually seize any one red-handed, were much disgusted with the performance. I think they were entitled to be, in view of a performance I once had the pleasure of seeing.

Joseffy, once famous as a professional magician and now an electrical manufacturer, came one evening to my home for supper. We were together for nearly four hours, during which time he not only did not leave the apartment, but did not leave my sight. At the end of the evening he picked up a table scarf, threw it over his arm, and drew from under it a bunch of roses—absolutely fresh, with the dew still on them!

The duplication of spirit phenomena by a magician is no proof that the phenomena copied are frauds, but I do think the spirits should be able to do as well by genuine means!

At first spirit phenomena were confined in their effects to the physical senses of the sitters. Then came a development (from America, like most spirit novelties) which recorded the presence of spirit visitors in imperishable form. In 1861, William H. Mumler, an engraver working for the Boston jewellers, Bigelow and Kennard, found unexpected extra pictures on amateur photographs of a fellow workman. Spiritualism was going full blast, and Mumler decided to make a business of "spirit photography." He did a booming trade, regularly getting extra heads and forms on pictures which he took of living sitters at his studio. The "extras" were recognized sometimes as dead celebrities, sometimes as deceased friends and relatives of the sitters. In February of 1863, however, recognition went too far—Doctor Gardner, a leading Boston Spiritualist, recognized some of the "extras" as living Bostonians. Although the Spiritualists still believed that many of the "extras" were genuine, Mumler's business was spoiled, and he went back to engraving or took up some other occupation until 1869. Then he turned up in New York, once more as a spirit photographer. Here he was promptly prosecuted for fraud by the municipal authorities. Livermore (Katherine Fox's materialization-séance sitter) and the ever-faithful Judge John W. Edmonds testified in behalf of Mumler (they had recognized some "extras"), and the photographer was finally discharged for want of evidence. He does not, however, seem to have played much further part in developing the art he had founded.

Once American ingenuity had shown the way, Europe followed. In 1872 a British medium named Hudson began to take spirit photographs. Some sitters brought their own cameras, lenses, and plates, and watched Hudson throughout the whole process of taking and developing the pictures. There were many recognitions of the "extras" on record. But before long leading Spiritualists grew doubtful; photographers among their membership discovered that some of the "extras" represented Hudson in disguise, and that many of the pictures were plainly double exposures.

Hudson was exposed in *The Spiritualist;* but the *Spiritual Magazine, Human Nature,* and *The Medium* came hotly to his defense: the marks of double exposure on the plates were simply signs of refraction from the spiritual aura. Hudson's business grew instead of ceasing; Stainton Moses quoted him as the chief evidence for spirit photography, and Alfred Russel Wallace, writing just after the exposure in *The Spiritualist,* said:

"Spirit photographs. We now approach a subject which cannot be omitted in any impartial sketch of the evidences of Spiritualism, since it is that which furnishes perhaps the most unassailable demonstration it is possible to obtain of the objective reality of spiritual forms, and also of the truthful nature of the evidence furnished by seers when they describe figures visible to themselves alone. . . . Most persons have heard of these 'ghost-pictures,' and how easily they can be made to order by any photographer. . . . But a little consideration will show . . . that the means by which sham ghosts can be manufactured being so well known to all photographers, it becomes easy to apply tests or arrange conditions so as to prevent imposition."

"Easy" is perhaps not quite the term, at least in the present state of photographic technic; in 1921 C. Vincent Patrick listed twenty-two fraudulent methods of getting "extras," and more have been developed since.

Shortly after the uproar about Hudson, a Parisian photographer, Buguet, made a professional visit to London. He was a much better photographer than either Mumler or Hudson; the extras were clearer, and the men who had detected Hudson's imposture could not catch Buguet cheating. Stainton Moses warmly endorsed Buguet in an article printed in May, 1875. In June, 1875, the French government arrested Buguet for fraud. At his trial he made a complete confession, and the police seized and produced his "spirit" doll and the collection of heads that fitted on it. In his confession Buguet said he had begun by using three or four assistants to pose as the spirits; but his business got so large that he was afraid of having so few different "extras," and he laid in a supply of heads.

At the trial a long succession of witnesses testified that they positively recognized the "extras," and in some cases they testified that the "extra" bore no resemblance to any of the dummy heads displayed in court. In short, they refused to believe Buguet's confession or the police exhibit, and when Buguet himself specified how he had duped a given sitter, the sitter clung to his statement that he could not be mistaken in recognizing his wife, sister, or other loved one.

The English Spiritualists sided with the witnesses, and indicated that the prosecution was a Jesuit, or at least a Roman Catholic plot to discredit Spiritualism. They said that Buguet plainly was a genuine medium who had been bribed to betray his cause.

Despite the defense, however, spirit photography declined for twenty-five years or more; then it took a new lease on life. Various innovations were made. One Wyllie, of San Francisco, got extras without a camera, simply laying his hands on the plate in the photographic dark-room. The faces, however, were not bigger than a thumb-print. The celebrated William Hope, one of the "Crewe Circle" of British spirit photographers, was the chief reliance of Conan Doyle, who had a large collection of spirit photographs which he wrote had never been "questioned." Doctor Joseph Jastrow, one of Doyle's most vocal adversaries, replied that every one of the collection had been questioned by competent authority. I asked my friend Pirie MacDonald, the portrait photographer of men, about this, and he said, "Sir Arthur brought to my studio one of his pictures of fairies. It was a photograph of a field and in the grass in the foreground were a number of little figures. To one who knew anything about photography it must have been obvious that something was wrong as the sunlight hit the field in one direction and hit the faces of the little figures from another direction. It was plain that a number of cut-out pictures had been stuck about in the grass and a photograph taken. The photographer had not cared, or did not notice that the lighting in the pictures was opposite to that of the scene. Sir Arthur was such a lovely gentleman I did not have the heart to disabuse his mind. I merely put the picture back in its paper and said, 'Very interesting.'"

I asked Pirie MacDonald if it were always possible to detect trickery by examining a photographic print. He answered, "A picture can be so well made that it is impossible to see the fraud from the print. Walter Scott Shinn demonstrates what a skilled photographer can do when he combines one negative with another. This is done in the case of a group, for example, where one child has moved in one negative and the rest of the group are well photographed; while in a second negative though the wriggly child is still the rest of the group are not so well portrayed. The head is taken out of the one picture and the head from the other substituted. The finished print does not show the substitution."

So far as William Hope is concerned, failing a confession like Buguet's it would plainly be impossible to show all his pictures frauds; but on one occasion at least he tripped over the wily precautions of an investigator with expert knowledge of photography. This was Harry Price, who has exposed so many tricky mediums. He brought his own plates as Hope always requested. Price, however, had taken the precaution to have the Imperial Dry Plate Co., Ltd., *x-ray* a mark on the unopened plates. When Hope got an "extra," that plate lacked the x-rayed mark. Hope was exposed again in 1932, but Conan Doyle, Price says, "abused me for years for exposing Hope."

Harry Price, incidentally, I understand, accepts the existence of certain phenomena; but of spirit photography he says, "There is *no* good evidence that a spirit photograph has ever been produced."

A celebrated colleague of William Hope's is Mrs. Ada Emma Deane. On Armistice Day, 1924, she took a picture of the Cenotaph, in London, showing the spirits of dead heroes hovering round. When the London *Daily Sketch* got hold of a print, the photographers copied and enlarged it. The spirits seemed to be heroes, no doubt, but not dead ones: they were portraits of living professional soccer players. As an English spirit photographer candidly told a close friend of mine, "It's 'ell to get the pitchers yer want to reproduce!"

Some of the most mysterious spirit photographs have been the work of persons hostile to the cause, who wanted to show what could be done by trickery. William Van de Weyde, a well known New York photographer, took some pictures for a group of investigators in New York in 1922, under the conditions laid down by Sir Arthur Conan Doyle as prerequisites for the acceptance of a spirit photograph. These conditions were, *a.* control of the photographic procedure by the investigators (they to buy plates, supervise exposure and development, etc.) ; *b.* appearance on the plate of a dead man's picture; *c.* resemblance of the picture to the dead man, but not to any known life portrait of him. All these conditions Van de Weyde complied with to the letter, and he got a spirit "extra" very definitely representing Professor James Hyslop, the well known psychic investigator, then dead. Van de Weyde admitted that the picture was a fraud, perpetrated to prove his personal disbelief in Spiritualism, but he made a hundred-dollar bet with Samri Frikell that Frikell could not discover the method. After a considerable amount of digging around, Frikell won the hundred dollars. The method was, as a matter of fact, much less subtle than some of those which spirit photographers have developed: he had in his files a photograph of Professor Hyslop which Hyslop had not cared to buy, and which therefore had never been seen by any one else; he bought a package of plates, carefully opened it, copied this unknown photograph on to one of the plates, repacked everything with the utmost exactness, and took the package to a photographic supply dealer. Here he asked one of the clerks to offer this particular package when he (Van de Weyde) and two other men came in to buy plates.

An even more impressive demonstration was given by C. P. MacCarthy, himself a spiritist, of Sheffield, England. Here the committee bought the plates, and Mac-Carthy was *never* allowed to touch them during the whole proceedings. Camera and slide were taken straight from a supply dealer's stock; the pictures were taken by a professional photographer; MacCarthy was searched beforehand, and was *handcuffed* while the picture-taking and developing went on. The plates were not faked beforehand, and there was no collusion of any kind.

Under these conditions five of the plates bore "extras," three of which were recognized by the sitters.

Afterward Mr. MacCarthy explained his method. First he hunted up some old photographs which looked like certain members of the committee. Mrs. William Ewart Gladstone was recognized by one of the sitters as his mother. Mr. MacCarthy managed by suggestion to get his own father to ask for a dead friend whose picture he had got hold of; this recognition, that is, was correct. He then made micro-photographs of the five pictures. Each micro-photograph was about the size of a pinhead. These he mounted in a special tiny projector for throwing ultra-violet rays, invisible to the human eye, but active on photographic emulsions. The projector was about the size of his little finger. Where he hid it during the search he would not say; but he got hold of it in the dark-room, and was able by careful practice to point the proper picture at the proper plate from a distance of eighteen inches. The handcuffs, of course, did not prevent him from pointing his finger, under which he had the projector attached.

It seems to me that this honest trick is almost as remarkable in its details as would be a genuine spirit "extra"! Certain magicians' tricks are more surprising when you know how they are done than when you do not, and I am inclined to put Mr. MacCarthy's performance in that class.

The spirit photographers who make their living by their work are mostly not in that class at all. One such man, "Doctor" William M. Keeler, pursued this career for some forty years, although he escaped exposure only by the most abject flight from any sort of investigation. When the Seybert Commission was trying to get sittings with spirit photographers, Keeler said he would give them sittings, but his terms would be $300 (his usual charge was $2 per sitting), and "if conditions made it necessary" he would insist on the sole use of the dark-room while developing the plates. Long after, from 1912 to 1919, he made the acquaintance of a wealthy Washington aristocrat, Mrs. Marguerite Du Pont Lee, and having once convinced her, allowed her to "get" the spirit pictures for herself. She would tie a package of plates, still in their black wrappings, to her forehead for an hour, and then black spots, curves and bands would appear on the plates when developed. These were later discovered to result from the fact that the black wrappings let through some light, while the mucilage and string cut it off in places. The pictures which most interested her were ordinary photographs taken by Keeler, showing "extras" of her late pastor, the Reverend Kemper Bocock. There were also plates on which such spirits as Bocock, Poe, Socrates, Henry Ward Beecher and Grover Cleveland would write direct. Many of the signatures were found to be exact copies, if not the real thing; but the messages, some of them quite long, were evidently in the hand of an amanuensis. After long and vain efforts to get even a sample of Keeler's handwriting, the late Doctor Walter Franklin Prince, then of the American Society for Psychical Research, managed to trick the man into sending a signature and a holograph note, and with the assistance of a handwriting expert he came to the well-buttressed conclusion that the amanuensis was William M. Keeler in person. Doctor Prince also took apart the pictures with the spirit "extras" of Bocock, some of which, to my possibly prejudiced eye, look extremely comical. Keeler was thrown into a panicky rage by the very mention of the A. S. P. R., and he neither answered their letters, nor would let any one connected with them come near his studio. That he should make a comfortable living for more than a generation is a sad commentary on spirit photography.

With less cautious mediums, exposures go on all the time. A sensational case in London was that of John Myers, a dentist, whom the Marquess of Donegall unmasked in 1932 with the assistance of staff members of *The Sunday Dispatch*, my friend Will Goldston, the magician, and the writer-conjurer J. C. Cannell. The simple scratching of corners of the plates brought by

Lord Donegall was a trap sufficient to ensnare Myers, although Lord Donegall also stated in print that he would take oath at law that he had seen Myers switch plates.

After the exposure was printed, the spiritist press came to Myers' defense. One of their allegations was that Myers was making good money as a dentist, and had no financial motive for fraud. To this Lord Donegall replied by reprinting an advertisement by Myers in the spiritist publication *Service*, with a list of fees for sittings. They ranged from 25s. for one sitter to 50s. for a group of six; Lord Donegall claimed to know that Myers always had as many customers as he could handle.

Keeler was not alone in producing photographic writing ("psychographs"); in fact William Hope, of the Crewe circle, did a better job. Hope's practice was to have people mail him packages of plates. These he would return unopened, and writing, usually in circular lines, appeared when the customer developed the plates. Sometimes he would get a message unmistakably in the handwriting of one dead. These, as Doctor Walter Franklin Prince pointed out, had a smudgy black background surrounding and separating the words, showing that the words were extracted individually from an actual letter, and rearranged to give the desired message. Another Hope psychograph cited by Doctor Prince contained the following Latin tag: "Ob mort-es nostr-orum fratr-um dob-emus." It "pretty effectually showed that he or his medium, in copying from a Latin grammar, did not know that the hyphens are simply to point off for beginners the case and tense endings."

An elaboration of spirit photography was the production of spirit paintings. The Bang sisters of Chicago were the most prominent American practitioners; their method was to have the sitter bring a photograph of the dead person to be painted, and the following day the spirits would paint the portrait in color on a canvas put in the window to catch the sun. David Duguid of Glasgow, on the other hand, specialized in little landscapes. Mechanical and chemical means were proved to have been used, where the mediums did not prefer (like Duguid) to use simple substitution of painted for unpainted cards.

Still another form of spirit portrait was the wax impression, at first of faces, later on of hands and even of feet. Some of the early impressions of faces appeared in wax in the medium's cabinet. These, according to the anonymous English author of *Confessions of a Medium*, were prepared beforehand from plaster casts, and were switched for the unprepared wax while the medium was manipulating the bowls of wax and hot water.

The most common form of impression was hands and feet molded in paraffin; usually there would be a complete paraffin glove, the wrist so small that the hand could not possibly have been pulled out. The procedure was to bring on a bucket of hot water, with liquid paraffin floating on the top. This would be carefully weighed, and then set in the center of the circle. After a long sitting, when the lights were turned up, there would be some of these paraffin gloves lying beside the bucket; when bucket and gloves were weighed, the result corresponded exactly with the original weight. Casts could be made from the hands, and a French investigator, Gustave Geley, printed many pictures of such casts in a book on clairvoyance and materialization.

Evidently M. Geley had not read or did not believe the description of John Truesdell, who told a good fraudulent method of producing such gloves. You simply wash your hand in strong soapsuds, and dip it into liquid paraffin again and again, until a thick coating has formed. You then make a cut at the wrist, allowing the hand to be withdrawn, and seal the cut parts again afterward by heat.

The actual process of smuggling the gloves in to the séance is fairly easy; Truesdell suggests that female mediums should pin them to their stockings under the skirt. The puzzle of the weighing is accounted for by the evaporation of a weight of hot water sufficient to make up for the gloves; this also explains why it takes quite a long time for the gloves to be formed.

Another method of making paraffin hands permitted the hands to be made during the séance. The medium brought an ordinary rubber glove concealed about his person. After the melted paraffin had been brought to the séance room, and the lights had been turned out, the medium took the rubber glove out of its hiding place and blew into it until it was fully inflated. Then carefully holding the wrist of the glove so that the air did not escape he dipped the glove into the paraffin until he had a sufficient coating. Then all that was necessary was to permit the air to escape and withdraw the glove from its mold. The one bad feature of this method was that the glove was smooth and therefore if an inquiring person were to break one of these casts he would find that there were no lines, or ridges, in the paraffin as might be expected from a hand. Some mediums, therefore, went to the trouble of having special rubber gloves made which were true copies of a hand—lines, ridges, and all. There does not seem to be any way of telling when a cast has been made from an actual hand and when it has been made from a true copy of a hand. Mediums scoff at the rubber glove idea for they say that many of the casts have the fingers formed into a fist and a glove would merely have each finger stick out straight. It is found in practice that after the first few dippings the fingers can be bent into any position desired without marking the soft wax. The glove is then dipped several more times after the thin coating has been allowed to cool and no mark of manipulation is left. The particular advantage of the glove is that once it is deflated it can be brought through a tiny wrist opening; one much too small to allow a real hand to be taken out without cutting the cast. After the cast has been finished the glove is returned to its hiding place.

From whole hands it was an easy stage (considering the state of popular scientific knowledge) to finger-prints. I shall have more to say about these later in this chapter; the most celebrated ones were made on dental impression compound, which leads one to wonder whether the next step in psychic progress will be tooth-marks! The actual technic of their production has not, so far as I know, been positively proved, but similar results have been got by the making of dies from wax impressions made by the thumbs of living persons.

As in war every new weapon of offense produces a corresponding defensive invention, so in spiritism every new phenomenon is likely to be accompanied by a further step in control of the medium. The Davenport Brothers were elaborately tied with ropes, from which they could escape with great speed when left alone for a moment. Then the dark-séance mediums had their hands and feet held or stepped on by sitters at each side. Palladino and others developed extraordinary adroitness in making "breaks" from this control. Early in the list came the medium and vaudeville performer Anna Eva Fay. She did a "mind-reading" act, which will be described in a later chapter, and also did a cabinet performance which in some ways improved on that of the Davenports. She was secured by means of a post fixed to the stage. There was a ring like that of a hitching-post hanging from this post. Miss Fay sat on a stool. Her wrists were connected behind her back by cotton bandages, which were sewn tightly on. The bandage link passed through the ring on the post. After the performance, the bandages were found still sewn, and this was the actual fact; she did not release herself from the bandages. While she was thus fastened, bells rang, a glass of water was carried to her lips, and so on. Her method of doing this has since become well known. All it amounts to is that the bandages would slip up her wrists some distance; the six-inch link between wrists gave extra leeway, and so did the ring on the post; all in all she could get a foot or more of play for one hand, and this was plenty for the manifestations she produced.

She shared with less skilful mediums the honor of being investigated and found genuine by Sir William Crookes. Sir William had her hold handles forming a circuit with a resistance coil and a galvanometer, and the galvanometer continued to register while manifestations went on. No real precautions were taken to prevent her from inserting a resistance coil in the circuit and merely pretending to hold the handles provided for her. Neither were precautions taken to prevent her from moving the handles from her hands to her armpits and thus freeing one or both hands.

Miss Fay lived far into her seventies, and Harry Houdini visited her in her retirement at her home in Melrose Highlands, Massachusetts. He reported that she was one of the keenest women he had ever met, and that she talked to him as to a fellow-vaudevillian, expressing complete agnosticism in respect to a future life.

There have been nearly as many types of restraint devised for holding mediums as there have been mediums who would permit restraint. Usually these methods were suggested by the medium and in the hope that once the sitters had secured the medium to their own satisfaction they would thereafter accept all manifestations which occurred during the séance as the work of spirits. Frequently, when one of the sitters had an idea of his own about fastening the medium, the excuse would be offered that it would injure the medium. However, it was very seldom that any one offered another method of restraint, for the way suggested by the medium would look to be so secure.

Among the various restraints used, other than being tied to a chair with rope, were handcuffs, and chains, pillories, and boxes, silken bags, and canvas mail sacks. Hundreds of methods were devised to escape from these bonds. Few persons know anything about the efficiency of a restraint and at times it was unnecessary to escape. For instance, though the committee would tie the arms and the body of the medium to the chair most securely they would not bother to tie the hands nor legs. The medium, though tied so that he really could not free himself without considerable trouble, was able to walk about the room—chair and all—and bring his hands close enough to the various objects to manipulate them. But when it was necessary to be entirely free the mediums were prepared. One of the cleverest of these trick releases was used when the medium was tied with ropes to a stool on which he was seated. The stool was so constructed that it came apart, when secret releases were pressed, so that the medium was free. At the end of the séance it was snapped together again and there sat the medium "securely tied." The handcuffs, and mail sacks, and bags belonged to the medium, although frequently presented at the séance by a confederate, and were prepared and tricked in a large variety of ways. The pillories had secret releases. The boxes too had false hinges and hasps, sliding panels and other secret openings, to permit the medium to free himself at will. I have literally hundreds of diagrams showing how all these things may be made. Some of them are most ingenious mechanically and some of them are ridiculously simple. An example of such simple means is the silken bag with a drawstring to be tied about the neck. As the bag is being put in place the medium secretly pulls a foot, or more, of the center of the drawstring down inside the bag and holds it tightly. The committee now pulls on the drawstring and ties it carefully about the neck so that the head only of the medium is outside the bag. The knots, usually, are sealed with wax and every one is satisfied that the medium cannot get out of the bag without injuring the fabric. Of course all that he needs to do is to release the loop of string he is holding and using this slack open the gathers at the neck until he can pull off the bag. Once he has conducted his séance he can reverse the process and be in the carefully-tied bag by the time the lights go up.

Church, a Kentucky medium, had a much easier way of convincing his sitters that he remained in one spot and quite away from the phenomena which occurred. He had the sitters sew the legs of his trousers to the carpet. One person sewed the outside of his right trouser leg to the carpet and another sewed the left leg. A variety of different-colored threads were used and each lady was asked to put some embroidery stitch in her work so that she could be certain of identifying it later. While Church was so fastened a guitar would be strummed as it floated about the room. The guitar was actually felt by sitters at the extreme corners of the room. An unexpected light one evening showed that the guitar was carried and played by the medium who had merely stepped out of his trousers.

Not only has there been a great deal of special tricky apparatus used to give the effect that mediums are so fastened that they cannot take any part in séances, but there also has been a wide variety of equipment made to conceal the various disguises used in materialization séances. I have diagrams showing how to construct hollow chair seats, hollow heels of shoes, hollow table legs, and hollow books. Other diagrams show the way to make secret wall panels and floor traps, and, in short, how to make almost everything about the room and the room itself give up its wigs and gauze. I have a contractor friend who, in his youth, worked on a job making double all the walls of a room in a house in a Middle Western city. Between the walls was space for a confederate to walk about and there were secret panels operating electrically so that he could aid the medium at various points of the room and at various points of the séance. It was quite a costly job but the medium had made arrangements for the contractor to wait sixty days for his money. In sixty days the medium had made quite a bit of money which he took with him when he secretly left town. It is not strange to discover that the contractor is an ardent anti-spiritist.

In secreting equipment for materializations, as with the releases from bonds, the simple methods were usually most effective. The old styles of women's clothing with the fullness of the material and the long skirts made it easy to carry secretly the equipment necessary for disguises for materializations. One confessed trickster-medium explained that she carried the muslin, with which she draped herself when appearing as a spirit, inside her "drawers where the examining committee's sense of propriety would keep them from looking." Another method was with a confederate who would hand the medium the disguises when no one was looking or else pretend to be examining the cabinet and at that time leave them behind. The confederate would have merely to take care that he was the last to enter the cabinet for its examination. These simple methods were particularly advantageous when the séance took place outside the medium's own rooms. However, the very fact that séances were held in the homes of patrons made the furnishings of those rooms free of suspicion. It, therefore, was easy to drop a small package of properties behind books, into a vase; or stick it under a cushion of a chair upon arrival. It was certain no one would think of examining the room before the séance.

As long as the style of restraint is chosen by a medium it may be assumed with justice that the medium can escape from his bonds. And as long as it is not assured that the medium cannot free himself and cannot have the aid of a confederate it also may justly be assumed that one may be suspicious of any materialization which occurs; particularly as séance rules forbid a close examination of the materialized form.

No attempt has been made in this book to give a list of all the various phenomena of the séance room, or to describe all the wide variety of ways trickster-mediums have produced manifestations which they hoped would be accepted as genuine. Neither does this book name all those who were at one time or another mediums. In most instances the first medium producing each type of phenomena is described. The attempt has been made to give the opinions of those who believed in them and the reasons why others did not believe. Usually both the believers and the scoffers upheld their opinions most ardently and held poor opinions of those who were on the opposite sides. This is particularly true of Margery.

Margery's mediumship is not something to study in the yellowing pages of some musty old report, for she began only in the spring of 1923. Neither is she some ignorant peasant living in a remote foreign town, for she lives in the city of Boston and is the wife of a surgeon. She does not charge a fee to attend her séances but rather puts them on a strictly invitational basis—those who witness her séances are guests in her home. At Margery's early séances the manifestations were the more usual kinds—raps, cool breezes, table-tipping—but owing to her social position this was enough for the newspapers and hundreds of articles told about her and the séances. The newspapers took from Margery her anonymity and published her own name, Mrs. Mina Stinson Crandon, and gave the name of her husband, Doctor L. R. G. Crandon. The newspaper stories were followed by many magazine articles, and a book, describing her powers. As each succeeding story was published it was seen that more and more phenomena were occurring at her séances.

Objects at a distance from the medium were pushed about sometimes without any connection with the medium and sometimes by a "teleplasmic rod" (made of ectoplasm) which came out of the medium's body. A bell contained in a wooden box and so arranged as to ring when the lid was pressed down rang even when at a distance from the medium. Equilibrium of a pair of chemical balances was maintained which had weights on only one pan. Musical sounds proceeded from no instrument known to be in the house. A variety of forms materialized; some invisible to the eye, but visible to a camera with a fused quartz lens; some which while they could not be seen were felt by the sitters; some which were visible and tangible. Lights, from pin points up to seven-foot columns, and perfumes were produced. During many of the séances there were both apports and deports. There were both trance and automatic writings. Paraffin gloves were made and finger-print impressions were left in the plastic compound.

At the very beginning Margery was aided by various spirits, such as is usual among mediums. Later she found herself almost entirely in the control of her late brother, Walter. Walter from his first visit took over the rôle of master of ceremonies of the séances. Even when he brings his spirit friends to help him he is always in charge. No change in the conduct of a séance could be made without the permission of Walter. According to reports Walter is frequently autocratic and not infrequently profane and talks almost continuously during the séances. To prove that she has nothing to do with the voice of her control Margery made use of a "voice cut-out." This was the invention of Doctor Mark W. Richardson, a friend of the Crandons, and was intended to make sure that the independent voice of Walter was not in fact produced by Margery. The cut-out was a U tube, half full of water, with a rubber tube and mouthpiece on one end. Each arm of the tube contained a luminous float. It was the intention of the inventor to prove that when Margery blew into the tube, disturbing the equilibrium of the floats, she could not take the mouthpiece out of her mouth without letting them fall back to the same level. It certainly was true that Walter's voice and whistling would be heard while the floats were out of balance.

The thing which had distinguished Margery from the start was the fact that instead of being an ignorant but slippery shyster, as disbelievers always paint mediums, she was an educated woman, trained in music and as a secretary, who professed herself willing to meet any sort of investigation from serious psychists. Doctor Crandon wrote, "Discovered accidentally in 1923, the mediumship has advanced rapidly and the phenomena which occur appear equally well at home or abroad. Margery enters a laboratory in Paris or London for the first time, and under conditions laid down by the most experienced men in the world, the phenomena begin within a few minutes."

Several prominent spiritists were quoted as saying, in effect, that spiritism stood or fell with the Margery mediumship. Here was a medium at whose séances a wide variety of phenomena occurred, a woman of position who gave literally hundreds of séances to satisfy the doubting world in the validity of spirit return. "Truly," a spiritist friend of mine said, "history will name her as the greatest woman of the twentieth century."

So much interest was evoked in the Margery mediumship that it was perfectly natural that the Committee formed by *The Scientific American* magazine to investigate psychic matters was asked to investigate her work. Every one was particularly interested in the Committee's report because the members had already investigated a number of mediums without finding one they considered genuine. *The Scientific American* was offering twenty-five hundred dollars to the medium who would satisfy the Committee as having produced genuine phenomena. The Committee did not sit as a whole but the members attended different séances and varying numbers of séances. The Committee consisted of Doctor William McDougall, head of the department of psychology at Duke University and at that time professor of psychology at Harvard and president of the American Society for Psychical Research; Doctor D. F. Comstock, formerly professor in the Massachusetts Institute of Technology; Doctor Walter Franklin Prince (since deceased), research officer of the A. S. P. R.; Hereward Carrington, and the late Harry Houdini.

The members of the committee made the following reports:

Mr. Carrington: "Many of the observed manifestations might well have been produced fraudulently—and possibly were so produced. . . . But I am convinced that genuine phenomena have occurred here."

Doctor Comstock: "Rigid proof has not yet been furnished."

Doctor McDougall: "As long ago as November, 1923, when I had enjoyed only a few sittings, I wrote Margery's husband, stating frankly that I was inclined to regard all the phenomena I had observed as produced by normal means, possibly with the admirable design of testing and exposing the gullibility of scientific men who venture to dabble in the field of psychic research. Since that date I have taken part in three series of sittings, eagerly looking for evidence of supernormal phenomena and doing my best to keep my mind open to such evidence.

"During this period the inclination described above has grown steadily stronger, in the main, in spite of some minor fluctuations, and now has become well-nigh irresistible."

Doctor Prince: "No sitting at which I was present was to me convincing. . . . In fact, I could write a chapter of indications which, in the absence of contravening proof, seem to tell the story of normal and deceptive production."

Mr. Houdini: "Everything which took place at the séances which I attended was a deliberate and conscious fraud."

By a four to one vote the committee voted against having found evidences of Margery's séance manifestations' having psychic causation.

There were five other committees largely made up of University professors who also brought in verdicts which ran from the mere statement, "Not proven," to the observation of fraud. No member of these other committees mentioned belief in any one of the phenomena.

Independent reports were also brought out. Doctor J. B. Rhine, of Duke University, "found ample reason to believe the whole séance to be premeditated and brazen trickery." W. T. Bell, formerly of Scotland Yard, reported that the lines on the inside of a paraffin glove supposed to have been cast on Walter's hand actually had a thumb impression identical with Margery's. Some of the investigators even went so far as to duplicate the things which happened at the Margery séances. One of these was Professor Grant H. Code, of the University of Delaware, another was the psychologist Doctor H. C. McComas. Doctor McComas even constructed a "voice cut-out" which looked exactly like Margery's but it could be made to hold the floats out of balance so that in his imitation séances he could use his voice as he pleased.

Many of the investigators were hampered, they felt, in making proper observations during the séances by the "arbitrary and irrational rules" laid down for the sitters. Sometimes these rules were made by Walter and often by Doctor Crandon.

The eminent scientist, Professor Robert William Wood, of Johns Hopkins, said to me:

"I saw nothing at the several séances I had with Margery that caused me to think for a moment that they were caused by any supernatural forces. You have to do things their way or not at all. For instance they would not submit to my request to hold a stethoscope to her chest during the time Walter was speaking."

It was said by those loyal to Margery that none of the committees had or could have observed any trickery. It was also said that the various ones who brought in unfavorable reports were ignorant, had some personal grudge which motivated their reports, and in one case flatly stated that a committee man was drunk.

Then a bomb shell was dropped on the Margery séances by the discovery by Mr. E. E. Dudley that the impressions of a thumb in the compound, which had been such a convincing proof of Walter's powers, actually were impressions of a living man. Not only was the man alive but he was Margery's dentist and the one who showed her how to handle the plastic compound which is used in making dental impressions. It was also shown that it was easy to make a die capable of reproducing any number of thumb-prints. A long list of experts agreed that the prints were the same: those made during the séance and those of the dentist's. Doctor Crandon had answers to all the accusations and even explained how a right thumb impression was made while photographs show Walter's left thumb making the impression. Doctor Crandon wrote, "Teleplasm being ideoplastic, Walter can make the thumb-print with his left or right hand, or his foot for that matter."

While many people still have complete belief in the genuineness of Margery's mediumship several scientific committees to investigate her work have brought in unfavorable verdicts. In a report, published by the Boston Society for Psychic Research, on the thumb-print duplication, Hereward Carrington, the only member of the Scientific American Committee to bring in a report favorable to Margery, wrote:

"Personally, I am strongly inclined to believe that, at the beginning of her mediumship, at least, Margery possessed some genuine telekinetic power, and I am frank in stating that some extremely puzzling phenomena were produced at that time, for which I could not account, after attending more than fifty sittings. This fact I have stated in my *Scientific American* summary. I am inclined to think that this modicum of genuine material was, in the course of time, constantly supplemented by other 'manifestations' of a more and more startling character, culminating in these preposterous thumb print phenomena—for the reality of which there is not, in my opinion, a shred of scientific evidence. I cannot but feel that these have thrown a cloud over the whole case which can only be dispelled, if at all, by a long series of rigidly controlled experiments given to a Committee composed partly of scientific men and partly of impartial magicians (and there are such). If such a series were given, and the results were favorable, serious psychical researchers would then be compelled to reconsider the case. As it stands with the séances all given in the medium's house, with her (unsearched) husband present and generally actually 'controlling,' with 'Walter' dictating the procedure, and with only a 'family party' of personal friends and complete believers being present, serious credence can no longer be given to this case by psychic investigators."

Among those mediums who produce physical manifestations—from spirit forms to tilting tables—there have been a pitifully small number who have never been exposed. An association of mediums in California even went on record to the effect that all those claiming to produce physical manifestations were frauds.

CHAPTER VI

VOICES

❨ 6 ❩

---

*F*RANZ ANTON MESMER, a studious Viennese doctor, evolved an idea he could not seem to develop. Many people saw in his work some diabolic aid while others were convinced he was a charlatan. He persistently maintained that he had no supernormal power or aid from another world. The medical groups scorned his theory of healing and scientists laughed at his ideas. He was turned out of one country after another by those who disbelieved in his cures. Though his idea lived, and has been followed along a number of paths, he died, a practically forgotten man, in a little town in Germany, a century and a third ago.

One of the most characteristic features of Mesmer's work was the state of somnambulism (sleep-walking) produced in some of his patients. While in this trance they would talk interminably on many subjects, often saying things which it did not seem possible they could have known in their waking state. Mesmer himself believed that somnambulists could foretell the future, particularly the course of their own bodily diseases. Followers of Mesmer, studying the somnambulistic trance, really discovered trance mediumship: "people possessed by the spirits of the dead."

The steps are logical and clear between; a mental case being put to sleep by hypnotism, a person in such a sleep talking, considering such talk a prophecy and diagnosis by God, forgetting God and considering the talk spirit-inspired. Some have also made the next step, which is forgetting the medium and believing the voice the spirits' own.

Today there are trance mediums who during their séances say they hear spirit voices and repeat to their sitter what they have heard. The Davenport Brothers, it will be recalled, claimed that power. There are others who in the trance state claim to become possessed by a spirit, or a succession of spirits, which use the medium's voice as their own. Whether these séances are the result of a living or a physically dead mind at work is a question with which some of the best minds continue to wrestle.

It is possible among some trance mediums to get perfectly astonishing phenomena where fraud in the sense of purposive deception is absolutely prevented. When conscious fraud is presented under the guise of trance mediumship, however, it is usually infinitely more difficult to discover than fraudulent physical phenomena, and harder to prove than it is to discover.

The classic case of trance mediumship is that of Mrs. Leonora E. Piper, of Boston. If you could call her a "medium" at all, she certainly was a private medium, a resident of Beacon Hill, and the mother of two daughters. Her sittings were under the investigation of William James, Richard Hodgson, Oliver Lodge, and people of like eminence, for forty years almost without interruption. Everything said was stenographically reported at first; in later years she got many of her messages in automatic writing, which provided its own record. Her chief point of similarity to the conventional medium was in having "controls," certain favorite spirits or personalities who purported to hand on the information she furnished. She first discovered her power after sitting with a medium in 1884, and some of the early controls (such as Chlorine, the Indian maiden) suggest that she began under his influence. Soon, however, she swung over to an "eighteenth-century French physician," named Phinuit. All efforts to trace the real existence of such a person have failed, and opponents of the spirit hypothesis are not impressed by his explaining that he could not speak much French because he spent his last years amid the English colony at Metz. But whether Phinuit was a spirit or a secondary personality of Mrs. Piper, he could tell perfect strangers the most astonishing things about their lives, families, and characters. The same thing was true of Phinuit's successors, G. P. (a young New York lawyer and writer who died in an accident) and the "Imperator group." William James, who began investigating Mrs. Piper in 1885, called her work "the most baffling thing I know," and he soon interested Doctor Richard Hodgson, of the Society for Psychical Research.

It was Doctor Hodgson and his suspicions that were the

undoing of Palladino at Cambridge (England), and Hodgson was the terror of physical mediums. From 1887 until his death in 1905, Doctor Hodgson took almost complete charge of Mrs. Piper, arranging all her sittings, getting the sitters, keeping the records, and so forth.

In 1889 he got the Society for Psychical Research to invite her to England, where she stayed as the guest of F. H. Myers and of Oliver Lodge. Here the precautions to prevent her getting surreptitious information were redoubled: the Lodges got a complete new set of servants the day before Mrs. Piper arrived, they opened her mail both incoming and outgoing, they searched her baggage, they put private detectives to work checking up. The sitters were introduced as "Mr. and Mrs. Smith" or were not introduced at all, and sometimes were brought in after the trance had begun.

Despite these precautions, and with astonishing consistency, Mrs. Piper would tell people about the diseases, feelings, character, personal peculiarities and thoughts of themselves and their friends: "their loves, hates, quarrels, sympathies, and mutual relationships in general; trivial but significant incidents in their past histories, and the like" (Podmore).

It was Mrs. Piper who converted Richard Hodgson to definite belief in spirit survival, and Professor James Hyslop too believed that this theory best explained her work. Some other investigators thought this was going too far for the evidence; but all agree that Mrs. Piper is one of the major puzzles of psychic science.

The particular difficulty in testing such a medium is to

make certain that he, or she, is not talking, like the oracles of old, so that his statements can be understood two ways. Another difficulty is to try to discover whether the medium is saying anything which is not either universally true, or something which can be guessed by observation of the sitter. Still another difficulty is to make certain the medium cannot have some advance knowledge.

It is amazing how many things are, for the purposes of the medium, universally true. People feel that they are not understood; that they have some marked talent which has not been developed, that they are good judges of character, that they are really exceptional, and that their experiences are unlike any other person's. The list of universal traits is long. This all makes good material for the medium and the sitters cannot reason out how the medium could discover these *unique* facts about them.

Comparatively few people go to mediums to make a study of their phenomena. Not many go for the solace of being in communication with a relative, or friend, who has passed on. The great majority go in order to get some information for themselves regarding their own affairs. The thrill seekers and other casual visitors need not be considered. Because the great majority do go for personal information they are satisfied when the medium gives them such information. It does not need to be accurate to bring satisfaction; it only must sound as if it were accurate. The easiest way to prove that you know about a person's future is to tell him something which he does not believe you know about his past, or present. Telling a person his name is always astounding; his address but little less so.

Strange that a person would feel that his name was a bit of secret information that a medium could not possibly possess. The human mind is so constituted that information which comes from the spirit of, for instance, a dead Indian seems more valuable than that which might come in a worldly way.

Usually at séances where there are many people it is required that each person write a question on a piece of paper. The medium then has all the papers brought forward and answers as large a proportion of them as time will permit. Each answer must of necessity be brief because of time. It happens to be easier to give the impression of knowing something for a moment than it does for a longer length of time. This again aids fraud. There are a variety of methods by trickery of discovering secretly what question has been written. The question often indicates an answer and even when no answer is made obvious it is a help to know the question. More about written questions will be given in the next chapter. When the question concerns the past the medium may answer it—with or without spirit aid—and be within the law. When the question concerns the future and the answer is given even by a spirit, it becomes fortune-telling. When done for a fee fortune-telling is illegal in many places. The vast majority go for an answer to a question relative to the future. They do not want to make decisions for themselves and hope to get an answer which will make it unnecessary for them to make an effort. Some few also have the bright idea that if they know the future they can cheat a little. If money is surely coming to you it is needless to work today. If you are to get a better job anyway, you do not have to work so hard to keep the one you have. If you are going to have a year of good health assured why not go out with the boys tonight?

Mostly, we forget the failures of prophecies and remember those exceptional times when they were correct. If, on the other hand, we do recall some prophecy which was untrue and inquire of a medium, we find that some ignorant or lying spirit gave the reply that particular time. I have a long list of prophecies which have been made on a wide variety of subjects, and very few of them ever came true. Mediums never fail to make prophecies about important, and much-talked-of events. In a good many instances there were only two possible outcomes, and yet the record of the medium is not right as often as would be expected if a coin had been tossed. A number of mediums bothered Colonel Charles A. Lindbergh at the time of his great tragedy. The Colonel told me that none of them had any information. He had each story checked, as he did with all the stories which came to his attention. Neither he nor anyone at his instigation acted upon information from mediums beyond the fact that no one claiming to have information was refused to be seen with the idea that they did not know how contact would be effected. In no instance do the records show that a medium had an iota of information to give. Not only were their statements carefully checked but they were watched by the police. A number of pages of recorded telephone conversations between certain of the mediums, at times when they were unaware of outside listeners, made it apparent that the mediums were conscious frauds. In the last several presidential elections mediums have given out information about who would win. There are several with the record of having told truly. But as there were others who also had picked the losing side, it is not surprising. I have a very low opinion of fortune-tellers no matter how they pretend to predict the future. Owing to the increasing number of cities which forbid fortune-telling unless done within the confines of a church, many of the old-line fortune-tellers have become Spiritualistic ministers. They had little difficulty making the change, as the fortunes are told in the same manner.

Not always does the fortune-telling medium ask that the question be written, nor does he necessarily read it when it is. People ask but few questions. The two main ones concern love and money. They usually ask when, instead of what. Health is a part of the question concerning love if it is another's health, and when your own, it is a part of the question concerning money. A person with any imagination can give answers, after sizing up his patrons, which sound plausible. They make the best answer they can and then change if they see the sitter is not satisfied. This is called "fishing" and it is amazing how satisfactory an adept at fishing can make his answers. If a medium has no imagination he can purchase books which give him excellent and very indefinite responses to all the stock inquiries.

If a person who consults one of these fraudulent mediums seems to be a good prospect financially, the medium will get advance knowledge about him. The patron may be asked to give his name when making the appointment for the séance. If such an individual is known to frequent séances, the medium will gather this knowledge in preparation for his first visit. When properly given out, a very small amount of information about a person is enough to convince any one but the most hardened skeptic that the medium has some gift if he is not actually in communication with spirits. To show how easy it is to make some little bit of information impressive, I have tried their methods. For instance, I met a man who, I had been told, spent his boyhood in China. That was all I knew about him as I did not catch his name when we were introduced. I suggested later that I should like to try an experiment in mind-reading which I had been studying. I asked the gentleman from China to think of a number of four figures. The trickery by which I discovered the numbers he had in mind is of no importance to the story, except that I was able to ascertain the numbers. I asked him to think of the figures very intently and I picked up a pad of paper and a pencil. I sat still and held my head down and my eyes half closed. Gradually I began to draw lines on the paper. I continued for several minutes very slowly and as if I were an automaton. Finally I dropped the pencil and slowly opened my eyes and held up my head. I looked around the room as if I did not know where I was. Then I noticed the writing on the paper and looked up at the man in great surprise. "Why, I asked you to think of figures and here are merely some meaningless scratches." He came over to the table, looked at the writing and said, "That is the most surprising thing I have ever heard of. Those are the four figures I had thought about but they are written in Chinese characters. I must have been visualizing them in that manner. You didn't know it but I was raised in China and spoke Chinese before I did English." He was completely convinced that I had read his mind because of the Chinese writing. The numbers from 1 to 10 are all the Chinese characters I happen to know. Before the evening was over he had me aside trying to get me to prophesy for him, and was annoyed when I told him I did not believe in prophecy.

Where do the mediums get the information? It is very easy. Look the person up in the telephone book. Talk to the corner grocer. Go to the house and try to sell a magazine subscription. Talk to the neighbors. Talk to the servants if there are any. If it is a small city go to the cemetery and look at the tombstones. It has to be done carefully but it is very easy. A man bet me one time that I could not find anything out about him within a half an hour. The reason for the time limit was that he had been to a medium and had a private séance, but had had to wait a half an hour after he had gotten to the medium's home. I picked up the man's own telephone and talked to his wife. I said that I was a photographer and because of her social prominence the papers wanted photographs of her and her family; that I was going to take these pictures free of charge and merely wanted her cooperation. She told me about her children, their ages, coloring, interests, and grades in school. She told me about her own clubs and those of her husband. In short, she told me infinitely more than the medium had told him. While I won the bet I doubt if the man yet believes that the medium had used any such method. I happen to know about that medium, however, and have learned that she not only has a very complete set of notes about all her patrons, but she keeps in her steady employ two people whose entire work is to collect information. When a sitter does not give his name it may be discovered in his hat, or he may have driven up in his car, and each state sells for a comparatively small amount a list of the license numbers of all cars, and the names of the owners.

One medium I was asked to investigate for a friend did not ask your name and did not require you to wait before seeing him. I could not see how some of the things told my friend, provided he remembered correctly, could have been discovered merely by fishing. I therefore went prepared for the method I thought might be used; the method John Truesdell had described. I had a letter in the pocket of my overcoat. Naturally I left the coat in an outer room. The letter was addressed to a name I had manufactured and which, incidentally, I have never found in any directory in the United States. I made it up, just as Kodak was made up to be unique. It was addressed to a street number which did not exist either. I had the envelope run through one of the cancelling machines in a big company, and then given back to me instead of being taken to the Post Office. There is no need to go into the details of the letter but they were manufactured items regarding the father of this non-existing man. At the séance I was told all the material of the letter and I was called by the name on the envelope. My friend did not recall that he had had a letter in his overcoat pocket. I looked at the overcoat. Inside the pocket on a label put in by his tailor was his name and address. He had never noticed it.

When properly presented a single nugget of information can be made most impressive, and in digging out information about a person it is amazing what comes to light. When, not infrequently, coincidence also plays a part, the result is beyond belief. For instance, the story of Fred. C. Kelly and the late Doctor James H. Hyslop. After one of Hyslop's talks on psychical research Mr. Kelly went up to Hyslop and asked for an explanation of a psychic experience of his own.

"While you were talking," said Mr. Kelly, "I visualized a man who looked like you, only much younger, in the act of sending a telegram. The message, it seemed to me, was about the death of the man's father. It was sent to a sister in a distant state, and she was requested to notify another sister living a few miles from her in the country. This message, according to the impression I have, was carried to the sister in the country by a boy on a bicycle."

Mr. Kelly asked if it had any significance. Doctor Hyslop said that it all tallied with the facts. When asked how he explained Mr. Kelly's having such a vision, Doctor Hyslop said: "I have no theory. The fact is, I never have any theory about any of the phenomena we find in these investigations."

The answer is very simple, as Mr. Kelly told Doctor Hyslop; Kelly had been the boy on the bicycle. Had Mr. Kelly been a pseudo medium rather than an honest writer he might not have told the truth at the end, and we would have another of those perfect stories.

After reading me that story from his book *The Wisdom of Laziness* my friend Kelly told me, "Just because a happening cannot at once be explained is no proof that supernatural forces are implicated."

One of the most important things necessary for these mediums who gather information about their sitters is to tabulate the information in some written record to make it quickly accessible. These records, or dope sheets, or blue books, are frequently traded among mediums. This is particularly helpful in making converts.

To list all the various methods which mediums have been known to use to get information about their clients would furnish material for a whole flock of detective story writers. In that way the material might be interesting, but a bare list of the methods I have in my files is not. The most interesting was mentioned by Travis Hoke in an article in *Harper's*. He wrote, "There have been quietly conducted prosecutions of insurance-company actuaries who sold to mediums information about wealthy policy holders."

When one understands how easy it is for a medium to get detailed information concerning one's life, it seems particularly foolish to accept some data about one's past as evidence of an ability to foretell the future. When it is considered how little value a charlatan's guesses could have about the future, it becomes doubly foolish to act upon such advice. It may do little damage in many cases, but too often the information sought is medical. To act upon a soothsayer's medical advice is quite criminally dangerous.

But provided one finds a true medium, should advice be taken then? From the number of wrong prognostications mediums have been reported as making, the advice can only be, No. Unless all prophesying mediums are fakes, and the spiritists will hotly deny this, the spirits, by the record, are no more able to know the future than we in life.

Mrs. Houdini told me that her husband's spirit has never come back to her either through, or without, a medium, despite the stories which have been circulated to the contrary. Doctor Joshua Allen Gilbert tried to get in communication with his wife through mediums. Before her death they had agreed upon a countersign to prove her communications were genuine. Two hundred and eighty-four mediums felt that they were in contact with Mrs. Gilbert, and each gave a countersign. All the countersigns were different and not one was right. I have case after case of this sort in my files.

When, as with Mrs. Piper, the medium uses a ouija board, or automatic writing, rather than the voice, the problem is very much the same. The only difference is that with the writing there can be no chance of some word being forgotten, for it is down on paper. It has been proven that when a medium does not know the order of the letters on the board, no message ever comes. It has also been proven by questioning under hypnosis that the medium writes only that which he knows. I am speaking now about the honest mediums, for of course, the dishonest ones know what they are going to write. The honest automatic writer is usually not conscious of either having the information or the experience which he describes. This test was made by Doctor Morton Prince and others.

In conclusion, this seems to be the most difficult branch of mediumship to investigate. The serious investigators believe that there are more indications of voice mediumship's being genuine than any mediumship of physical phenomena. The exposures show that a very large proportion of such mediums are proven frauds. The psychologists show that even a perfectly honest amateur medium can unconsciously bring from his mind forgotten facts and experiences. I repeat that the utmost care must be taken by those who visit mediums to insure that the mediums do not have full biographies of them.

CHAPTER VII

THOUGHT WAVES

EVERY ONE has had the experience of saying the same words at the same instant that some one else said them. There is a traditional ceremony children go through when this happens. The Chinese have the term "heart lightning" for this incident of the same thought striking two hearts at the same time. The Western people, according to their individual bent, ascribe such an occurrence to coincidence, or to mind-reading.

Many people have also had the experience of thinking of a name which had not been mentioned, or thought of, in ages and almost immediately afterwards meeting that person, getting a letter from him, or possibly merely hearing his name mentioned. When this happens fewer will ascribe it to coincidence although large numbers of people cannot accept it as evidence of mind-reading.

It does not look intrinsically improbable that one can take the thoughts from some one else's mind in view of these events, but whether this probability of mind-reading is real or specious is a question which finds the scientists of the world in active disagreement. Those who believe in mind-reading very often believe that one possessed of this power is also clairvoyant. Many also believe that mind-reading is one of the evidences of power of a medium. Since they do so, mind-reading becomes a part of the study of spiritism.

There are countless stories of mind-reading, or mental telepathy, told about the American Indians, the Negroes of Africa and the West Indies, the Tibetans, and other peoples who do not have telephonic or other modern mechanical methods of long-distance communication. A village would know all about a traveller long before he would arrive with his caravan. No outsider would come to a camp and yet all the bearers would have minutely detailed information of an event which occurred at some distant point.

Outside of these stories of travellers and explorers I can find no instances recorded of detailed stories coming regularly to any mind-reader or telepathist, in either Europe or America, prior to the demonstrations of the stage performers. True, there are many instances recorded of a person at a distance receiving the thoughts of some loved one who was ill or in some great trouble, but the records show that these instances are neither daily nor dependably regular.

Stage mind-reading was first presented as a demonstration that a person on the stage, sometimes blindfolded, could instantly describe any object shown to his, or her, associate by members of the audience. While a few people will always believe that this is a demonstration of telepathy, the majority realize that it is an exhibition by two highly trained actors whose art keeps hidden their real method of communication. It was not until the basic design of the act was changed to give the effect that the person on the stage could read the thoughts of the audience that any large number forgot that they were witnessing a performance in a theater by actors, and accepted the demonstrations as evidences of mind-reading. One of the first, if not the first, of these acts was given by Samri S. Baldwin and his wife, Kitty. Not only thousands of people, but the press of the world endowed Mr. and Mrs. Baldwin with true psychic powers.

Samri Baldwin was born January 21, 1848, in Cincinnati, Ohio. Kitty was English. According to his own story, he first became interested in magic while a medical student by attending a performance given by the Davenport Brothers and Fay. He attended many of their demonstrations and watched their methods. After Baldwin was certain that he knew all the tricks of the Davenports, he practiced until he could duplicate them to the complete mystification of his friends. He combined the study of theology with his medical school work but gave both up to enlist as a drummer boy in the Civil War. After the war, he went to New Orleans where he began following the profession of mystifying instead of either the ministry or medicine. He travelled far over the earth's surface with his show of illusions, and he was quite as much at home in Melbourne as he was in London or San Francisco.

Baldwin attempted to avoid arguments with those who

felt that the part of his performance which he gave with the aid of Kitty Baldwin was a demonstration of some supernormal power. He did not claim power nor, on the other hand, did he specifically deny using a sense that the majority of persons do not possess. He permitted the audiences to make up their own minds on the subject after subtly confusing them with his choice of words. He called this part of the performance "Somnomancy," a word of his own devising, which he said meant "sleep reading or dream portrayals." Mrs. Baldwin was brought on the stage and "hypnotized" by her husband and while seemingly hypnotized told various members of the audience incidents of their past, present, and future. The newspapers gave incident after incident which Mrs. Baldwin described correctly, and about which it was agreed that she could in no natural way have discovered the data. In Brisbane, the paper carried the story that she had described where a man could discover his late father's will. The next morning the reporter for the paper discovered that she was right. She rightly told a ship captain, according to a Hong Kong newspaper, that his brother had been lost when the clipper ship *Grey Eagle* had burned six years before. In Cape Town, again according to the local paper, the police credited Mrs. Baldwin with the discovery and the arrest of a murderer.

Samri Baldwin said of his wife that "she is the possessor of gifts that belong to few organizations." While this was understood by many to mean "psychic gifts" he could point out that what he meant was that she possessed many costly gifts from the Royal families they had appeared before. He called himself "The White Mahatma" but at the same time said that he was "an illusionist and escamoteur." His opening introduction should have warned every one that his demonstrations were not psychic.

"I am giving entertainments with the idea of mystifying and bewildering while pleasing and amusing the public. I am a skilled entertainer and theurgist, and will use all the means at my disposal to make my séances a mystery and puzzle to my audiences. I regard all means as fair and legitimate that will conduce to this end. Do not believe me if I tell you anything foolish or that seems untrue. Use your own common sense in estimating the value of anything I may say to you, and unless it is sensible, rational, and in accord with the teachings of science, then don't believe me. In fact, it is well to distrust all I may say, and use only your own common sense as a guide—for I admit that I will illusionize you whenever I find that by so doing I can add in any way to the mystery, interest, or realism of the entertainment I am presenting for your approbation."

Samri Baldwin was among the first to say that if there were any branch of psychic phenomena to study it was the mental side. He held a low opinion of physical phenomena. He wrote, "I have attended at least two thousand spiritual séances, and I am more convinced now even than I was in my early days, that under no circumstances do disembodied spirits return to this world to produce manifestations of any character." He also wrote, "I do not assume or claim the possession or use of any miraculous, occult, superhuman or supernatural powers whatever."

While he believed mind-reading to be possible, he at the same time admitted that what he showed in his performances was not mind-reading. He wrote several booklets exposing mediums and publicly demonstrated the methods of tricky mediums throughout the world, and yet he was credited time after time with the possession of supernormal powers by newspapers and by a large proportion of his audiences.

I attended one of Baldwin's last public appearances in company with several people who were convinced that he had read their minds. I went backstage after the show to call on him and told him of the belief of my friends. He smiled and said, "Isn't it strange what some people accept as evidence?"

Baldwin lived in retirement for several years before his death on March 12, 1924. He had lived an adventurous life, associated with many of the most famous people of his day, was praised from the pulpits of three continents for his exposures of fake mediums, and died to be remembered as a psychic.

According to some records, Kitty R. Baldwin was English and the wife of Samri S. Baldwin; according to other records Julia Clara Mansfield Baldwin was the wife of Samri S. Baldwin and was born near Carthage, Missouri, on July 7, 1852. Perhaps the White Mahatma was married twice, which is of little moment to the story except that then each wife had the gift of making people think that their minds were as open books.

Many people followed the Baldwin type of stage mind-reading with its question answering, and not a few suc-

cumbed to the lure of straight fortune-telling. Anna Eva
Fay, mentioned before, was one of the stage performers
most widely known for her mind-reading.

Miss Fay did not, however, follow the same methods
as any of her predecessors. Her method was so simple
that after it was exposed in newspapers she went right
on with it, for no one believed that she would have the
effrontery to use it. She answered questions, which she required in writing. All that one did was to write a question
and drop it in a basket which, supposedly, later was taken
on the stage. That basket, however, was not taken to the
stage but behind the scenes where Miss Fay would read
the questions and pick out those to which she thought she
could give interesting answers. Another basket filled with
blank pieces of paper was taken on the stage and left to
stand in full view of the audience.

My friend George W. Stock told me much about
Miss Fay's "séances." Mr. Stock is a magician, and the
son of a magician, and particularly well posted on the
methods of magic. When he was a young man Anna Eva
Fay needed an assistant. Some one who, all unknown to
the audience, would be skillful enough to attend to the
backstage part of her mysteries. George Stock got the
job and travelled with her for a year. He told me that
she had great charm and that it was a pleasant job, but he
is quite certain that Sir William Crookes' endorsement of
her psychic powers was a grave error.

Stock still recalled the words of the "lecture" by which
Miss Fay was introduced. "Just a few words before introducing Miss Anna Eva Fay. The results may be put

before you in this manner; if you think that these experiments are produced through strong will-power, animal magnetism, odic force, electricity, spiritualism, or mind over matter, you have that privilege: these results are simply demonstrated for your kind consideration." It is rather like Baldwin's introduction in that no claims are made and the audience was left to discover, if it could, any possible meaning in the words.

What made Anna Eva Fay stand out was that her séances, to quote *The New York Herald*, "are of a high order, and appeal rather to the intellect than to the risible faculty." Another point in her favor, according to *The Boston Herald*, "She gives her séances in the broad gaslight without resorting to trickery of a darkened room." While some of her audiences doubted that she actually produced spirits they did believe that she could read minds and, in all probability, had other unusual powers.

There is no more interesting and puzzling figure among the stage "psychics" than Washington Irving Bishop, the New York muscle-reader. He was the originator of the "pin test," and caused a sensation with his "blindfold drive" and other performances which seemed to transcend the natural. The pin test consisted simply of hiding a common glass-headed pin somewhere in the theater. Bishop would seize the wrist of the man who had done the hiding, and would race about the theater, eventually leading the man straight to the pin, which he would find. An elaboration was to give a spectator a dagger, and ask him to touch some one with it and then to hide the dagger. Even though he would allow himself to be blindfolded, and only holding his hand above that of the "murderer," instead of grasping the wrist, Bishop would find the dagger, the person touched, and usually the spot on his body at which the dagger had been pointed. The blindfold test was simply the same hide-and-seek with the addition that the object was hidden in another building, and Bishop would drive blindfolded through the streets in a carriage, avoiding car tracks and the like to find the thing.

"Muscle-readers" are people who are able to follow the almost imperceptible and totally unconscious volition of a person who is thinking of some action he wishes performed. This type of work is done most easily through the sense of touch but it is quite possible to do it by sight. It requires the thought to be one of action. Muscle-readers can choose the correct color from among several colors displayed by that method, but they cannot name a color thought of when none are shown.

Washington Irving Bishop wrote a book describing the methods of mind-readers in detail. In the introductory chapter he wrote: "There is, indeed, much reason in favor of an explanation of Clairvoyance, because knowledge of the process is still sufficiently obscure to enable unprincipled persons to use the influence that this supposed power gives them for improper purposes. Nothing can be more detrimental to morals than the prevalence of superstition; and there is scarcely a phenomenon in existence which operates so largely to the encouragement of superstition as the supposed power of Clairvoyance. It is always associated in the vulgar mind with the power of prophecy and divination. The many inquiries made of me as to the process of mesmeric exhibitors and Clairvoyants proves how widespread is the curiosity on the subject. The absence of any explanation gives rise to the belief among weak people that there is something supernatural in the matter, and that, in fact, the supposed professor of the power of second-sight is working under the influence of some occult force."

Bishop was slight, nervous, and liable to fall into cataleptic trances. What more natural than to think this neurotic-looking young man must have psychic power? As a matter of fact, Bishop used to tell a publicity story about old Commodore Vanderbilt, who, he said, was a well-known Spiritualist. The Bishops, he said, had lived near Vanderbilt, and had sometimes taken part in family séances with him as a friendly gesture, although the family was strictly High Church. At these séances Vanderbilt would ask Bishop for messages, produced by automatic writing. The messages often dealt with the stock market, and were not unlikely to be right. Bishop claimed that this proved not the spirit hypothesis but his own ability unconsciously to read Vanderbilt's shrewd mind, giving back to the financier his own opinions. For striking cases of trance vision on Bishop's part, we have unfortunately only the word of his own advance agent.

The fact of Bishop's performances is that he may have been peculiarly skillful in them, thanks to long practice and some degree of "hyperesthesia," but in general any one not too unobservant and horny-handed can do the same sort of thing. The performer seems to lead the assistant to the pin, but in truth the assistant, by involuntary hesitations and other signs, leads the performer. The performer always insists that the assistant must concentrate intently on the hiding-place or the thing to be done, and in this kind of performance (unlike almost all other "mind-reading" tricks) the concentration is really essential. One noisy and boisterous joker in an audience can spoil the trick.

Bishop's sensational death was a fitting end to a sensational career. The actual facts seem never to have been legally proved, but many people believed the charge by Bishop's mother that he fell into a cataleptic trance while giving a show at the Lamb's Club, in New York, on May 12, 1889, and was pronounced dead and cut up alive for autopsy within a few hours by three "medical Jack-the-Rippers."

Bishop was successful in England as well as in America, and an English coworker, Charles Garner, led a prosperous career doing Bishop's tricks for many years under the name of Stuart Cumberland. Cumberland was a frequent investigator of physical séance phenomena, and exposed a number of fraudulent mediums. Cumberland declared that "consciously at least" he had no supernormal powers, and that his achievements were merely a matter of acute perception of detail, trained by practice, and of quickness in putting small indications together to form a deduction. He died in St. George's Hospital, London, in 1924.

Neither Bishop, Cumberland, nor their many imitators claimed spirit aid in their performances, though some Spiritualists attributed it to them, nevertheless. It was

otherwise with Charles H. Foster, the "ballot test"*
medium.

In a pamphlet called *All About Chas. H. Foster the
Wonderful Medium* is written: "Mr. Foster says unhesi-
tatingly that they (the phenomena) all take place through
spirit agency, of which agency he is a mere instrument,
and that he does not cause the phenomena any more than
he could prevent them."

The same pamphlet quotes *The Boston Herald* for
July 13, 1873. In the quoted article Foster is coupled
with Home as the most widely known exponent of modern
Spiritualism. The article also mentions that he continually
smoked a cigar during the séance, which will be amusing
to recall when reading the next paragraph. The article
ends by saying that "The Spirits may not have any part
in the wonderful things done by Foster the 'Medium,' but
any man who sees his performance and thinks they are
done by any sort of jugglery is an idiot of the most
hopeless kind."

The simplicity and openness of Foster's séances were
reminiscent of his contemporary, Henry Slade. He, too,
had two principal tricks. One was the reading of questions written and folded up by spectators.* The other was
causing answers, names, etc., to appear in letters of blood
under the skin of his arm. Both of these tricks were done
in full light, without the customary hymn-singing and
talk of possible injury to the medium, and there were no
"negative séances." As a matter of fact, Foster was a
fat, jovial man who constantly puffed at a cigar through-

*Usually in spiritistic circles known as the billet test, or billet reading.
A billet is any small piece of paper on which a question is written.

out the séance. The redoubtable John Truesdell visited Foster on three occasions, and discovered that the cigar had a purpose beyond that of most tobacco: it was constantly going out, and Foster's efforts to light it again enabled him to read ballots palmed in the hand that held the match. When Truesdell brought questions already written on pieces of red paper, unlike the slips Foster had ready for substitutions, no reading resulted. Foster, like Slade, once exposed by Truesdell, talked affably with him of his methods.

A year after Truesdell's exposure, some one else believed he had caught the ballot-reader cheating in Boston. This provoked the following reply from Epes Sargent, in the *Banner of Light:* "The coarse blunderer who can set down the amazing evidences of clairvoyance which Mr. Foster gives in such wonderful profusion, as mere 'Swindling' is simply an incompetent investigator of phenomena to the genuineness of which many of the most intelligent persons in England and America can bear witness."

Foster was born in Salem, Mass., about 1835 or 1840, and died of softening of the brain in an asylum on December 15, 1885.

An even more adroit message-reader, who claimed to have worked with Foster, and is considered to have surpassed him in performance, was the late Bert Reese, a Polish Jew who spent most of his long life in New York. Houdini once got him to admit in private that he was no medium, merely an entertainer; but in public Reese stuck to the shrewd custom of the Davenports, and said nothing. His sitters did that for him.

[207]

What Reese did claim was that he had a gift of X-ray vision which had come to him at the grave of a friend he had loved as a boy. He even warned people to mix the papers on which they had written questions so that they did not know the question which any given paper contained, in order to convince them that he was not performing mind-reading. Many people felt that he was a medium and went to him for advice. Many others did not believe him to be in communication with spirits, but at the same time did not think him to be merely a trickster. The most eminent of those who trusted Bert Reese was Thomas A. Edison. He wrote a letter of protest to the editor of *The Evening Graphic* after that New York newspaper had printed an article by Samri Frikell describing Reese's sleight-of-hand methods.

In the letter Mr. Edison said:

"I am certain that Reese was neither a medium nor a fake. I saw him several times and on each occasion I wrote something on a piece of paper when Reese was not near or when he was in another room. In no single case was one of these papers handled by Reese, and some of them he never saw, yet he recited correctly the contents of each paper.

"Several people in my laboratory had the same kind of experience, and there are hundreds of prominent people in New York who can testify to the same thing."

Of course it is not possible to say that Reese did not do all that Mr. Edison believed that he did. However, many people believe that it was not possible for Mr. Reese to read the writing on any paper he had not handled. The

Berlin attorney, Doctor Bruno Birnbaum, and the famed psychologist, Professor Moll, exposed, before the German Psychological Society, Reese's manipulation, whereby he opened and read the papers secretly. And finally Samri Frikell was not only able to follow Reese's trick but learned to perform it to the complete bewilderment of a number of people who had also seen Reese. Every one whom I have known who understood the methods and psychology of mystification, and who had seen Reese's demonstrations, agreed that he was not only slick manipulatively but that he was extraordinarily clever in misleading and confusing his subjects regarding what really happened.

Naturally Mr. Edison was interested in Bert Reese's performance merely as a demonstration of what might be a peculiar power. The great majority of those who paid Reese for his services felt that because he gave the effect of knowing questions he had not read his "power" would also permit him to know the answer. They went to him for his answers and acted upon them. Those who kept track of his answers said that he had an extremely high average of wrong guesses. Bert Reese died abroad in 1926.

I was never so fortunate as to attend one of Reese's performances, but at one of my lectures after his death I had an odd contact with him. I was answering questions about fortune-telling methods and a lady got up to ask what I knew of Bert Reese. I said that, so far as I could find out, he was an extraordinary sleight-of-hand performer; certainly nothing more.

The lady said, in a loud, piercing tone, "You lie!" and

sat down. To this I replied, "You asked for my opinion and I gave it to you. Next question, please!"

After the lecture she came back-stage. She said, "I want to apologize for making such a fuss; you see, the whole party I was with knew I was Doctor Reese's housekeeper for many years, and so I couldn't say anything else."

Shortly before his death Reese was arrested in New York City for a supposed violation of the fortune-telling law. The magistrate before whom he appeared dismissed the case after Reese told what the judge had written on several pieces of paper. Reese declared that he did not profess to tell fortunes but merely that he could tell a person's thoughts after that person had written them on slips of paper. When a person, who professes to be a mind-reader, demands that the thoughts to be disclosed must be written, he is a reader of script, in all likelihood, rather than a reader of thoughts. As this type of pseudo mind-reading is most amusing, it would hardly be fair to the reader to describe the methods of discovering what has been written, for it would take away the reader's amusement when next he saw such an entertainment. May it suffice to say that there are hundreds of methods used to discover what may be written on a piece of paper without the writer's being aware that his writing has been read. So-called mediums, who require those who attend their séances to write the questions they wish to have answered by the spirits, frequently call attention to how impossible it would be to get an answer to the question merely by reading the question. However, I have never received an answer that was not indicated by the question asked and frequently after having written a question which could be read two ways got the obvious though incorrect answer. I do not claim that all mediums who require questions to be written actually read the questions before having them answered, but I do claim that if they know one or more of the methods they can read them without their sitters' knowing they have done so. Once you have written something on a piece of paper you may believe with complete confidence that the mind-reader can, if he wishes, read your writing without your knowledge.

One of the most famous mind-readers who did not require anything to be written was Julius Jensen, known on the stage as Julius Zancig. In one of the numerous pamphlets he wrote he said, "Never write your questions, no matter whom you visit, and you will get a more honest reading and be better contented with it no matter how little there is to tell."

Julius Zancig was born in Copenhagen on March 7, 1857. He first became famous on the public platform in company with his extremely quick and clever hunchback wife, Agnes. Her deformity was offered by many people as proof of her psychic powers, unbelievable as that may seem when put down in cold print. Some of the others who described Mrs. Zancig as a possessor of some supernormal sense gave reasons which seemed quite as weird to Zancig. He, by the way, was a member of The Society of American Magicians, as well as the Magicians' Club of London, and at meetings of those organizations used to tell with glee of some new convert to his "power." J. Hewat McKenzie, in his book, *Spirit Intercourse*, wrote that he had clearly proved that Mr. and Mrs. Zancig gave their exhibitions by "soul projection and not by thought transference." Mr. McKenzie came to this conclusion because when he handed Zancig a box of matches, Mrs. Zancig not only described the box but also told the number of matches the box contained. Mr. McKenzie believed that not only Mr. Zancig but no one else was aware how many matches were in the box. Also quite convincing to Mr. McKenzie was the demonstration in which Mrs. Zancig told the exact words on a given page and line of a book in another room. Here again the tester felt certain that no one knew just what those words were. I asked Zancig if he had actually given these tests, and he told me that in so far as the effect went he had. Of course, one magician never asks another the secret of his tricks, but as Zancig and I were such close friends, he did offer me an inkling of his method. "You know, John, I am right smart, for I can open a match box and count the matches. And many people never imagine, with my broken English, that I can read in English, though I can read quite rapidly from a printed page." He was most skillful in concealing when he counted the matches and when he read the given line in the book.

Mr. McKenzie suggests that what Mrs. Zancig did was to project her soul to get the required facts, and then transmit them to her "physical brain through the psychic umbilical cord, which stretches unseen between the object of the soul's investigation and the medium." Mr. Zancig said, "We don't claim that our work is supernormal, nor do we claim that we read your minds; but we do claim that what one of the Zancigs thinks, the other thinks; what one of them sees, the other sees—an apt illustration of our phrase, 'two minds with but a single thought.' We never claim, and never have claimed, any occult powers."

Another indorsement of Zancig's work which amused him was given by Sir Arthur Conan Doyle. Zancig, of course, realized the great value for a public entertainer of a testimonial from so famous a person as Sir Arthur. He had photographic copies made for the press of Doyle's script and gave one of them to me. This is what Sir Arthur wrote, "I have tested Mr. and Mrs. Zancig today and am quite assured that their remarkable performance, as I saw it, was due to psychic causes (thought-transference) and not to trickery." Later when I met Sir Arthur, I asked him why he had called Zancig a psychic when he was admittedly a magician, who claimed no powers. Doyle's answer was that when he saw him Zancig was a psychic and did no trickery, for had there been trickery he would have seen the tricks. I could only quote Zancig to Doyle, naturally, for I did not attend the séance Doyle had alone with the Zancigs. Zancig had said, "We did our regular tests for Sir Arthur." Several years after this conversation with Sir Arthur I told Gilbert Chesterton about it. He said, "Mr. Mulholland, it has long seemed to me that Sir Arthur's mentality is much more that of Watson than it is of Holmes."

Not only was Zancig a magician, and, as far as the methods went, only a magician, but he taught a number of people his methods. When his first wife, Agnes, died, Zancig was left without means to earn his living. She had been a Dane and Zancig was also Danish and they had worked together for thirty years. Had they really had some method of psychic communication he would have had great difficulty in getting a new partner, but because he had a system which required merely a good memory and close attention to details, he shortly found a young man for his act. He called the young man his son and went about as before with his entertainments. The "son" was offered a better job and so Zancig was again left alone. For his next partner he took the son of Theodore Bamberg, a close friend of his and mine. David Bamberg was only a boy, but owing to his being very intelligent and quick to learn, Zancig was on the road again within two weeks. I attended one of the first performances where David appeared as the "son of Zancig." He was really a beautiful child and had such large, dark, soulful eyes that every one in the audience, except myself, was sure the demonstration of mind-reading must be genuine. David, the young scamp, thought that I, too, should be impressed. When Zancig got near me, David started to describe a hunting-case watch which was in my pocket and which I had not shown to Zancig. He then said that Zancig would find the watch in my pocket. I was impressed, for I felt quite certain that Zancig had not seen my watch, at least that day, and had certainly not asked David to describe it. Several days afterwards I visited David's father's home. Theodore Bamberg said, "I understand that David described your watch the other day in Zancig's performance. He thought that you would probably not recall that you had shown it to him when he was much smaller, and he could tell by your face that you were impressed. You know, John, Julius did not like David's adding to the act. Actually, I think that he was as surprised as you were." Young David, now grown up, is one of the greatest magicians in the world. He and I have laughed many times over his stunt.

David Bamberg had a chance to go to Europe and once more Zancig was left without a partner. Once more he taught his system, but this time to the second Mrs. Zancig, an American. Her name was Ada. They continued to go about the world "transmitting thoughts" until his death on July 29, 1929, in Santa Monica, California.

Among the things handed to Julius Zancig for him to "send a thought description" to his wife were, the toe of an ostrich, wood from Napoleon's coffin, the petrified finger of a man, a glass eye, and a live snake. All these things could be transmitted with ease by Zancig's system. Although, as far as I know, his two wives and his two "sons" were the only ones ever to work publicly with Zancig, he described his methods to others. I have a signed copy of his system and while he gave it to me, I know that he sold many other copies for fifty dollars apiece. Many others also do mind-reading and mental-telepathy acts today. One of the cleverest of these teams are the Zomahs of England. A. Zomah holds high offices in several magical organizations and appears as an enter-tainer, but many have attempted to tie psychic tags to him and to his wife.

Outside of their own personal experiences, which might be ascribed to mind-reading, few people have had the opportunity to witness demonstrations other than seeing a "mind-reading" act on the stage. When they read an endorsement of the psychic powers of the stage performer by some well-known person they would naturally believe that they were witnessing a true exhibition. Few people ever stop to think about whether the opinion of a famous person is backed by knowledge or whether he is completely outside his field.

Some spiritists not only accepted mind-reading as proven but began to wonder how much the medium received thoughts directly from the minds of his sitters, and how much depended upon a spirit reading the sitters' minds and then passing on this information to the medium. Either method is believed to show occult power on the part of the medium.

Many scientists who have fully realized what could be done by magicians, and at the same time were not impressed by the theories of the spiritist, have felt the subject worth studying. These scientific studies have been going on for many years. The reports do not help the layman to make up his mind even after fifty years of research.

In the last century, Professor C. S. Minot wrote in an article in *The North American Review*, "After a thorough examination of the evidence adduced, I am brought to the conclusion that thought-transference, even as a hypothetical explanation, is a superfluous conception." Early in this century in *The London Daily News*, Professor W. F. Barrett wrote, "Thought-transference . . . is not, in my judgment, a subject of controversy. It is established beyond the possibility of challenge to those who will really read the evidence."

Doctor Alexis Carrel told me that he was convinced that some few people had the power of thought-transference although it was very rare.

It was suggested that mind-reading was a subject for study by psychologists. A number made long studies. A number accepted the hypothesis; many more did not. Professor Joseph Jastrow said, "I regard the acceptance of telepathy as an established phenomenon, as absolutely unwarranted and most unfortunate."

Several college studies were made. The University of Groningen in the Netherlands had three members of the Department of Psychology conduct an experiment in which the subject was to choose one number out of a group of forty-eight numbers. Although the experiment was conducted less than 200 times, the result, according to those who were impressed, was far above the mathematical expectations of chance. Those who were not impressed pointed out that in so small a number it was not at all against the laws of chance that a high run was made. All that the laws of chance say is that out of so many tries such and such a result is probable so many times. It does not contend that such results have to be spaced at any given intervals nor to come at any set time.

Then further experiments were carried out in the Harvard Psychological Laboratory. Some of these experiments were just what would be expected by chance and a few were above mathematical chance expectations. However, all those who had high scores gradually "petered out," which again may be said to be the chance expectations.

Still more experiments were conducted from the Division of Psychical Research of the Department of Psychology of Stanford University. These experiments were under the direction of the psychologist, the late Professor John Edgar Coover. Ordinary people were tested with "negative results" and the psychics who were tested fared no better, for "the statistical results are obstinately negative." These results were particularly interesting, for the tests were the most carefully and scientifically conducted.

About this time my friend Albert Edward Wiggam wrote that "the kind of a person who believes in telepathy on the flimsy evidence so far accumulated is the kind of a person who likes to believe in telepathy."

The experiments in universities left mind-reading just about as much up in the air as it had been before they were made. The journals of psychology and other scientific bulletins kept their pages quite free of the question of mind-reading. The journals of societies for psychical research were about the only place one could find that investigations still continued. Once in a while a newspaper would run an account of a person getting another person's thoughts at some distance great enough to make it news; or perhaps the newspaper account would be of a candidate for elective office running his campaign by sending out thought waves. These stories would be under the same freak category of news interest as a ground-hog's prediction, or a hen that crowed. Almost all interest in mind-reading had gone, and it was generally believed by scientists that there was nothing to it. It, therefore, took a large amount of courage for Professor Joseph Banks Rhine to begin another university experiment to discover the validity of thought-transference.

Doctor Rhine began his experiments by making tests to discover whether any one had the ability of perceiving beyond the limits of the known senses, or clairvoyance. He carefully chose his subjects, and those whom he did not believe to have any indications of such ability he stopped testing. With those who did seem to him to have some ability he continued his tests. His test was simple. The subject was asked to name the designs on the face of twenty-five cards which were back up on the table and which were in a shuffled chance order unknown to any one. The cards were especially designed for these tests and were marked with simple geometrical designs. There were five cards of each design in each pack of twenty-five. Doctor Rhine carefully calculated what the chance expectation of correct guesses should be and feels that because many of his subjects ran above this chance expectancy the tests are indicative of clairvoyant powers. He also made the same type of test to discover thought-transference, or mind-reading, abilities. In these tests the cards were looked at by the tester before the subject made his choice of cards. Again Doctor Rhine feels that the tests are indicative of power. He has grouped both clairvoyant and mind-reading abilities under the general term of "extra-sensory perception." In his fascinating book, *New Frontiers of the Mind*, Doctor Rhine describes many of his methods of testing.

As a magician, I am constitutionally opposed to accepting anything the reasons for which I do not understand, and Doctor Rhine does not feel that it is proper as yet to offer conclusions. I told my attitude to Doctor Rhine—not, be it distinctly understood, that I had any qualms about either his great ability or his integrity—and he most genially sympathized with me.

The thing that most bothered me was mathematical-chance expectancy, for I had an experience, the chance expectancy of which mathematically expressed needs so large a number that it dazzles by its size. I was to give an entertainment for the benefit of the church of a friend. In order to advertise the show, he asked me to go to lunch with him at a luncheon club in a near-by town. At lunch he gave a sales talk about my abilities as a magician—glowing, as sales talks always are. I was introduced, said a few words and sat down. After the lunch was over and the group was going through the lobby, one man came over to me and said that if I were anywhere nearly as good a magician as I was said to be, he wanted me to get the jackpot in a quarter machine over in a corner of the lobby. This machine was an automatic gambling device in which a quarter was put, a handle pulled, and wheels spun around. These wheels had designs on them and, according to how the designs matched on three wheels when they stopped running, the machine would give out varying numbers of quarters—or, on the other hand, one might (and probably would) lose his own coin. Once in a fantastically large number of times the wheels would stop so that a certain three designs would match. These designs appeared but once on each wheel. All the other designs appeared several times on each wheel. When these single three designs matched, all the quarters in the machine would be released, and this was called the "jackpot." I tried, without any effect, to explain to the man that that was not my brand of magic. He insisted. Finally, to quiet him, I decided to lose a quarter and play the machine. But instead of losing the quarter, I did just what he had asked me to do—won the jackpot. Incidentally, all the seats for the show were sold on the theory, I am quite certain, that I was a true magician.

Having had that experience, I began to question the likelihood of any given event's being mathematically predictable. Of course, I realize that the mortality tables of the insurance companies do not say which man is going to die in any year. They merely hold that in all likelihood so many men out of so many will die during a given year. Furthermore, the insurance statisticians, by study, know that the presuppositions fit the situation.

I took my troubled views to Professor Walter G. Pitkin, who pointed out to me that what I had in mind was clearly expressed by mathematicians. They hold that it is fallacious to believe that, when you get a long run, it implies anything whatsoever in connection with the mathematics of chance. It is not implied mathematically that a run will or will not come at any given time. All that is said is that out of n events the chances of a particular type of event occur so many times, but there is nothing inconsistent in any run.

Doctor Rhine chooses his subjects for his tests, which

of course is quite right, for he is testing those who are supposed to have special abilities. However, as I understand his method, when the answers of one of his chosen subjects fall to mere chance expectancy, he drops that case. Is it not a possibility that what Doctor Rhine's subjects have done is to name cards in but a segment of events enormously larger than he realizes, and that because high runs come closely together it seems to prove a point? There is nothing in chance expectancy that says where in time, in a long run of events, given events come. Perhaps when a subject in his tests seems to lose his powers, which sooner or later they all seem to do, it would be fairer to continue the tests and merely record that there was no run of striking accuracies in the next thousand tries. Perhaps then the total results would more nearly agree with mathematical chance.

Doctor Rhine made studies which showed that fatigued subjects made low scores, and those given caffeine made very high scores. This would seem to make his case much stronger unless hyperesthesia or some outside influence enters into the picture.

Professor Pitkin and I were interested in seeing what true chance might bring. We therefore asked aid from the International Business Machines Corporation. We not only asked aid from the company but dropped our problem into their lap. While we knew what we wanted, we were most anxious not to have anything to do with getting it, so as to eliminate any possible chance of psychic cause. Jointly we wrote the following letter to the company:

"The interesting experiments of Professor Rhine, of

Duke University, in 'parapsychology' seem to show that some people are, in a sense, clairvoyant, while others are televisual. The entire country has been following the card-naming tests which Rhine and his many friends have been conducting. A few scientists still suspect that something in the method or in the interpretations of results requires clarifying. We happen to be of this opinion.

"In recent discussions we have advanced two lines of thought, both so closely interrelated that we have decided to invite your company to conduct one or more fairly simple tests on your machines by way of clearing up a fundamental issue.

"This issue has to do with the structure of long runs of presumed chance events. The so-called 'laws of probability' in their purely mathematical form assert nothing as to specific sequences in the space-time order that we call the real world. All that is asserted is that, out of a given number of events, presumably determined by an indefinitely large number of variables, certain relative frequencies tend to occur. When any particular frequency arises is not known; nor is any unusual frequency regarded as evidence that a 'special cause' is at work.

"In common thinking, however, another practice is followed. People regularly assume that any striking series of similar repeating events implies the 'probability' of a special 'cause.' 'The rule of common sense' or 'the lesson of experience' is invoked here. It seems to us that the parapsychologists have not given due consideration to certain logical weaknesses in this practical type of inference.

"For instance, we should like to compare minutely a

very long Rhine sequence with a correspondingly long one made by a method which is incontrovertibly 'pure chance' in the mathematical sense.

"Such runs would be strictly comparable to the total of tests made by all the parapsychologists. The important question would then be directly answerable; it is this:

"Do the right answers recorded by the parapsychologists' subjects relate to the total answers in a manner significantly different from similar coincidences of events mechanically produced?

"Our doubt would then be solved one way or another. We feel that the parapsychologists, by casting out all the persons who answer according to the 'law of probability' and by talking solely about the rare cases who show abnormal correctness in answering to the card draws, distort the picture gravely. Here we agree thoroughly and would like to see a full intercorrelation worked out between total guesses, right and wrong, in the Rhine experiments, and a large series made mechanically."

The International Business Machines Corporation, under the direction of their skilled operators, ran two hundred thousand numbered cards. The first hundred thousand cards were white, and each card carried digits from 1 through 5. There was an even distribution of those digits. Twenty thousand cards carried 1; twenty thousand 2; and so on. The white cards were mechanically shuffled and run through a machine which printed the numbers on paper in the order in which they happened to come. The second hundred thousand cards were red, and these also had an equal distribution of the first five digits. These, too, were mechanically shuffled, and their numbers were printed on the paper. The finished job, as sent to Professor Pitkin and myself, consisted of page after page with printed columns of numbers—one column from the white cards and one from the red. Just as with Doctor Rhine's test there was one chance in five of the pair of digits in any given line being the same—that is, matching. But, with our test, there was no possible chance of mind-reading or clairvoyance as a factor. In getting a true picture of pure chance, a run of 100,000 is a small number, but it is a large number to work with; for instance, there are not that many words in this book. Of course, as we expected, we got what seemed to be most exceptional runs and lack of runs. When mathematicians say that an event is likely to happen but once in so many times, they do not mean that it has to happen, or that it can't happen more than once in any given series. No segment and no particular time are referred to in the mathematician's statement. If we knew how to state the possibilities of special events, they would cease to be possibilities and would become certainties.

We got some amazingly amusing results. For instance, there were as many as thirty-two lines of figures in sequence without one matching pair. Of course, by chance we might expect to get six matched pairs. Again, there would be runs of matching pairs. Professor Pitkin made a most astonishing discovery about these runs. Runs of five matching pairs in sequence fell 25 per cent below theoretical frequency, while runs of six rose to 25 per cent above theoretical frequency. Runs of seven jumped still higher to 59 per cent above chance expectancy, and with runs of eight we went to 780 per cent above theoretical frequency. Now, if we were to use our short-test run illogically, we might infer that in any long run the tendency is for the striking coincidences to occur oftener than called for by the mathematical formula. And the longer the coincidental run, the higher its frequency as compared with mathematical requirements. Obviously, this ends in pure absurdity. Another amusing freak deviation from theoretical distribution was that in the first forty thousand pairs there were almost three times as many runs of five as there were in the next sixty thousand, while with the runs of six it was just the reverse. And neither of these series of runs was to be expected.

We also found that when we arbitrarily selected segments for their high frequency of matching pairs, we would find twenty-five and twice twenty-five with half the pairs matching. These runs were above chance expectancy in 100,000; but in an infinite number they were to be expected. All that we had was a series of numbers in which these matched pairs happened to come.

Totaling the number of "correct guesses" in each thousand of our pure-chance run, we found that twenty-four thousand came within 2 per cent of mathematical expectancy; thirty thousand went above and forty-six thousand went below theoretical chance. The total number of pairs in the entire one hundred thousand was less than 2 per cent away from what was to be expected. The total, by the way, was under mathematical expectancy.

Perhaps Doctor Rhine has proved that a certain few

people have mind-reading or clairvoyant powers, but so far the tests do not seem to me to be conclusive. I know that he will agree with me fully in stating that, even granting that there are people who have extra-sensory perception, it is a most uncertain and undependable ability.

Fallacious isolation is so easy in dealing with psychological studies. My mother has been amused for years because of a book in which the author pointed out my extremely youthful identification of music. The author based his opinion on personal observation and on the answers my mother gave to his questions. He saw me get quite excited in a dining room in a hotel when the orchestra began to play a march by Sousa. I was but a baby in a high chair, and he was quite astonished to hear me call out "Sousa!" He came over to the table and asked my mother if I had actually said "Sousa" when the orchestra began to play, and she replied that I had. He then asked for my name and age, and both were given him. It so happened that my baby name for music was "Sousa." The professor had merely failed to ask the right question.

So far, nothing has convinced me of any one's ability to read minds, but then many other people do believe. My mother not only does believe mind-reading possible but bases her proof on the number of times I have read her mind. I think the probability is that on a few occasions I have outguessed her and, mother-like, she has unconsciously multiplied the number many times.

CHAPTER VIII

SPECIAL DISCOUNTS FOR QUANTITY

"*O*UR EXPERIENCE during the past thirty years in supplying mediums and others with the peculiar effects in this line enable us to place before you only those which are practical and of use, nothing that you have to experiment with. Please note the large number of absolutely new and original feats that have been added, and in considering all, remember that we guarantee everything just as represented. We have no agents or representatives, and do not sell on commission to any person. Our prices are net, except where quite a number of effects are ordered at once, when we allow a certain amount, according to agreement. All of our effects are equally suitable for ladies or gentlemen except where mentioned.

"We wish you to thoroughly appreciate that, while we do not, for obvious reasons, mention the names of our clients and their work (they being kept in strict confidence, the same as a physician treats his patients), we can furnish you with the explanation and, where necessary, the materials for the production of any known public 'tests' or 'phenomena' not mentioned in this, our latest list.

"You are aware that our effects are being used by nearly all prominent mediums, entertainers and others of the entire world, and you can, therefore, be assured of receiving fraternal and honest treatment in all transactions. To those who have not dealt with us would call your attention to the fact that in listing many effects the word 'Spirit' is used in describing them. It should be borne in mind that this is only the customary name used to explain the effect, as 'Spirits,' in the general acceptation of the name, are not a factor in their presentation, although, 'for the good of the cause,' that impression has been fostered by many. There are, as you are aware, sporadic attempts at exposure of mediums, and of slurs in the press at the same and at ourselves. We do not countenance or support the former and utterly ignore the latter.

"In our mental feats are found much to ponder over, and prove the truth of the immortal Goethe's history of the friendly philosophers in his wonderful work on 'Electoral Affinities,' while in our mechanical appliances the work is absolutely faultless.

"TERMS.—Remittance to accompany all orders of $10.00 or less. Large orders, one-half with same; balance collected on delivery. Prices net. Please remit Express or Post Office Money Order or Registered Mail."

With this introduction in a well-illustrated printed catalog one of the old supply houses of equipment for tricky mediums offers seventy items. Many mediums claim that they have never heard of the existence of such firms, although there are a number of them not only in America but in all the other countries where there are mediums.

I have many such catalogs and the total number of "effects" they offer run well into the hundreds. Although the dealer whose introduction is quoted above promises to keep the names of his customers secret, he, in all probability, kept a record of the names and addresses of the mediums he dealt with as well as a list of their purchases. When one knows such a dealer well it is not hard to get permission to inspect his list of patrons. One such dealer in a Mid-Western city allowed me to go over his list most carefully. The list contained two thousand names of mediums of various degrees of renown. It was particularly interesting to me to note that in many cases a description of their séances read quite like the description in the catalog of the "effects" which they had purchased. A number of the mediums were well known in various associations of mediums and spirits. I took the trouble to go to a few of them and to mention that the manifestations of their séances were most reminiscent of the tricks of my dealer acquaintance. All but one of the mediums protested their ignorance of the dealer and declared that it was utterly impossible to duplicate fraudulently their manifestations. The one medium told me that he knew the dealer and as a matter of fact had purchased several pieces of his apparatus in order to be quite familiar with the methods of "those fakers whom every true medium despises."

I shall not list either the name or address of any of these dealers, for I do not want to be put in the position of advertising their strange businesses. However, I have shown the catalogs to several directors of Charles Scribner's Sons in order to prove their existence. I know that I shall be called a variety of names for suggesting that the equipment advertised in these catalogs was ever used by any of the better known and trusted mediums but that such is the case I am absolutely certain.

In order to give an idea of the variety of phenomena these dealers have in stock I have picked out a few of the items advertised and print them in the dealer's own language.

"Raps! Here!! There!! Everywhere!!! For a number of years we have not listed any effect for spirit rapping, leaving the production of such phenomena to our clients that have strongly developed psychic powers in the line of such tests as used by D. D. Home and others. Of late, however, we have had so many inquiries that we have decided to list same. With this you can produce raps at any time while standing or sitting, in light or dark, and in any room or circle, as often as you like. It is the only perfect means of its kind for this effect period. No inconvenience in using it. You know what you can achieve with it. Price—$18.00."

"Spirit Rapping Table. This is particularly for mediums who have their own apartments, yet is easily used in any room where the table can be placed. In appearance it is an ordinary finely finished library table; bears minute examination, and is portable. When circle is formed around table it emits raps as desired. Can be used at any time, no previous preparation necessary. Infallible in every respect. Price—$50.00."

"Spirit Table and Chair Lifting. Unexcelled. By placing hand in center at top of table, chair, stand, box or barrel, you can lift same up and carry it around clinging to palm of hand. Done everywhere, in light or dark and if desired can have sleeves rolled up. Borrow any gentleman's stiff hat, place palm of hand over it and it will cling to your hand, owner of hat can remove same from your hand, without being able to detect how you do this. Both methods as described above, complete, delivery charges prepaid to any address for $1.00."

"Spirit Table Lifting. Same effect as above. Larger table used, and when started to move two or three persons cannot hold the table down. Requires operator and one assistant, suitable for gentleman only. Can be done anywhere with sleeves rolled up. Price—$12.50."

"Spirit Bench for Rope Test. This is a finely finished small portable bench to which the medium is securely bound by wire, rope or tape, yet can release himself at any moment. Price—$25.00."

"Telescopic Reaching Rod. A very useful article for mediums working in the dark. They go in pocket and extend from four to six feet, fine workmanship, will pick up or bring to you any ordinary small object, float a guitar, etc. Any size to order. Medium size closed $8\frac{1}{4}$ inches, extends three feet when open. Price—$4.00."

"Self Playing Guitars. Indispensable for mediums. Finely finished guitars. In dark séances they play without medium's hands touching them. Price—$25.00."

"Spirit Lights. Beautiful weird lights, which appear and disappear, causing a ghostly and mysterious effect. For dark séance. Price—$2.00."

"Full Form Materialization and Dematerialization. For

dark circles. A small, light spot is first visible near the floor, which gradually grows larger and larger until a full formed spirit stands in plain view. After a few moments the form begins slowly to dematerialize, growing smaller and smaller, until only a small spot of light is visible near the floor, and this finally vanishes completely. After the form has appeared the lights can, if desired, be partially turned up, when all can see the features of the spirit. Complete. Price—$12.00."

"Manifestations in Full Light. Several instruments, paper, pencil, etc., are all examined and placed on examined table. Performer stands at side of table and holds up a large handkerchief by two upper corners, so instruments are hidden from view. And in full light the instruments are played up, appear above top of handkerchief, messages written, and other marvelous tests take place. No assistants or confederates. First time offered for sale. A corker. . . . Price—$10.00."

"Foster's Marvelous Blood-Writing. The performer bares his arm, washes it in water to prove there is no preparation, and allows any one to hold his wrist. Now a name is seen to slowly appear on his arm *under his skin, in his own blood*. A marvelous test. Price—$1.50."

"Bona Fide Sealed Letter Reading. A number of envelopes and blank cards or paper are given out or can be brought by audience already sealed and sewed around on a machine, thus proving the impossibility of opening envelopes. Letters are collected in a borrowed hat, from whence they are taken out, read in full view of audience, one at a time and given after each reading untouched and undisturbed, to owner. New and fine effect, especially for mediums or private tests. Price—$5.00."

"Washington Irving Bishop's Sealed Letter Reading. His original manner of reading sealed letters in presence of the audience. Our instructions are all that is necessary. Price—$1.00."

"New and Mysterious Slate Writing. With this you can write on any slate at any time or place, and even while the end of slate is being held by investigator. Requires some skill; most suitable for male mediums. Price, complete—$5.00."

"Our Unexcelled Spirit Slate Writing. This excellent manner of producing a message on an ordinary slate that can be thoroughly examined and cleaned is one of the very best in existence. Slates are closely inspected and then held underneath any ordinary table by both operator and the sitter, or the sitter alone, and upon replacing them on table a message is found thereon, as full and complete as the operator desires. It can be easily produced in any room, at any time, by either lady or gentleman, and even in the presence of several sitters. Slate or slates can be taken away and be kept by the sitter if desired. Price, complete—$10.00. Extra slates per dozen, size 4 x 6, $1.00; size 7 x 11 inches, $1.25."

"Clairvoyant and Psychic Readings for Private Sittings. In view of the fact that nearly all of the old time methods employed by mediums for producing various phases of psychic phenomena in private sittings or readings have been more or less 'written up' by the press, many letters of inquiry have been coming to us from mediums in all parts of the world asking if we could not supply them with a method of obtaining communications which would be impossible of detection, and could be produced, or rather obtained, under the severest conditions. Several very clever professional mediums who have been in the profession for twenty years or more have recently told us that in many of the best sections of the country it is fast becoming impossible to use the old methods, and that even those now in use among some of the most successful readers in the profession are fast becoming worthless. This request having come to us so strongly we have devised and can now offer you absolutely the best method of obtaining communications for use in private readings ever brought out or even thought of. The sitter enters the medium's parlor and is seated anywhere. He is requested to write his questions on an ordinary piece of paper, and keep same in his possession, the medium is not necessarily present during the writings, yet he, in a few seconds, is in full knowledge of what was written, although he does not handle or touch the paper on which questions were written. It is certainly the most wonderful effect of its kind ever produced and simply startles all skeptics alike. There are a few mediums who have been using this method during the past year with phenomenal success, and the closest investigation by the most clever people in the country fails to solve the mystery. There is no particular skill or preparation required. We wish to impress upon you that in this there is nothing used that has been made use of in somewhat similar effects in times past. This is absolutely new and reliable. Those now in possession of it would not sell except at a fabulous price. We offer same to you under certain written conditions only, and cannot recommend it too highly. Price—$25.00."

"Clairvoyance, Psychometry and Platform Tests. There is at all times a good demand for a clever and intellectual lecturer or medium who can give good and genuine tests from the platform. Nearly every issue of the Spiritualistic journals contain inquiries for just such mediums. We can furnish you the only reliable system, complete in every detail, which will enable you to at once take up this interesting and remunerative branch of the profession. With this you can satisfy the most captious audience, and all the tests are genuine.

"This method is boundless in its scope, and is the only one you can rely on. It is suitable for either lady or gentleman and is being constantly used by many of our mediums. We have for many years supplied this to our clients, to whom it has given perfect satisfaction. It is so perfect that at a few days' notice you can fill satisfactory engagements in any ordinary-sized town in any part of the country. Our former price was $100.00. We now offer it to you for $25.00. For those who desire a special lecture to use with it, we furnish an excellent one for $25.00 additional. It is the usual custom to occupy about an hour for the lecture and forty to fifty minutes for the tests, though longer or shorter time can be used."

"A Complete Spiritualistic Séance. A combination outfit for spirit work. For parties who wish a first-class collection at a reasonable price for giving a fine séance in small halls or parlors we recommend the following collection:

Catalog item numbers, 2, 17, 22, 29, 32, 36, 47, 54, 65, 78, 81, 104. As a special offer we include the Medium's Fire Test, which enables you to handle heated lamp chimneys, with bare hands, hold fingers, handkerchiefs and neckties in blaze of a lamp without injury to yourself or the articles. All of above complete, with special and explicit directions for every effect, express charges prepaid throughout the United States, Canada and Mexico for the very low price of $25.00."

After one is known to these dealers in spooks it is comparatively easy to get them to talk about the business of mediumship as well as its secrets but an unknown investigator has to be particularly artful to draw them out. My friend Will Irwin had an amusing experience with a dealer which he described in his excellent series of articles in *Collier's* on *The Medium Game*. He found the dealer in a little store down beside the railroad tracks.

"When I told him that I wanted to buy some silicate flaps and a reaching-rod, he protested that he was out of the 'Spook' business. 'I was exposed,' he added, 'and there is nothing in it for me now.' But he was eager to gossip; it was plain that spirit apparatus is the vocation of his heart. He said that my forehead was mediumistic; he knew me for a psychic the minute I came into the room. Learning that I came of late from New York, he wanted to know how I found the spook business throughout the country. 'Some think that Christian Science has taken a crimp in it,' he said, 'but I don't think that will last. Spiritualism gives them something for the money.' He thought that Spiritualism had a lot to learn from Theosophy.

"The inwardness of his game began to dawn on me.

" 'Say, iron out your face and drop that talk with me,' I said suddenly. Roman augur looked into the eyes of Roman augur, and he laughed. 'Well, you can't be too careful,' he said. Forthwith, out came the tricks. First he showed some effective 'spirit light' cards for use at the end of a reaching-rod. The hearts, crosses, and stars of luminous paint are covered with paper flaps. A flip of the reaching-rod covers or uncovers them, making their appearance and disappearance instantaneous. For three dollars he sold me a wax hand which may be fastened on a black cloth to impersonate your right hand while that is employed in spirit business elsewhere.

"After I had declined to pay twenty-five dollars for a black envelope clairvoyant card-reading trick, we fell to talking of the Bang Sisters and their 'spirit paintings,' famous since Isaac K. Funk 'bit' two years ago.

" 'You bring 'em photographs of your spirit friend,' he said, 'and come back next day. They put a blank canvas in the window. The light shines right through it and there is nothing in sight. While you watch, the picture begins to grow on the canvas. If they have put a red necktie on your spirit friend and you'd rather have a blue, you only have to say so. The picture will fade right out and come on again, with a blue necktie this time. I don't mind telling you that I am something of a chemist, and I'm dead onto that trick. When you get settled in your own place, send to me and I'll fix it.'

" 'How much?' I asked.

" 'It would make a hundred dollars look small, and it

would be worth the money. I'd give a hundred any day to get onto their slatewriting trick. It's the best ever, something new and original. That's the way to do high-class work—invent your own stuff and keep it to yourself.' "

As mediums can save money by buying equipment in quantity so, in many instances, can sitters get rates for a series of séances. This is particularly true at many of the summer camps. One has to pay a twenty-five cent fee for single admission to either the morning or afternoon session of lectures and messages while season tickets, good for all lectures and messages, sell for two dollars and a half.

These summer camps are most interesting and are conducted in a manner similar to that of camps run by the various Protestant Churches throughout the country. There are all sorts of outdoor games, swimming pools, and golf courses; there are teas, and dances, and bridge parties; there are musicales and dramatics. Many families have their own cottages and go back year after year. The transients are taken care of in hotels and boarding houses. In the Protestant camps there are many sessions where hymns are sung and there are frequent prayer meetings. In the Spiritualistic camps there are also séances, message meetings, and lectures. Those who visit these camps are in the main most devout followers of Spiritualism as a religion. The psychic investigators very seldom attend. The mediums in many instances seem to be just as devout as their followers but some of the camps also have the most blatant fakers.

Most of the camps have their "Authorized Mediums" and those not passed by a board are forbidden to give séances within the camp grounds. One camp charges one dollar for a permit to each medium passed but also requires that the mediums have a minimum price of one dollar for private readings and charge no less than twenty-five cents apiece for "circles." Among the authorized mediums are found, in classified lists, "trumpet, slate writing, materialization, blind-fold ballot readers, trance, independent writing, clairvoyant, and healer." A newspaper exposé of trickery or even, in a few instances, court convictions do not seem to influence the boards of some of these camps against a medium. Granting that many of the mediums are honest and religious people, as fakers also are working at some of these camps a visitor is unable to know whether a spirit be spurious or genuine. My friend, Virginia Swain, exposed in a series of syndicated feature newspaper articles a number of mediums at one of these camps but the next summer found them back at the old stand. The largest of these camps brought to its own grounds the Hydesville farmhouse where the Fox sisters began. The "Fox Cottage" is one of the major points of interest for visitors. Even though the body of the murdered peddler was not transported with the house, visitors, who pay their twenty-five cent admission fee, can hear the knocks sometimes even today. When my wife and I heard them there, by the way, they made misstatement after misstatement.

A number of years ago the celebrated magician Harry Rouclere with his wife toured one entire summer as "the celebrated English mediums, Ellington and Cooke." Every time they got near one of these camps they would give a series of séances. No one ever guessed that their manifestations were all spurious. Just before they would leave a camp they would challenge the other mediums to prove their genuineness. Their manager would go to the newspaper in the nearest town and leave at the office two thousand dollars in cash to back Ellington and Cooke in their challenge. After waiting a reasonable length of time for the challenge to be accepted the deposit would be taken back and the couple would go on to start the whole thing over again. The challenge was never accepted although many of the papers ran articles similar to that of *The Jamestown Sun and Standard* which, after pointing out that it had been the only newspaper of any importance to back the local camp, said that the challenge is so worded that it cannot be ignored without serious reflections upon the legitimacy of the workings of the camp's mediums. The paper also printed: "We are personally acquainted with the wonderful and almost superhuman gifts of Ellington and Cooke, know them well, and therefore feel convinced that they are genuine and real spiritualistic mediums who perform all they claim."

My friend Rouclere and his beautiful wife never made up their minds which one was Ellington and which Cooke and, as they travelled about, he was first Mr. Ellington and then Mr. Cooke as his wife became Miss Cooke or Miss Ellington.

Perhaps the most surprising business connected with spiritism is that done by a number of organizations, many of them incorporated bodies, bartering certificates of ordination, including the degree of "Doctor of Divinity" and "Bishop at Large" for the best obtainable price.

In a printed advertisement "The Spiritual Psychic Science Church" notes: "The following fees for Ordinations are in effect:

First Degree (Ministry) $10.00   Yearly assessment $2.00
Second Degree (D.D.) . . $ 5.00   No assessment
Third Degree (Bishop) . $25.00   No assessment

No percentage fees or other dues required by the Parent Body.

"A commission of 50 per cent will be paid to any Ordained Minister of this Church for properly recommended and signed Applications for new Ordinations of Minister forwarded to the Parent Body with above fee.

"No commission paid on the 2nd and 3rd Degrees or on Assessment fees."

The advertisement also notes "Over 1000 Branches in U. S. A., Canada, Mexico, British W. Indies, and Australia."

The application blank which must be filled out and accompany the fee for ordination in this church lists five articles of faith which the signer must agree to indorse. The first four profess a belief in God and in "Spiritual Laws" while the fifth is, "We believe in all forms of philosophy that tend to the upbuilding and betterment of society."

The blank also contains the following promise:

"I herewith specifically stipulate and agree not to use the authority herewith vested in me by the Spiritual Psychic Science Church, Inc., of California, in any unlawful or illegal acts, in disobedience to the Statutes of my

State, or the Ordinances of the City or County in which I reside or engage in business of any kind.

"That in the event of such disobedience, I exonerate from all responsibility for same the said Church, and abide by my own personal defense for such unlawful act."

The space for signature is followed by space for two references. The blank carries in capital letters: "Their personal signatures not necessary." In case of mischance, however, there is the further instruction: "If unable to get reference, have a local Notary Public notarize instrument. Ordinance Certificate will be mailed to you immediately upon your return of this instrument and election to the Pastorate by the Board of Directors."

On the back of the application blank is printed:

"The Parent Body of the Spiritual Psychic Science Church, Inc., is desirous of establishing Schools of Philosophy and Religion in the Parishes of the Doctors of Divinity of the Church, and to facilitate this end and the further work of the Church, has now presented in neat printed form, several Courses of Lessons on various subjects, suitable for Class Work or individual instruction, under the following Titles:

1. Religious Philosophy
2. Practical Psychology
3. Scholastic Theology
4. Spiritual Science
5. Theo-Therapy or Divine Healing
6. Fundamental Astrology
7. Spiritual Mediumship
8. Science of Numerology

"These Courses consist of about 12 Lessons each, and can be obtained singly or in groups of four or more at

25 cents a copy. Reduced rates to Teachers using them in classes of their Church. Quantity prices obtained for resale by Correspondence or otherwise."

There are many such organizations. Usually the fee is the chief religious qualification. Two prestidigitator friends of mine, Caryl S. Fleming and Edward Saint, invested in the title of "Reverend" with the accompanying dividends of fees for marriage and burial services and special rates for the clergy; another, Fulton Oursler, allowed himself the added luxury of becoming a bishop. Fleming and Saint wanted to have evidence of fraud which would hold up in a court of law. They were satisfied that their own credentials had not been investigated as they had given Erik Weiss for reference. Weiss was Houdini's real name and Houdini had been dead for several years. They sent in names of other applicants, among them Lou D. Squaller (loud squaller), and Drake Googoo, the Persian Mystic. Googoo, by the way, is a duck owned by a famous comedian. For one of the ordinations a dog was given in part payment. They got the data and the district attorney got the conviction and the faker was put out of business and no more ordinations were sold by him. However, there was no retroactive action cancelling, or nullifying, ordinations, or degrees, which had been granted prior to the decision. In many cases the certificates of ordination were recorded with the proper county or state officials, making them of extra legal record. So, legally, the duck and my friends are still "Reverends" and, legally, can marry, or bury, or get minister's rates on railroads.

CHAPTER IX

DAYS IN COURT

W̶HILE THERE is no law against calling on
spirit aid, or against talking to spirits if they answer
the call, even mediums are forbidden to get money under
false pretenses, to practice medicine without a license,
and, in many localities, to pretend to tell fortunes for a
fee. Also, while loath to state that anything is impossible, scientists believe that any one claiming to do something beyond present scientific knowledge should be asked
to demonstrate and prove his claim. Many mediums have
been brought before the courts of law and many before
the courts of science.

Some of the most interesting, though not the pleasant-
est, stories of "mediumship" are to be found in court
records. It is a thoroughly unfortunate fact for serious
psychical research that spiritism seems to draw a large
share of such characters. On the other hand, the unregen-
erate reader may find more entertainment in reading
about the proportionately few facts of Ann O'Delia Diss
Debar than about the career of a Mrs. Piper.

Ann O'Delia Diss Debar, alias Editha Salomon, alias

Baroness Rosenthal and Countess Landsfeldt, alias Editha Lolita Montez, alias Vera P. Ava, alias Mrs. Paul Noel Messant, alias Mrs. McGoon, alias Mme. Swami Viva Ananda, alias Laura Horos, alias Mrs. Frank Dutton Jackson, was the greatest rogue that ever used spirits to defraud. No doubt a number of her aliases are missing from the above list, and no doubt many facts of her life are missing from the account below; she was consistent in only one story about herself, and that a lie; that she was the daughter of the notorious dancer and adventuress, Lola Montez, and the King of Bavaria.

The best evidence (the Salomon family Bible, produced in court, according to *The New York Times*, in 1888 in connection with the Marsh fraud trial) indicates that this versatile woman was born in Mercer County, Kentucky, on February 9, 1849, the daughter of John C. F. R. and Eliza Salomon. Even before she left home in Louisville, probably in 1869, she made herself unpopular with her family. A man named George C. T. Salomon, whose claim to be her brother was never disproved, said in an affidavit in 1888, "It would be necessary for others to see her as all her family have to comprehend the depth and magnitude of her many villainies. Whenever she enters a house peace departs and with it everything portable. Nothing is safe in her hands. As an intriguer she has few equals and no superiors. I would not believe her under oath under any circumstances."

Between 1869 and 1871 she lectured in New York, professing to be the daughter of Montez and the King of Bavaria; this period of her existence was terminated by a spell in Ward's Island insane asylum, from which she was freed by a Doctor Messant, who married her. By him she had a daughter, originally named Alice, and later apparently rechristened Lola in honor of the suppositious grandmother. From her first New York period dates an affidavit which she swore out against the celebrated Victoria Claflin Woodhull (who once ran for President of the United States before women were allowed to vote) for alleged conversion of property. The complaint, signed by Editha Gilbert Montez, was dismissed. It seems to me fairly typical of a rather surprising trait in Diss Debar's character —her lack of finesse in villainy. How she could have expected to get the law on her side against any one so prominent as Victoria Woodhull is more than I can see, particularly since she herself had done nothing beyond posing as an illustrious illegitimate.

About 1879 she picked up the man by whose name she has become familiar to history—an elderly surveyor, "General" Joseph H. Diss Debar. This weak old man was born near Strassburg, Alsace, in 1820; was a Roman Catholic; had a wife and family in Philadelphia. He was the author of a handbook for West Virginia immigrants, in which he is described as State Commissioner of Immigration without salary, resident at Parkersburg from 1864 to 1870 or later; he was a very bad portrait painter; otherwise history is silent. I do not know where he got his title of General, or whether he merely assumed it. Ann O'Delia had a daughter by him too; and now the stage is set for the big act.

After a career as a hypnotist, she became a spirit me-

dium. She did slate-writing and other commonplace manifestations, and managed to get along all right until she
encountered Luther R. Marsh, a distinguished and prosperous lawyer prominent in civic life. Marsh's wife had
died not long before, and Diss Debar's new profession of
Spiritualism seemed made to suit him. She and her "husband" soon moved in on Marsh, converting his house at
166 Madison Avenue into a Temple of Truth. Under
spirit advice he went so far as to deed the house to the
mediums. Meanwhile the Diss Debars were working hard
for their take; they produced messages on slates and
pads of paper, but better yet they, like the Bang Sisters,
got spirit paintings by such persons as Raphael and Rem-
brandt. One, described in *The New York Times*, represented a dead friend of Mr. Marsh's. It was in plain black
and white, with the form clothed in spirit drapery; the
face was an exact copy of an engraving from a book in
Marsh's library. There were great quantities of such
paintings, which were supposed by skeptics at the time to
have been executed by General Diss Debar during his
spare time in Marsh's attic; experts later testified to their
artistic worthlessness, but to Marsh they were priceless.
Albert Bierstadt, the painter, had a sitting with the Diss
Debars at 166 Madison Avenue, at which they put a cardboard on his head, and the cardboard later bore a picture.
They were so careless, however, as to do the manifestation in view of a mirror, and Bierstadt saw General Diss
Debar take the blank card from Ann O'Delia, handing
her a painted one instead.

Bierstadt was a particularly nasty observer. A much

nicer attitude was shown by ex-Judge Nelson Cross, whose testimony is thus reported by *The New York Times*: "He was a Spiritualist, he said, and believed in Mme. Diss Debar's powers as a medium, although about ten years ago he had detected her in throwing a slipper across a room during a séance. The slipper was supposed to have been propelled by the spirits. He afterward accused her of being a fraud, and she placed upon his head a slate, saying, 'Let the spirits decide whether I am a fraud or not.' In a moment he took the slate down, and there was written upon it the word 'Fraud.' Still, he believed in her because this showed her powers. He had had paintings come on canvases held over his head since then, and was a firm believer in the genuineness of all of Mr. Marsh's pictures."

When Marsh deeded his home to Mme. Diss Debar, it caused considerable sensation. Action followed: John W. Randolph, a theatrical agent, and George C. T. Salomon, who said he was Mme. Diss Debar's brother, made affidavits charging her with fraud. Randolph was her manager for a very short time, during which, according to his sworn statement, she told him almost in so many words that she was swindling Marsh and offered Randolph a share of the loot. She tried to short-change Randolph a week or ten days before he made out his affidavit, and he thereupon abandoned her.

On the strength of the two affidavits, Mme. and General Diss Debar were arrested (April 11, 1888), together with two minor assistants, "Doctor" B. M. Lawrence and his son, Franklin Lawrence. These two were later released when it became evident that they did not live at the Temple of Truth and did little but operate Diss Debar's magic lantern. The principals, however, had to sit through a trial that provided New York with a better show than many of the theaters.

They were defended by John D. Townsend, who had successfully defended Mumler, the spirit photographer, against the charge instigated by Mayor Oakey Hall. Mme. Diss Debar rather took charge of him at times during the trial, and though she sometimes scored off witnesses in this fashion, she was hard to handle. As a witness, she herself was not first-rate; she skipped around, often lost her temper, and produced such an effect on the non-Spiritualist public that *The Times* described her as a "fat confidence woman." An example of her changes of front concerned her brother George. In court she admitted writing letters which he produced, addressing him in terms of affection and asking him for money. Afterward she told a police inspector who was prominent in the prosecution that George was not her brother; then she said he was her brother, but that she knew enough about him so that he would not dare testify against her (plainly a ridiculous statement, because he had already done so); these conversations were repeated in court, and then she denied talking to the inspector at all. She also turned against General Diss Debar, and he against her.

While the trial was going on, she had a spirit message from "Cicero and his colleagues in the Council of Ten," instructing her to return to Mr. Marsh the deed to the Temple of Truth. This she did.

Throughout the trial, Marsh's faith in Mme. Diss Debar's spiritual powers did not give way; he insisted that his paintings and messages were genuine, no matter how many fraudulent duplications were shown him by skeptics. But he was really upset by the discovery that Ann O'Delia and General Diss Debar were not married. If he had known this, he said, they would never have been admitted to his house. He did not want persons of such character around him; he was disappointed in them as people, but as a medium she was remarkable just the same.

The prosecution introduced my friend, the late Carl Hertz (Louis Morgenstern), a professional magician, who duplicated in court some spirit-writing tricks which Diss Debar had used on Marsh. Marsh was as mystified by Hertz's act as by Diss Debar's, but quite rightly refused to accept this as final proof that Diss Debar was a fraud. One Carvalho was introduced to make spirit paintings, which he did by spraying a blank canvas with an atomizer. There was great triumph on Mme. Diss Debar's side when he said he could not do it without spraying the canvas. Apparently her method was the easier one of simple substitution.

After wranglings, recriminations, and columns of space in the newspapers, the jury returned to court on June 16 to say through the foreman, "May it please the court, we, the jury, find the defendants guilty of the charge made in the indictment, with a strong recommendation to mercy." On the 19th, *The Times* said, "The fat confidence woman, who has been so prominent in the proceedings of Part II of the Court of General Sessions during the last fortnight as the Princess Ann O'Delia Salomon, and her consort, J. H. Diss Debar, were sentenced yesterday morning by Judge Gildersleeve to six months' imprisonment on Blackwell's Island on the charge of having conspired to defraud Luther R. Marsh."

Ann O'Delia's career for the next dozen years was less sensational, though hardly more praiseworthy, than her earlier period. She got two years for larceny at Geneva, Illinois, under the name of Vera Ava, being sentenced on March 25, 1893, and sent to the penitentiary at Joliet. She claimed to have married a Mr. McGoon, who died in 1896. A marriage certificate produced in court in London showed her to have been married November 13, 1898, at New Orleans, under the name of Princess Editha Loleta, Baroness Rosenthal, Countess of Landsfeldt, of Florence, Italy, to Frank D. Jackson, of Fond du Lac, Wisconsin. Her bridal bliss was disturbed by her expulsion from New Orleans on May 7, 1899, as a suspicious character, and her incarceration there on May 16 for thirty days, presumably for mediumistic practices.

She and Jackson then went to England, and thence to Cape Town, where she had a considerable spiritistic and hypnotic business under the name of Mme. Swami Viva Ananda, assisted by Mr. Theodore Horos (formerly Frank Dutton Jackson, as she did not announce). *The Cape Town News* had a rather favorable notice of her establishment, but apparently some of the other papers disagreed.

At any rate, 1901 found the couple in London again. They set up an occult organization called "The Theocratic Unity," to which, as a sort of gratuitous insult, they later added "and Purity League." *The London Times* of September 27, 1901, under Court news, said: "At Marylebone, Theodore Horos, aged 35, and Laura Horos, aged 47, described as lecturers of Park-road, Regent's-park, were brought before Mr. Curtis Bennett, on a warrant dated September 20, charging them with unlawfully conspiring together, by false pretenses and subtle devices, to cheat and defraud Vera Croysdale of her jewelry and money." Inspector Kane, who did the police work for the prosecution, said, "I have a criminal record for the woman from Chicago, and I produce her photograph and the particulars of her dimensions. These show that she is a convicted thief, a swindler, and a fortune-teller."

So far it was mere run-of-the-mill stuff for Editha Lolita Ann O'Delia Laura; but in October the Treasury, conducting the prosecution, put in a further charge of rape on the person of Daisy Pollex Adams, sixteen years old, a more or less involuntary member of the Purity League. It then appeared that Horos (by this time discovered to be Frank D. Jackson) had recruited his League by matrimonial advertisements under assumed names, to which certain trusting and apparently rather ignorant girls replied. He would take them home to Ann O'Delia, whom he introduced as his mother, and he would pretend he was soon going to marry the victim. He would then seduce her, often in the presence and with the assistance of his amiable wife, first hypnotizing the girl if necessary. At the same time he was laying hands on whatever little money the girl might have. Daisy Adams, a

[259]

child of sixteen, would not yield like Vera Croysdale, and the useful "Swami," Laura Horos, held her while Theo attacked her.

The various victims, though temporarily annoyed, seem on the whole to have gotten along well enough with the Horoses, and they wrote affectionate letters, which emboldened the prisoners to deny the charges of immorality as ridiculous. Theo asserted he was a eunuch, that the whole affair was a frame-up, and demanded medical examination to prove his statement. The official medical examination showed nothing of the kind.

Naturally the case, though modestly headlined in *The Times* as "The Charge of Conspiracy," was a huge sensation. Street peddlers coined money with a pamphlet, "Horrible Disclosures in the Horos Case." A newspaper report said, "When the prisoners were removed at the adjournment for luncheon they were hissed, and the man turned to the public and shouted, 'Just keep quiet, you reptiles.' " Two days later: "The prisoners were hissed as they left the court. The man shouted, 'Now, you Lilliputians, don't judge a case until it has been heard.' "

After all the preliminary hearings, the prisoners were committed on November 30 for trial. The trial came up on December 20 before Mr. Justice Bigham. From *The Times* report:

"The Solicitor-General [Sir Edward Henry Carson]— Do you claim to have visits from the spirit mother?

"The prisoner—I claim that I have spiritual communications from what I call a guide—my spiritual wife, who only visits me through a medium.

"The male prisoner said that spiritism was part of the teaching of the Theocratic Unity. . . .

"The jury retired to consider their verdict, and after an absence of five minutes they returned into Court, finding the male prisoner *Guilty* of rape and the female prisoner *Guilty* of aiding and abetting him in the commission of that felony."

Mr. Justice Bigham, sentencing Jackson to fifteen years' penal servitude, and Ann O'Delia to seven years, said he thought the verdict absolutely justified by the evidence.

No other medium has perpetrated the all-round villainy of the Kentucky belle; but the passing of years has brought a few new ideas that Ann O'Delia never got around to.

According to *The New York Times* of July 19, 1936, "A stock-selling woman spiritualist and a promoter, represented by her during séances as a reincarnation of the man who built the Pyramids, were temporarily enjoined yesterday by Supreme Court Justice Charles B. McLaughlin from selling 'Super-Utilities' stock in this State."

Miss Alma Nelson, "former waitress and teacher of mystic philosophy," gave "truth sittings," at which she sold stock for the promoter, Charles B. Lingelbach. She was charged with doing this for a 20 per cent commission. At one of the sittings, according to an affidavit attached to the Attorney General's complaint and reported in *The Times*, "The voice of Sudah, 'Son of the Solitude of the Lost Isle of Atlantis,' spoke through the medium in a deep bass voice and declared that Lingelbach was a master engineer and the reincarnation of his (Sudah's) brother, who had built the pyramids." Assistant Attorney General Ambrose V. McCall said, "Lingelbach, when questioned at his office, . . . testified that he had aided Henry Ford in developing the Model T motor, helped Edison over some rough spots in the development of the phonograph and worked with Steinmetz in the General Electric Company. Other claims made by him or on his behalf by his associates were that he had designed the front-line trenches for the American Army in the World War, had been asked by President Theodore Roosevelt to build the Panama Canal, had developed the process for extracting sugar from beets and the machine for sewing seams in the back of stockings. He said he had received an engineering degree from Georgetown University and had held at one time an airplane pilot's license." Mr. McCall declared both these assertions were untrue.

A different aspect of mediumship was aired in a story in *The New York Sun* of March 24, 1936:

"Mrs. Eleanor B. Stevens insisted today that when she wrote love letters to Homer Curtiss, founder and president of an organization known as the Order of Christian Mystics, she did so as a medium under control of the spirit of his wife, who died in 1922.

"Supreme Court Justice Julius Miller didn't seem to believe this or other denials on the part of the elderly looking woman, for he granted a divorce from her to Herbert Rennel Stevens, British broker.

" 'When you addressed him as "my darling" and called

him your lover, you were under Mrs. Curtiss's influence?'
asked the Justice.

" 'Yes,' said Mrs. Stevens, "Mrs. Curtiss felt she could
not express herself and she chose me out of many to write
to her beloved through me. She even wrote a book through
me.' "

In 1924 and 1925 *The Los Angeles Times* was active
in instigating and assisting the prosecution of one William
A. Jackson and his wife, Lois A. Jackson, as heads of the
National Independent Spiritualist Association, Inc. The
various cities of California either licensed or forbade
clairvoyants, mediums, fortune-tellers, etc., but excepted
ministers of religion in the exercise of their clerical func-
tion. The business of the Jacksons was the sale of "ordinations" in their "church" for sums from seventy-five to
two hundred dollars. These ordinations gave immunity
from the license regulation. It was brought out at the
trial, however, that neither self-confessed unsuitability of
candidates nor the most unfavorable references from other
Spiritualists would prevent ordination. Two of the "reverends" on the rolls of the organization were Michael
Angelo Crespo, B.S., M.S., Ph.D., and Charles Newman,
alias Harry Y. Cohen, alias Professor Belmont, alias
Professor Lewis.

Crespo was a Porto Rican, thirty-two years old, who
taught Spanish for a while at a junior high school, practiced drugless healing, and then was ordained by the
National Independent Spiritualist Association. His Ph.D.
degree came from the University of Oskaloosa, Oskaloosa,
Iowa, a mail-order institution which sold degrees but no

real correspondence courses. As a Spiritualist minister, Crespo made a specialty of getting Mexican divorces for people; he also sold charms, love philters, did crystal-gazing, card-revealing, and thought-reading, and in fifty-two days was alleged to have taken $1611.50, in amounts from thirty cents up. On November 12, 1924, he was convicted at Los Angeles of violating the State Medical Practice Act.

Cohen, alias Newman, specialized in marriage ceremonies and licentiousness. According to *The Los Angeles Daily Times* of November 8, 1924, "Cohen . . . was arrested September 27, 1922, and found guilty January 25, 1923, of contributing to the delinquency of a minor. He appealed and lost in the District Court of Appeals, but when officers sought him to start him serving a sentence of two years in the County Jail, he was not to be found.

"Newman had more than 1500 women clients, the police judged from a list in his pocket. Reports that young women had been lured to his office and coaxed into posing in the nude led to his arrest and the breaking up of the Newman Spiritualist Temple, 705 West Sixth Street; also certificated and registered by the National Independent Spiritualist Association. . . .

"Newman . . . in 1900 . . . started as a medium and fortune-teller in Minneapolis, under the name of Professor Belmont. For ten years he dodged trouble, then got into hot water and moved to Waterloo, Iowa. As Belmont and as Lewis he operated in Waterloo, Cedar Falls, Fort Madison, Muscatine and Oelwine. In 1913 he appeared in Cripple Creek, Colo., as Prof. Lewis. Then he went to Hot Springs, Ark. In 1914 and 1915 he was at Americus, Ga., and Decatur, Ala., still as Prof. Lewis.

"In 1915 he left Morgantown, W. Va., just ahead of an investigation of the manner in which he induced two women to 'invest' $10,000. In 1917 he was heard of in the vicinity of Kansas City, and then came to California. He operated in Santa Cruz before appearing in Los Angeles.

"Besides the charge on which he was convicted, Mrs. Angelina Coons, a divorced wife, charged him with failure to support an adopted child and asserted he had threatened her with death if she came to Los Angeles to testify against him."

William A. Jackson, the ingenious head of the N. I. S. A., was also secretary and treasurer of the California League, "an educational organization of voters incorporated for the purpose of preventing as well as correcting freak legislation, legislative blunders and other matters of public interest." "Inquiry of those well informed politically," said *The Daily Times*, "revealed that the organization is little known in political circles." Jackson was listed in the city directory, as a dealer in investments, and as president of the Los Angeles Joint Fraternal Association, Inc., and secretary-treasurer of the California Fraternal Association, Inc. But alas for his grandeur, William A. Jackson, Lois A. Jackson, and Gertrude Hull, as president, secretary and director of the N. I. S. A., were found guilty of criminal conspiracy by Police Judge Pope on February 26, 1925. They did not even go down with all flags flying; among the material seized by the police at N. I. S. A. headquarters and in the course of the prosecution were fake playing cards that had different denominations according to which end up they were fanned, a book on conjuring, and explanations of stage "mind-reading."

Stock-selling as a Spiritualist perquisite has developed to some dimensions since the time of Ann O'Delia Diss Debar (if these be not still her times—nobody seems to be sure she is dead, though she would be an old lady now). I have mentioned the ingenious sellers of Super-Utilities, Inc.; Harry Houdini told a Congressional committee in 1926 of his success in convicting one H. E. Parker in Chicago for selling Wilcox Transportation Company stock, which was worthless; and new schemes crop up all the time. Only the spirit smoke-screen remains permanently the same.

As much as worthless stock may annoy the person to whom it is sold, it is not as vicious a practice as selling bogus medical treatment. I have heard mediums during séances announce that their controls were definitely against an operation on an absent relative of a sitter. I have heard other quite as outrageous medical advice offered, although I have never been to one of the séances where, without diagnosis, the medium claims to be able to cure any disease the sitter feels that he has. However, the New York City Police have had their trained and clever policewomen get such evidence at many such séances—evidence which brought about convictions. The work against fraudulent mediumistic practices in New York City is but part of the work of the policewomen, who are under the able direction of Officer Mary A. Sullivan. This group during 1937 arrested, and got convictions for, one hundred and fifty mediums within the city of New York. Only part of the arrests were because of giving medical advice and cures, but it was a large part. Many were arrested because of selling predictions. Two things are particularly interesting about the number of arrests: first, only those mediums about whom the Police Department had complaints were investigated; second, some of the mediums convicted were members of the various "approved" associations of mediums. Yet one official list names but ninety-eight psychic churches within the city limits.

The ordinance in San Francisco makes it unlawful to tell fortunes "for or without pay," which makes it easier for the police of that city than in New York, where, to get a conviction, proof has to be given that a fee was paid. Both cities, like many others, specifically exempt from this law regarding fortune-telling duly accredited ministers, provided they do not take a personal fee. I heard, at a meeting of spiritists, advice given by one of their officers. He said, "We won our case in court when one of our ministers was arrested for telling fortunes. We showed that he was a minister ordained by us, and that every message was given in Church atmosphere. That is our cue. Use a banner and a vase of flowers to give Church atmosphere."

The police of various cities are not the only ones to interest themselves in disclosing fraudulent practices by mediums, for a very watchful eye is kept on them by the Better Business Bureau and by Chambers of Commerce. The Better Business Bureau, in its bulletins, has time and again warned against mystics and soothsayers, particularly in answer to personal questions. In one of their warnings they write: "First there is the matter of economic waste. Although the original amounts requested in the soothsayer's copy may be small, it is frequently merely a prelude for what is to follow. Even more serious is the damage that may be done to those who heed the advice that they purchase." One of the favorite stories told by the officers of the Better Business Bureau is about the Texas trance medium who claimed to tell the past, present and future. This medium asked the Fort Worth police to help her find her fur coat, which had either been lost or stolen—she couldn't tell which.

One thing that so many investigators never seem to understand is that a thousand Diss Debars and Jacksons do not weigh one iota against the theory of genuine mediumship. Even though it were proved—and it is not— that every one professing to be a medium is *ipso facto* a swindler and libertine, there would still be the question of whether these swindlers and libertines can communicate with the dead.

Mediums' morals are weighed by courts of law; mediums' scientific honesty is tested by the devotees of psychical research. But this opens up a whole new wrangle: who is to test the psychical investigators? Thomas Low Nichols said in his book, *Forty Years of American Life:* "Professor Hare, a distinguished chemist and electrician, and a thorough materialist and sceptic, commenced to investigate Spiritualism in the expectation of being able to explain it on scientific principles; but he failed by

becoming converted to a belief in the verity of manifestations, and by the same means lost, with sceptics, his credibility as a witness. Judge Edmonds, a distinguished jurist
of New York, failed in like manner; Governor Talmadge,
of Wisconsin, met a similar fate. Professor Mapes, of
New Jersey, and Judge Tilton, of Ohio, from investigators became converts. Indeed, a great number of persons,
from whom the public expected enlightenment, became
unfitted even to give evidence on the subject, from the
fact of their becoming believers. Those who denied the
reality of the phenomena called loudly for investigation;
but, as those who investigated were converted, nothing
was gained. The unbelieving public could not take the
testimony of believers. . . . Great numbers of scientific and
literary men are also believers. This fact destroys their
credibility. There seems no way but that every one who
has any interest in the matter should make his own investigations. On such a subject men will not be satisfied
with any amount of testimony. They must see for themselves."

I tell in another chapter what this seeing for yourself
is really worth—*i.e.*, nothing. The subject of physical
manifestations has now become so complicated, and the
adroitness of fraudulent mediums so extraordinary, that
a layman trying to test a medium is simply inviting
hoodwinking. It has come to the point where the British
psychical investigator, Eric J. Dingwall, has thought it
necessary to publish a pamphlet, "How to Go to a Medium." Harry Price, writing on "How to Test a Medium," says, "If I were asked to give, in a few words, some

sound advice to a prospective investigator of psychic phenomena, I would say, 'Believe nothing you see or hear at a *séance*.'"

Sir Oliver Lodge said, "Full control must be allowed to the observers—a thing which conjurers never really allow. I have never seen a silent and genuinely controlled conjurer; and in so far as mediums find it necessary to insist on their own conditions, so far they must be treated as conjurers." Doctor Walter Franklin Prince, in quoting Sir Oliver's statement, said, "I regret to add that, whatever may be the experience of others, I have had the good fortune but once to be present when investigators of mediumistic physical phenomena were untrammelled throughout, and that in this instance the results were entirely disastrous to the claims presented."

Some of the best observers have, in fact, come to the conclusion that all the *physical* phenomena ever produced have been in some way fraudulent. This naturally brings the Spiritualists to their feet, demanding to know why scientists (with the exception of the enthusiastic converts like Crookes, Hare and Lodge) will not take Spiritualism seriously. A partial answer is furnished by the late Doctor John E. Coover, in his paper, in "The Case For and Against Psychical Beliefs," edited by Carl Murchison and published by Clark University.

"The distinction must be made," he writes, "between (A) parlor observations under séance conditions, that yield at best but anecdotal evidence, and (B) scientific observations under laboratory conditions, that yield evidence acceptable to 'official science.' We must regard the scientific method.

[270]

"A. Under séance conditions, proper observation is precluded by the

- *a.* Multiplicity of phenomena,
- *b.* Unexpectedness of each event,
- *c.* Distraction of synchronous phenomena or discourse,
- *d.* Demand on attention for several hours continuously,
- *e.* Dim light,
- *f.* Lack of essential instruments,
- *g.* Lack of control of the conditions,
- *h.* Emotional atmosphere,
- *i.* Taking of inadequate notes while phenomena are occurring.

"The observer cannot be prepared to observe a specific occurrence, for he doesn't know what is coming next; any observation is consequently incidental, out of the tail of the eye, or in peripheral vision. Incidental observation in poor light for two continuous hours, amid distractions addressed to both eyes and ears, and attention often misdirected, favors inference in description and becomes malobservation. With the medium in control of the conditions, no instruments to assist the senses can be used to certain advantage. The report at best can be but anecdotal.

"B. Under laboratory conditions, proper observation is carefully provided for by

- *a.* Selecting as simple a phenomenon as possible,
- *b.* Providing a definite moment for its occurrence,

c. Excluding as much distraction as possible,

d. Limiting the time for concentrated attention,

e. Adapting most favorable lighting,

f. Utilizing all essential instruments,

g. Keeping complete control of the conditions,

h. Excluding emotional elements,

i. Recording correctly after the phenomenon has occurred.

"The experimenter is prepared to observe the specific event at the moment it occurs. He gives concentrated attention, and his attention is directed to it. Immediately after he 'observes accurately,' he 'records correctly' by taking care to exclude inferences from his description. With the conditions of experiment under his control, he can vary them at his pleasure and repeat the experiment as often as is necessary to reach a decisive, a reliable, result. His report is scientific.

"The attitude in the séance is that of blind faith; in the laboratory, of precaution. The closer the scrutiny, in the séance, the less you learn; in the laboratory, the more you learn. Cooperation in the séance is simulated; in the laboratory, effected. The purpose in the séance is to conceal causes; in the laboratory, to reveal them.

"The charge has often been made, and in itemized detail, that the rules of the séance enforce the conditions precisely favorable for fraud. And it is a curious fact, briefly suggested in the contrasted lists above, that if all the requirements in scientific method are formally set down in a list, and their opposites are then formally

set down, the second list gives the method of the séance.
. . . The 'obstinate incredulity' of 'official science' must
be largely attributed to the séance method of investigation
to which metapsychics has been almost wholly confined."

Of course, not everything can be brought into the laboratory and tested. No scientist doubts that lightning
does occur; but, even knowing that it is about to happen,
it takes a quick eye to follow its course.

Science realizes the difficulties of making tests but has
not given up. Doctor Karl T. Compton, president of the
Massachusetts Institute of Technology, told me: "This
has been a problem that so many people have worried
about for so long that it would seem to be advisable for
some recognized organization of scientists to undertake a
co-operative investigation. There are some obvious difficulties in having an individual conduct such experiments.
Perhaps the investigation might be taken up by some
such organization as the National Research Council."

In America there have been several bequests made to
colleges and universities for investigations into psychical
matters. Mention has been made previously of the Seybert bequest and the Thomas Welton Stamford bequest.
Other grants have been made to other institutions, the
principal one being made by a number of contributors to
Harvard University to commemorate the life and work of
Doctor Richard Hodgson. No one of these institutions is
as active as the University of London Council for Psychical Investigation founded by Harry Price, which constantly publishes reports of its scientific studies. Harry
Price, using every means within his extremely wide knowl-

edge and with the assistance of eminent men of science, attempts to stop fraud during his investigations, but at the same time tries to make the conditions as nearly as possible like those the mediums say bring the best results. He has made many exposures of trickery and found some things which he feels should be investigated further. I understand that he has not found anything like satisfactory proof of any phenomena being caused by spirits. His reports not only show his understanding of the subject but also now and again, between pages of statistical reports, have a deft touch which makes them interesting reading even for a layman. For instance, in describing the technic they were compelled to employ when investigating the German medium Rudi Schneider, he noted that it was "unfortunate" and went on to say: "The fact that we have to sing, talk, count, and be 'lustig' during a séance does not help us to observe or examine the phenomena and is very tiring. There is something undignified in having to bawl 'Three Blind Mice' and to confess that we did so looks ridiculous in a report." Even though the conditions were unfortunate, he was nevertheless able to disclose the methods that Rudi used.

There also have been formed a number of independent organizations for psychical research. Many of these have done excellent work, while others have acted merely as advertising agents for mediums, some of whom were of questionable integrity. Not even excepting the advertising organizations, I have no record of any one of them having become convinced that they have seen or heard anything which they need assume were spirits.

So far the court records show thousands of convictions by the police, and, even where indications of abnormal phenomena are found, the courts of science find no evidence of spirit causation.

CHAPTER X

THE CONFUSING PROPHETS

·THE HOME OF THE FOX SISTERS AT HYDESVILLE N.Y.·

·THE BIRTHPLACE OF MODERN SPIRITUALISM·

MARCH 31. 1848

⟨ 10 ⟩

BY THIS time the reader will have noticed that not every one agrees on the reality of psychic phenomena. It is also apparent that there are varying shades of belief on the subject. Each side points with pride to the eminence of its members and usually chooses to ignore the noted persons on the other side. There are three main points of view: first, that phenomena do exist and are caused by disembodied spirits; second, that while phenomena do exist the causes are unknown; third, that no genuine phenomena exist at all. Many of those who believe in the spirit causation see in mediumistic phenomena demonstrations of great religious value.

In making up a list of quotations regarding the validity of spirit manifestations I undoubtedly shall be accused of carefully picking those quoted. As a matter of fact I have; but only because I felt that each person's statement was interesting and furthermore expressed a viewpoint held by many.

In answer to my request for his belief, my friend Hendrik Willem Van Loon wrote, "In all my historical studies I have never come across a ghost story that could really be authenticated. Some of them seemed reliable enough but upon close investigation they proved to be either deliberate or accidental frauds. I cannot make this statement definite enough. I have done my best to find one single honest-to-goodness ghost story. I have found a lot of bad cases of indigestion but invariably a liberal dose of bicarbonate settled the ghost."

On the other side is Professor William McDougall. In a paper read at Clark University, at the conference on "The Case For and Against Psychical Belief," Doctor McDougall said: "In my opinion there has been gathered a very weighty mass of evidence indicating that human personality does not always at death wholly cease to be a source of influence upon the living. I am inclined to regard as part of this evidence the occurrence of ghostly apparitions; for it seems to me that, in many of these experiences, there is something involved that we do not at all understand, some causal factor or influence other than disorder within the mental processes of the percipient."

In London at a dinner arranged by Harry Price for a group of noted persons interested in psychic research the main address was given by Professor René Sudre, the French scientist and psychist. He said in his address, "I ask you to believe me when I say that my stand against traditional spiritism is purely on scientific grounds. I say so, not without sadness, but certainly with emphasis: there is no scientific evidence for survival. I admit that some people are content with certain assumptions and thereby acquire a spiritual faith. It is a religion and, as such, I respect it. But in that case let us speak no more of science! The words 'scientific spiritualism,' of which you often read, are in my opinion utter nonsense and a contradiction in terms." The scientist's viewpoint is so unlike that of the medium. At the convention in New York City of the General Assembly of Spiritualists in 1935 Felice Crossley, a medium from California, said: "Notwithstanding the fact that Modern Spiritualism has been the object of false and malicious slander nothing less significant could have inspired the revolutionary changes in religious denominations. So great has been the influence, despite the relentless persecution of its enemies, that those theologies which could not stand the test of reason have begun to crumble under the impact of historical and scientific research. Since the epochal event in the Fox Cottage, Hydesville, New York, March 31, 1848, psychic phenomena has engaged the attention of the entire world, particularly those masses who are too honest to let their lives be governed by a faith they no longer hold."

As we have seen, professed Spiritualists today believe that the Fox sisters were genuinely in communication with the dead when they produced the "Rochester rappings," but that they were under the influence of liquor and poverty, and quite untrustworthy, when they claimed to expose their séances. The believers have never wavered in their reverence for the first rappers, although the manifestations obtained by some later mediums have been subject to much less suspicion from outside.

The original house at Hydesville has been removed

bodily to Lily Dale, New York, a center of Spiritualist activities in this country. While on a visit to Rochester, however, Sir Arthur Conan Doyle suggested that a memorial ought to be placed there to the Fox sisters. He contributed substantially toward a fund for the purpose, and in 1926 it was realized.

The monument chosen was a twenty-five-foot granite shaft, placed on the lawn of the Plymouth Spiritualist Church in Rochester. It bore a tablet with an inscription, and above this a bas-relief of the Hydesville house. At the unveiling, performed by Mrs. M. E. Cadwallader, general Chairman of the World Committee for the memorial, there were representatives from fifteen American States and Canada, and emblems from eighteen foreign countries. Mrs. Cadwallader was escorted in a procession by the Mayor of Rochester. "Owing to the cold weather," says the newspaper report, "the ceremonies on the lawn lasted but a few moments." Inside the church, however, the Reverend Walter Foss, the minister of the church, read the following letter from Conan Doyle:

"I send my hearty congratulations to the Spiritualists of America for having raised a monument in memory of what posterity will recognize as the greatest event that ever occurred upon American soil. It came, as Christianity came, in a lowly form, and it suffered as Christianity suffered, from the opposition of the high priests and the wealthy and the powerful. But there was always a brave minority in every country who had the brains to understand and the courage to proclaim that the veil of death had been rent, and that the outlook of human life would never again be the same. The knowledge has spread all over the world and has tinged all religious thought, even when they do not admit the source from which it comes.

"The ultimate merit of that revelation, which came in so humble a shape, will be the simplification of religion, the breaking down of the barriers between sects, and a universal creed which will combine the ethics of real Christianity with direct spiritual communication, receiving our teaching not from bygone traditions and documents, but from actual contact with beings higher than ourselves. I pray that God may bless you, and that the great cause which is committed to your care may ever progress, discarding its lower manifestations and extending its higher ones, until the divine purpose has been fulfilled."

Arthur Conan Doyle believed what he said in spite of what Margaret Fox wrote in a signed story in *The New York World* for October 21, 1888. In the story she said, "Spiritualism is a fraud and a deception. It is a branch of legerdemain, but it has to be closely studied to gain perfection." Sir Arthur did not believe her. Neither was the confession of fraud by Margaret Fox acceptable to Henry J. Newton, the president of The First Spiritual Society of New York. His reply to the Fox article was, "Nothing that she could say in that regard would in the least change my opinion, nor would it that of any one else who had become profoundly convinced that there is an occult influence connecting us with an invisible world."

Doctor George Sexton, in order to prove that no legerdemain was used in producing spirits, made, what he called, an oration at the Cavendish Rooms, London, on the

Sunday evening of June fifteenth, of the year 1873, to prove his point. He called his oration "Spirit Mediums and Conjurers" and in it said, "Mediums are not conjurers; they are, as a rule, persons whose past life has been very unfavorable to learning the mysteries of this, or indeed of any other art. They are frequently ignorant, uneducated, and withal most diffident and modest. When we see certain phenomena taking place in their presence, we are perfectly sure they could not have produced them."

Horace Greeley was said to have been very much interested in spiritism and, it will be recalled, he sent Katherine Fox to school. I have a letter of his in my collection which shows that at least he had some faith in the Fox girls. He wrote the letter from New York, on November 19, 1851, to Obediah A. Bowe, the man with whom he had learned the printer's trade. In one paragraph he said, "What have you seen or heard about Spirit Rappings? Now don't stiffen your (unshort) ears, for *there's something in 'em!* What it is, I am not yet sure, but it isn't knee joints nor toe snaps—notwithstanding the wise pill-peddlers of Buffalo."

Unless, by the way, I have the script, the authorized published statement, or heard the opinion personally I am not quoting any one. I feel that this is necessary even though I must leave out some of the best stories. For instance I have heard many times that Abraham Lincoln admitted having gotten the text for his Gettysburg Speech from a spirit and through a medium. The only basis for the story that I can find is that long after his death his spirit came back and made that statement to a medium. I am only quoting statements which were made during life in this world. I still do not know whether Lincoln was a believer even though I have read the pamphlet, published in 1891, titled "Was Abraham Lincoln a Spiritualist? or, Curious Revelations from the Life of a Trance Medium." The claim has been made that Lincoln held séances at the White House, which I believe to be true from the records I have seen. While Franklin D. Roosevelt was Governor of New York State the Associated Press carried the following story:

"Albany, Feb. 17.—Mrs. Franklin D. Roosevelt revealed today that a party in the Executive Mansion for members of the executive staff last Saturday night resulted in a reading for her by a spirit medium.

"It was her first such experience she said, and she admitted asking about the Governor's presidential prospects. The medium communicated for a moment with her 'spirit control' and replied:

" 'Well, there are two other strong contenders for the nomination, but he will probably get it.'

"And if nominated, would he be elected?

"The spirits were quite confident that he would."

To attend a séance does not prove one a Spiritualist and I have no knowledge of the number of people in public life who are believers. The brilliant journalist and reformer Thomas Low Nichols, previously mentioned as a lecturer for the Davenport Brothers, says in his panoramic book, *Forty Years of American Life*, "In America, probably half the members of Congress and the State Legislatures are spiritualists." His book was published in 1864 and he even may have been wrong then. But America is not the only country to have had men in public life interested in the subject. M. Thiers, ex-President of France, said, "I am a Spiritualist, and an impassioned one, and I am anxious to confound Materialism in the name of science and good sense."

Camille Flammarion, convinced of the facts of psychic phenomena, said, "Although Spiritualism is not a religion but a science, yet the day may come when religion and science will be reunited in one single synthesis." A large number who hold this view still attend some church not spiritistic.

For a long time I have had a report of a statement of the president of a spiritist's association to the effect that good and bad spirits alike come and possess men and women. In this manner, according to the statement, bad spirits are helped to a better life. I had doubted that this statement had been made until I attended the annual meeting of The General Assembly of Spiritualists in New York City. (I went as an accredited reporter for *The New York World-Telegram*. This gave me an excuse to take everything down in black and white as it was said. A regular staff writer, E. E. Titus, accompanied me and all our notes were found to be identical.) One medium made the statement that, "There are liars over there, just as there are liars in this world. It is quite possible for a clairvoyant to contact an unreliable informer while in a trance state, if he is the sort of person who makes a daily habit of associating with prevaricators and chiselers." Shortly after this statement a medium went into a trance and both

Titus and I had the ill fortune to be put in touch with a lying (to use the medium's own word) spirit.

Titus and I filled page after page of notes of verbatim reports of the meetings. One medium from the colored section of Harlem, notorious for its policy, or "numbers," gambling, said:

"It should be adopted as a rule that no one should have messages or give out numbers in a Spiritualist church without first having a song and prayer. There's no good in having people come to church just to get numbers. If she can't, I won't go. Let them know and let them go out into the world and say that 'Spiritual' is a religion, not a fortune telling."

Another medium said that the spirit world was socialistic and had apartment houses and that all a person needed to do for new clothes was "you think of a suit and there it is." By the way, the mediums do not agree on descriptions of the land of spirits. Still another medium in explaining the comfort Spiritualism was to the living said, "A girl whose sweetheart has been dead three years has a psychic affair with him." I was unable to discover just what that meant. But perhaps it may be understood by the motion which was passed at a Spiritualistic Convention in Philadelphia as reported in *The Banner of Light* for April 21, 1877. The resolution was that society has no right to punish any individual because "what to a man seems evil, to the angel world and God is but undeveloped good." Or, on the other hand, it may have had to do with the resolution passed at the Michigan State Convention of Spiritualists in 1877, "that the only open door out of our difficulties is the entire abrogation of all merely man-made marriage laws, leaving the sexes free to seek harmonious association under the laws of nature."

Regarding free love I again quote from Thomas Low Nichols' book: "The influence of spiritualism upon morality is not very easy to estimate. It is claimed that the influence and admonitions of spirits and the belief in immortality have reformed many drunkards and profligates. On the other hand, it is known that numbers of spiritualists have taught and acted upon ideas of the largest liberty in social relations. They have adopted individualistic and 'free-love' doctrines. Husbands have abandoned wives, and wives their husbands, to find more congenial partners, or those for whom they had stronger spiritual affinities."

Doctor Nichols' remarks are particularly interesting because he and his wife were ardent Spiritualists, and also former member of a "free-love" colony at Yellow Springs, Ohio. In all fairness I must point out that I have not heard free-love advocated by any medium whose séance I have attended and while I have heard suggestions made which, to me, were of questionable ethics, it may be that I was either not with a "true" medium or that one of those "lying" spirits was at work.

There are many different codes printed for conducting séances. In the rules set down by J. Burns for the conditions for a Spirit Circle he stressed the "Mental Conditions." He wrote, "All forms of mental excitement are detrimental to success. Those with strong and opposite opinions should not sit together; opinionated, dogmatic, and positive people are better out of the circle and room.

Parties between whom there are feelings of envy, hate, contempt, or other inharmonious sentiment should not sit at the same circle. The vicious and crude should be excluded from all such experiments. The minds of the sitters should be in a passive rather than active state, possessed by the love of truth and of mankind. One harmonious and fully-developed individual is invaluable in the formation of a circle."

Disbelievers say the various rules are conducive to fraud and that the conditions of many séances make the discovery of fraud almost impossible. The Associated Press quotes Doctor William J. Mayo, of Rochester, Minnesota, as saying that the person who attends a spiritual séance in a darkened room surrenders 95 per cent of his intelligence so far as obtaining accurate knowledge is concerned. He went on to say:

"They remain there in the dark, expectant, until their nerves are jumpy. And they imagine they have the same means of investigation that they have in their laboratories. They haven't as much chance to detect a fraud in that darkened room as a hound dog would have. The hound dog could tell something by his sense of smell. The fakir in those séances has less than 5 per cent of the intelligence to combat, there in the dark. And out of such séances come such men as Sir Arthur Conan Doyle, Sir William Crookes and Sir Oliver Lodge to become propagandists for spiritualism."

But not only the skeptics are against darkness, for D. D. Home, medium and spiritist, wrote in October, 1875, that he advocated the suppression of dark séances. He went on to say, "Every form of phenomena ever occurring through me at the few dark séances has been repeated over and over again in the light, and now I deeply regret ever having had other than light séances." Many other spiritists agree with him.

Many people, wholly apart from mediums, have had psychic experiences. For instance Ignace Paderewski, in his autobiography,* wrote that as a youth away from home he had a premonition of some great change at home. When he returned he found that his grandfather had died the day before. He wrote further: "I have had several such experiences. I often had them as a child. Now I use more logic. Perhaps I am not so wise as I used to be, because now I apply logic to my intuition, and logic and intuition do not go hand in hand." His statement makes interesting that of Lloyd Testor, the English Spiritualist, who wrote: "Many a so-called 'genius' has been simply a more or less perfect instrument upon which or through which another played. Many a writer of brilliant 'fiction' has been but the 'pen' of some great mind-entity, without whom he may have been a very ordinary person."

My friend Father C. M. de Heredia has spent his life studying mediumistic phenomena. He wrote: "Without a consideration of the natural credulousness of man and his desire to be deceived, the tendency of a medium to satisfy their desire, the ease with which an ordinarily accurate scientist can be fooled, the total dissimilarity between a séance and the regular scientific investigation, and the inclination of observers to imagine and distort and misin-

*The Paderewski Memoirs, Charles Scribner's Sons, New York, 1938.

terpret, a convincing study of Spiritism cannot be made. As in few other scientific problems, the investigator must bear in mind the variations and weaknesses of the human factor." The viewpoint of the spiritist is well given by Morell Theobald in his book. In speaking of mediumistic manifestations he said: "Such phenomena can never be received until faith in accredited narrators and reliance on the commonplace integrity of ordinary reputable people is admitted as one of the canons of scientific attestation." Still on the same topic Albert Edward Wiggam wrote: "The human mind is so constructed and it operates in such a way that all general impressions and beliefs about matters of fact and the laws of nature which have not been corrected and tested by that particular way of thinking called science are bound to be wrong."

A bulletin published by a Spiritualistic Church notes: "All psychic manifestations are really the demonstrations of Spirit. It is useless to ask science to prove this because science knows nothing of Spirit." Another side is given by what Thomas A. Edison wrote: "The psychic forces are merely words for perfectly natural forces which as yet we do not understand." The third viewpoint is found in the writings of Houdini: "I have been an ardent investigator of Spiritualism for thirty years, during which time I have witnessed more than 5000 séances, but never once have I detected any phenomena that would lead me to believe in the existence of a spirit sphere. Not one of the mediums I have encountered in all those years has satisfied me with the genuineness of his psychical phenomena. To the contrary, I have never failed to detect fraud, or at least a possible solution on a perfectly rational basis."

Some accept one type of phenomena as having been proven satisfactorily to them and refuse to accept another. Others will attest to belief in the type of phenomena dismissed by the first. Still others believe it all sham. Will Irwin kindly wrote his belief for me: "I spent several years in my youth investigating commercial mediums —some of them undoubted frauds. I saw nothing which would lead me to believe in the spiritist hypothesis—although occasionally, I did encounter phenomena and performances which are hard to account for except on the theory that certain people possess the faculty of clairvoyance. The sixth sense—if it really exists—does not necessarily have anything to do with the existence of disembodied spirits and human communication with them." Another friend, Hereward Carrington, wrote: "Physical phenomena of a supernormal character are undoubted! I hold that this will be proved to the satisfaction of all, before many years have passed." Elmer P. Ransom wrote for me the skeptic's view: "Even after watching mediums for more than sixty years, amongst them those of the highest reputation, I have never seen anything that was not produced by the human efforts of the medium. Furthermore no one of them would submit to a satisfactory test. Nevertheless I still hold an open mind."

Spiritualists say that their teachings offer the proof of survival while the orthodox churches offer only uncertainty. They point out that the Bible frequently mentions mediums and spirits. Doctor Harry Emerson Fosdick told me that, "All references in the Bible to mediumship attack it." And as Doctor Raymond C. Knox told me: "In ascertaining the meaning of any particular term in the Bible—as for example the 'Spirit of The Lord'—you have to see what the phrase signified in its latest and highest usage. 'The Spirit of The Lord' meant something entirely different at the time of Christ than it did at the time of Samson. In the highest development 'The Spirit of The Lord' meant the spirit of ethical love—and that only. This is not a disembodied spirit but an expression of a personal relationship to God."

Professor John Dewey told me that: "Leaving out the elements of fraud in spiritism, what interests me is the psychology of the people interested in the subject. It is a good example of the will to believe."

There are hundreds of people who have opinions on one side, the other, or astride the psychic fence. Somehow when read one after another the beliefs of our teachers do not help us to form a clear picture. The prophets of spirit matters are confusing, for the statements, even those in regard to the same phenomena, are so conflicting that one cannot go by the record. Then belief resolves itself into a matter of personal experience.

CHAPTER XI

WITH MY OWN EYES

(11)

Huck Finn, in one of Mark Twain's books, said: "Why, I had eyes and I could see things, but they never meant nothing to me. But Tom Sawyer was different. When Tom Sawyer seen a thing it just got up on its hind legs and talked to him—told him everything it knowed. I never see such a head." Huck Finn rightly was surprised for few people are possessed of a mind which registers what their eyes can see.

Almost no one notices unimportant details. His eyes can see, and in many instances have seen many times, things which his mind discards. Almost no one, including professional typists, can name the order of the letters on a typewriter keyboard. In those cities where there are dial telephones I have never met any one who could name the numbers and letters in each hole of the dial. Yet I have asked people who use the telephone constantly and do their own dialing. Very likely the reader does not recall whether the numerals on the face of his watch are Arabic or Roman. Few know how many steps are in front of their homes, whether the right shoe is put on before the left one when dressing, or, unless it is a very small town, the stores passed on the way to the bank. Few of those who use the dictionary regularly have the foggiest notion where the thumb index for any given letter may be found. People who play cards constantly do not know which of the court cards have profile pictures and which full face. Even if they happen to guess rightly that a certain Jack, for instance, is pictured in profile they do not know which way he is facing. A man's coat buttons on the right and a woman's on the left though few of the opposite sex ever notice. The bow of ribbon on a man's hat is on the left side while it is on the right side of a woman's hat of the mannish type, though few realize that fact. Unless a man is a tailor he is probably unaware how many buttons he has on his waistcoat, or how many he has on his sleeves, or his trousers. Most men use every pocket in their clothes, and unless they count, have no idea how many pockets they have. Women do not know how many eyelets their walking shoes have, nor do they know how many stripes run down the back of each glove. Even women who wash their dishes do not know that the water running out of the sink always swirls to the right, though they have seen it happen three times a day. Few wives could describe the type of letter with which their silver is marked. We see all these things but our minds decide they are not worth noticing.

Literally thousands of times I have heard, "I know it must be so for I saw it with my own eyes." What people really mean is that among the things which they saw certain things seemed, at the time, important and they attempted to remember them. The picture they give is a most incomplete picture. Furthermore, as they didn't notice all the details, what they attempted to remember was a series of disconnected bits of the complete picture. It is utterly impossible to recall any long series of unrelated details, and therefore what their minds pleased to notice was not described in full.

Memory in intelligent persons is purposive. It retains what is useful, what can be related to knowledge or made to serve an aim. It is trained to discard what is unrelated or valueless. So it is the more baffled by events that are purposeless or disconnected.

Take a simple example. You see the word "deconstitutionalization," and I ask you to look away from the book and recite the letters. You do it, of course, accurately, after a single glance, because these twenty-three characters relate certain patterns of association which are imbedded in your mind. But if I show you the letters "sqwloehgvpzrcxatdmebzfk," it will take you perhaps half an hour to memorize them in sequence, precisely because there is, for you, no logic in their appearing in that order. Furthermore, even in the memorization, you most likely will not notice which letters of the alphabet are missing or if any appear more than once. Yet in both examples there are just twenty-three letters. In each instance your eye has the same chance to see but you have never been trained to memorize a series of items which are not logically sequential.

Blackstone pointed out how dangerous it is to accept the testimony of eyewitnesses, for twelve persons observing an event would give twelve distinct and often contradictory accounts of what happened. They did not all notice the same details; they did not all consider the same details to be important among those they noticed; and lastly they did not remember all they did think important. Man's objective memory is astonishingly faulty.

Most of the followers of mediums have become convinced of the reality of the phenomena because they "saw it with their own eyes." During meetings of spiritists people give testimony about what they "saw," and "heard" during a time when the medium was "under complete control." I am perfectly willing to have the people believe that they are accurate in their impressions but as a magician I state that I am in a position to prove that they cannot know.

A magician depends upon the fact that if something which he has to do can be made to seem quite unimportant, no one in his audience will see him do it. For instance, many times I have wanted to look at my audience before being called upon to make my appearance. At a banquet it is particularly easy, for all that I need to do is to put a folded napkin over my arm, and as a waiter no one pays any attention to me. I have, to the assembling diners, become so unimportant that I am invisible. No one notices that I am not correctly dressed to be a waiter, and as far as that goes, few people know what constitutes the difference between evening clothes and a waiter's uniform.

In a theater if I saunter down the aisle holding a program where it may be seen, I am merely another patron, and no one stops even to discover whether I am a friend.

In a magician's performance the same psychology holds true. The magician by his acting stresses certain details of the performance and minimizes others until they become invisible.

Another element in making things either invisible or important is time. If an action is expected at a certain time the audience will see the magician make that action even if it is false. Were it done out of time, every one would recognize it to be merely simulated. Because the observer is alert, his imagination jumps ahead of the magician's operations. The timing of a magician's work is very important. It is very easy to demonstrate but hard to accept merely from a description. Perhaps it may be explained most simply by saying that the magician seems to be acting to the cadence of a waltz, for example, but actually the rhythm of his work is off beat as in swing music. The minds of the audience are led in some regular time, and the magician does those things which he wants to pass unseen either before or after the beat. In timing, magic is rather like baseball batting. The batter must not only swing his bat to the right spot, but he must swing it at the right instant, or the ball will go by him.

The magician depends upon the mental habits, distraction of attention, and preconceived opinions of his audience to work his wonders. It is a recognized fact that most of our knowledge is accepted upon authority and indeed rightly so. It would be quite impossible for any human being to discover for himself all the information necessary to his complex existence. But authoritarianism is a dangerous way of knowing unless it is guarded, since authorities can generally be invoked to prove either side of a dubious question. Even proverbs have their opposites. Absence makes the heart grow fonder. Out of sight out of mind. Live not for today alone. One today is worth two tomorrows. Penny wise and pound foolish. Take care of the pence and the pounds will take care of themselves. Then, too, authorities have a trick of slipping their leashes —"the transfer of authority," as it is academically known —and making pronouncements in fields unrelated to their special knowledge. Outside of his own field an authority may know no more than the man in the street.

Besides tricking the mind the magician also uses cunningly devised apparatus and manipulative skill, but 80 per cent of his success depends upon psychology. It is not necessary for him to know that it is psychology. He may, by trial and error, have discovered that when he did something in one particular way no one ever saw him do it. The magician's skill has nothing to do with speed— the hand is very decidedly *not* faster than the eye. Even if it were possible to make motions so fast that the eye could not follow in detail, the eye would still see that a movement had been made. That would be all the audience would need to lose all interest. Movement attracts attention—witness our moving signs—and the last thing a magician wants to do is to attract attention to his secret movements.

When any one says that a medium cannot be a magician because he does nothing rapidly, that is merely another way of saying that the person has no knowledge of the way a magician works. When the argument is offered that a medium cannot be a magician because he had no opportunity to learn a trick and never had any lessons in magic, it is just as meaningless. There are, on the stage today, magicians, and very successful ones, who never had a lesson and never read a book on the subject. However, it is easier to learn the art of deception through a teacher, and there are many places, as I have pointed out, where one may learn the tricks of the séance.

Mind you, I do not say that all mediums use trickery. I am only attempting to point out that: first, it takes a large amount of knowledge and special training to observe correctly a mediumistic exhibition; second, that the layman's opinion of the way a magician works is not according to fact; third, that merely because one does not suspect that a medium knows how to do tricks, or that he has had an opportunity to learn them, is not proof that he is not a trickster.

People believe the evidence of their senses, yet nothing is more deceptive. Even those trained to observe certain things may be faulty in the observation of other things which they have not studied. A person assumes that what he believes he sees is just as he sees it. A person seeing a diamond ring in Tiffany's window is satisfied he has seen a real diamond because of Tiffany's reputation. It is an inference that he depends upon, not his eyesight. Were his eye that of a trained jeweller he might notice—provided that Tiffany were to go in for practical jokes—that it was an imitation. On the other hand, were his eye that of a trained doctor, for instance, he would in all likelihood "see" a diamond.

Because I have spoken about the fallibility of sight only does not mean that the other senses are more to be depended upon. One cannot tell the direction from which a sound comes in the dark. That has been proven beyond question, in the laboratory. If you have the idea that you can tell one thing from another by taste when blindfolded you will enjoy testing yourself. Pick out those things which have no odor and go ahead. You will not be able to tell the difference between tea and coffee and chicken broth. You will find that cold mashed turnips and apple sauce are quite alike. Now another blindfold test will show that the sense of smell is a liar too. In comparison with the rest of the senses the sense of touch is really good. But at that, you cannot tell in the dark whether ice is hot or cold, or whether you are holding your wife's hand or the hand of some one else merely by the sense of touch.

This fallibility of the senses is not some new theory I have just made up to write about. It is the basis for all magicians' performances. Magicians, however, are not the only ones to study the subject. It has been a university study for many, many years and has been convincingly proven. Then as long as one cannot trust himself to know true phenomena from false, how is he to find out about the subject?

Let me interrupt to mention an article by the late Richard Hodgson on the *Testimony of Conjurors*. Doctor Hodgson pointed out, and I agree with him, that because one who knows nothing about magic says that something can't possibly be caused by conjuring, his statement is worthless. He also pointed out, and I still agree, that a magician's statement is just as worthless when he says that everything must be trickery. A magician is trained in his subject and he is apt to notice indications of trickery that a person knowing nothing of either the psychology or method of magic would pass over. He cannot make a blanket statement, however, and have it mean anything more than any other blanket statement would mean.

Another thing I feel should be noted is that because a magician seemingly can duplicate a phenomenon, the medium is not thereby proven a fraud. An oasis is no less real because some people think that they see one when all they see is a mirage. When, however, a medium can produce his phenomenon only under the conditions necessary for the performance of a feat of magic, it seems to me that he is asking for a stretching of credulity when he desires that it be accepted as genuine. A mirage is no less a mirage because some one is able to prove the existence of an oasis.

One more thing which should be mentioned is that while our senses are most untrustworthy there are occasionally found people with some sense particularly acute. These people have developed a sense which was naturally very sensitive. I have seen and tested people who could, by the sense of touch alone, tell how many playing cards or tickets they held. Any number might be given them from a half-dozen to two hundred and they would tell the number by touch as fast or faster than it could be done by sight. Even these people cannot rely on their sense of touch in other matters. I have known people with particularly keen, and, furthermore, trained sight, and others with such acuteness in hearing. I mention this because when one of these persons, without acknowledging the fact, uses his gift he will seem to one who does not possess it to have knowledge which he could not obtain by natural means. If he then trains his memory too he can perform miracles. For instance, a person with very exceptional eyesight, trained perception, and with trained memory can see and remember after a mere glance details which another would never realize he could get in that manner. Many mediums have trained their perceptive faculties and memories. This makes another point to beware of in visiting a medium.

Whose word should one take about the existence of spirit manifestations? Because a person is sincere does not mean he is scientific. Because he is a scientist does not mean that he may not, under conditions which he cannot control, find his senses unreliable. Because he is honest does not mean that his opinion of another's honesty is to be accepted. In spiritism we cannot avoid the emotions, and when emotions are brought into play reason is left behind. The only proof which would be acceptable generally would be after a scientific investigation of the simplest phenomena. Scientific proof would be attained if by careful observations, or measurements, a collection of facts were arrived at which would be fitted by one explanation and would not be fitted by any other proposed explanation. The judges of the proof must be familiar with the technic of the observation, or measurement used, and with the significance of the explanation. One of the principles of scientific investigation is that no complex explanation is acceptable until all of the simple ones are tested and found wanting.

The great difficulty is to find the proper investigators. They must not be so open minded as to be credulous. They must not go to find proofs of their preconceived beliefs.

One of the most difficult things to accept with the spiritists is their jargon. Page after page is completely meaningless even to them. That was proven when Charles R. Flint and several friends wrote an article which they had labored over so as to have it entirely without meaning. The article was printed in a leading spiritist paper and frequently quoted. (An account of this hoax is found in Mr. Flint's book *Memories of An Active Life*.) The spiritists ask that they be accepted by science and then they fill their books and papers full of meaningless phrases which no self-respecting scientist would countenance. As long as they attempt to fool with words, or are so ignorant that they think they are saying something, the only followers will be those who wish an occult rather than a scientific explanation. Their "literature" has probably led more people away from spiritism than all the exposés of fraudulent mediums.

Another hurdle the spiritists have to jump is caused by some of the group who insist that all and sundry must certainly be mediums. Doyle and others have written at length in an attempt to prove that Houdini's performances were demonstrations of mediumistic powers. The very tricks which they picked out as evidence were left to his brother Hardeen, who performs them today with the same methods Houdini used, and those methods are definitely not mediumistic. Cumberland was accused of being a medium without knowing it. His answer was, "Permit me to be the best judge as to how I do my own experiments." Many people have stated that I, too, have mediumistic powers but surely I, who do them, know how my tricks are done. None of my tricks require psychic powers. Many of us in magic have had the opportunity to "confess" we are mediums. Of course we are in a bad position for wishful believers end all arguments supporting their claim by saying, "You can not prove that you are not mediums. Other true mediums have resorted to trickery."

Not all spiritists, by any means, countenance the patter some use. Many feel that attempting to draft magicians into the mediumistic ranks is insufferably silly. Many are fully aware of the fallibility of the senses and yet feel that they have convincing proof by demonstrations of the ability of spirits to return to earth.

CHAPTER XII

UNANSWERED

(12)

M ANY PEOPLE have weird experiences, or witness strange events, which have nothing to do with séances or mediums, unless, as some believe, the people themselves, unwittingly, may be mediums. Some think that these experiences are evidences of some strange force at work; not the work of spirits but merely some natural force not as yet understood. A great many believe that these experiences make amusing stories but are entirely meaningless except to show how fallible is the human memory and what strange tricks it plays when given impetus by coincidence.

My own best story is about an experience which occurred in broad daylight. When I was fourteen years old I spent a summer on a farm in Massachusetts. One morning, late in the summer, with the farmer's twenty-seven-year-old son I rode to town on a farm wagon filled with grain. On the way to town we had to pass a graveyard. The farmer's son was in a grouchy mood and very talkative. His particular complaint was about an "old skinflint" who had died several years previously. The man had been, the son said, both shrewd and crooked and had amassed a fortune by tricking the farmers. "And what did he do with the money?" Said the farmer's son. "Built himself a fancy tomb—that's what. There it is there. I wish it would fall apart and his coffin fall to pieces." We had just come to the cemetery and as he expressed his hopes he pointed at the tomb. The moment he pointed the huge metal door began slowly to swing open. He was so amazed that automatically he pulled on the reins and stopped the team. We both sat watching the slowly opening door. We were badly frightened and speechless. Finally the door was wide open and stopped moving. That instant there was heard a dull boom and a cloud of dust came out of the door and hid the tomb from our sight. Slowly the dust settled and everything was as before except that the door was still open. My curiosity made me want to go up to the tomb to see what had happened but I was too frightened to go alone. It was fully five minutes before I could coax the farmer's son to tie the horses and go with me. At the tomb we discovered that the coffin, which had been on trestles, had just fallen apart. We could see no reason for the door to have swung open but decided that the fresh air had caused the rotten coffin to fall apart. The trestles still stood and a part of the bottom of the coffin was on them. The body was on those boards and a part of the top of the coffin was flat on the chest of the body. We had seen enough and were happy to leave the tomb. Once we were outside we swung the heavy door closed and braced it with a large stone. It makes a weird story but even if during the years which have passed

I have remembered the details correctly, which I probably haven't, I see nothing in the experience except coincidence.

A story which I have been told many times is about Malena Harned's vision. Malena was an American-born girl of pure Dutch descent and she and her Dutch forebears not only had never been addicted to visions but there is no other record of any of them ever having one. On the night of her vision her husband, Samuel Harned, was away. He had taken a flock of sheep to town and expected to sell them for a considerable sum of money. The town was so far away from his Pennsylvania farm that once he had sold his sheep it would take him all night and far into the morning to drive home. Shortly after midnight Malena wakened her eldest daughter Sally and asked her to get dressed and look after the four younger children. Malena explained to her daughter that she had just had a vision and that she was going to the neighbors for help. In the vision, she told Sally, she had seen Samuel lying, badly injured, in the ditch by the road near a clump of trees by a cemetery about ten miles away. It was not supposed that he could have gotten so near home by that time. Malena ran to the nearest neighbor and repeated her story and persuaded him to drive her to the spot. They found Samuel where she had described seeing him in her vision. His head was bashed in and his money gone. He was rushed to the doctor who said that had he been left alone he undoubtedly would have been dead by morning. His injury was very serious but by covering the hole in his skull with a piece of silver and with careful nursing he was brought back to complete health. The reason that Samuel was so near home was that he had sold his sheep more quickly than he had expected and had started sooner.

Malena Harned was my great-grandmother and Samuel my great-grandfather. My grandmother, Sally, was twelve years old at the time of Malena's vision. She told the story many times and it was corroborated by my great-uncle Henderson G. Harned who was one of the younger children. My great-uncle was a Methodist minister who felt that exaggeration was not permissible even to make a story better. Of course 1834, when this was supposed to have happened, was a long time ago but many members of the family believed the story in all its details.

Whether they are viewed as occult or as examples of what amusing tricks the mind can play these stories still are interesting. One continually runs across stories of this kind in biographies of famous people. Of course I have long been interested in the subject and have heard many people describe their experiences. Those whose stories I have liked best have been kind enough to write them for me. They follow:

Phil Stong

I've never seen a ghost and I shan't worry about it if I never do; I have had three or four experiences, however, which have seemed definitely outside the bounds of normal experience to me. There is, for example, a member of my wife's family who indubitably can be "willed" to perform trivial acts like sitting in a certain chair, turning a given lamp on or off, moving a book, etc.; this, blindfolded and without any kind of contact. John Mulholland suggests unconscious and normally imperceptible noises, respiration, the creak of a chair; this is, of course, nonsense.

I do believe in extra-sensory perception of sorts and I most certainly do not believe in awareness of events that haven't yet occurred, or premonition, even though a premonition of my wife's probably kept me out of the great New York subway wreck ten years ago, or thereabouts.

I was working for the newspaper trade journal, *Editor & Publisher*, at the time, as an associate editor. It was a splendid shop, with a most congenial staff, but like any efficient publication it insisted on punctuality. We were all at our desks within a minute or two of nine o'clock in the morning; two or three minutes before five in the afternoon we reached for our hats, unless it was one of the days when there was some special work, and hit the door right on the dot.

We were on the seventeenth floor of the Times Building; we took the express elevator down and most of us then walked on down through the arcade to the "B'way-7th Ave. Express." I lived in Greenwich Village—a garden apartment at 259 West 11th Street—so I rode down to Fourteenth Street and took the local one stop to Sheridan Square. Office-going New York is so paced and routed that I suppose that seventy-five evenings out of a hundred I bought an evening paper at the newsstand in the arcade at three minutes after five and caught my express three or four minutes later.

About a quarter of five one hot summer evening my wife called me and asked rather anxiously if I was all right. It struck me as not only extraordinary but particularly silly so I answered too sarcastically that my regularly robust health hadn't declined much since morning.

She hesitated for a moment and then said she wished I would "drop by" the office of a friend of ours and get a beach robe his wife had borrowed a week-end or two before.

I pointed out that Ed's office was eight blocks in the wrong direction, that I was tired and hot and Seventh Avenue was crowded with people getting off work, that there weren't any beaches around Twelfth Street and that we could walk over to Ed's and Betty's any evening and pick up a Scotch and soda and the beach robe.

Virginia insisted and I grew increasingly bitter—I asked her if she had gone off her nut; I said I would see the beach robe in the seventh circle of Hades, and finally I got mad and hung up on her, so I didn't dare to go home without the beach robe.

She called me again in ten minutes and told me not to forget the beach robe because she had told Ed I was coming for it. I hung up on her again.

My sympathetic colleagues, two married and two unmarried, said women were all dopes—they took notions but you had to put up with them—it was a tough life and married men really didn't live longer—and so on.

When I got to Ed's office he agreed with them and me. He said he'd told Virginia that he'd be glad to drop the robe at the office, which was on his way home, but that she'd said I was going to come up. We went to a refreshment stand and had two glasses of cider. We cursed women, the climate, General Motors common and everything. We shook hands feelingly and I went into the Fiftieth Street subway kiosk.

The gate was closed.

I put a handsome glaze on the Seventh Avenue concrete as I tramped on back to Forty-second Street, where there was the worst mob I had ever seen, even in a subway station, milling at the turnstiles which were all capped.

This was too much. I shoved up and past the guard—I had a press card in my pocket and knew I could get away with it—put a nickel on the closed coin machine and hopped over the chains. I might have started a lot of trouble but I didn't think of that till afterward. The poor old guard yelled at me three or four times and then said disconsolately, "He didn't hear me."

Underground around Forty-first Street I came on fire hoses strung down into the tunnel. At Fortieth Street a woman scrambled up on the platform. Her face was black with the greasy dirt of the tunnel and she was crying. I started after her to ask if anything was wrong and if I could help her but she went into a Ladies' Room and my press card wasn't valid there.

I decided some one must have been killed in the tunnel and stopped a train and the woman had gotten hysterical and walked back. I thought I might wander down the tunnel as a distracted passenger and get an exclusive, but people are always butting at subway trains in New York and delaying traffic, so it wasn't worth the trouble and I was hot and madder than ever.

The Fortieth Street exit looked like a log jam on the Pacific Ocean, but people got out of my way and stared at me with my beach robe rolled under my arm. I steered out of the jam to Eighth Avenue and started plodding toward the Village. Around Thirtieth Street it was possible to get back on Seventh Avenue again and then I heard the continuous chorus of emergency cars and ambulances shrieking up and down. At Twenty-third Street there was a policeman at the kiosk and I asked him rather petulantly, I'm afraid, what the deuce the Interborough was doing with its subway trains.

He said there had been a big wreck—nobody knew how many killed. This quieted me down a good deal. At Fourteenth Street they knew that two cars had been smashed and picturing the indecent, brutal crush of bodies into those cars at the rush hours, I did have the ordinary humanity to wish I had gone down into the tunnel as I'd thought of doing to see if I could possibly help—no, probably just in the way.

I got home at six-thirty and my wife was on the day-bed crying. She said, "Where was the subway wreck? What happened?"

I was startled because I knew that even the then extant *Graphic* couldn't have put its staff together and hawked an extra in the fifteen or twenty minutes since I'd heard the first spot news, and the crowds around Fortieth Street had known less than the policeman at Twenty-third. The ambulances screamed into St. Vincent's, three or four blocks away, but we had grown almost oblivious to that sound.

I said, "How did you know? They haven't got out an extra yet?"

[318]

She said, "I took a nap at two o'clock and woke up crying. Something awful had happened or was about to happen. I didn't want you to take the subway. I thought if you got my beach robe you'd come home in a taxi."

I said, "Here's the beach robe."

P. S. I never gave Virginia a medal. I always used the middle ramp which put me well forward of the middle of the train. The wrecked cars were far back. But I'm just as glad I got the beach robe.

Note to neurologists: Mrs. Stong had never been psychic before and hasn't been since, except that she likes lamb chops and carrots; her only abnormality.

Henry Pratt Fairchild

This happened a good many years ago out in a little town in Nebraska. A group of eight or ten young people, of whom I was probably the oldest by two or three years, was amusing itself with a planchette. We were all in a more or less facetious mood, as people are likely to be under such circumstances, and while the planchette was performing some mildly interesting stunts nothing very significant had been produced. All of a sudden I proposed that we make a serious attempt to see what the little instrument was really capable of, and, strange as it may seem, the other members of the group agreed, abandoned their frivolous attitude, and settled down to a sober test. The plan we decided upon, and carried out, was this:

We sent one of the girls, whose name was Esther, out of the room. We then agreed to ask the planchette a question, the answer to which we would all know but which would almost certainly be unknown to Esther, and then to concentrate intently on this answer while Esther operated the planchette alone. I suggested the question and told the others the answer. Having arranged all this, we called Esther back. She put her fingers on the little heartshaped table, and I asked her, "What is the name of the man my younger brother is working for?" The planchette scratched aimlessly for a brief moment, and then proceeded with complete legibility to write out the name—Mundt.

There was no conceivable way by which Esther could have known this name, and in fact afterwards I questioned her on the subject and she assured me that she had not the slightest idea what the planchette was setting out to write. My recollection is that it wrote the name upside down as far as Esther was concerned, and that she did not even know what it was writing until it had finished; but on this point I am not positive.

George M. Cohan

Late one night I got up from the desk in my den and walked down the hall to go to the kitchen for a glass of milk. I had been working on a play—hadn't had much sleep in several days and was awfully tired. Down at the end of the long hall I turned on the light right by the door. The door had a glass its whole length. Looking at the glass in the door I saw my father. That didn't seem at all surprising but I wondered, how did I happen to think that I was my son. That did bother me. I turned out the light for a moment and then turned it on again. Once more I was myself. After the glass of milk when I started back up the hall again I found myself peering up the hall to see if I was sitting at my desk. Of course I was tired and all that but it was a very real experience.

My father definitely felt that he had talked with spirits. I remember one story he told me about waking up one night and finding three old cronies in his room. These men had been doctors in the Civil War with my father when he was just a young doctor's orderly. This visit happened when my father was about sixty-five years old and the doctors, who were much older than father, had been dead for years. Father said that he did not feel any surprise at their being there and drew up chairs and had them sit down. He recalled telling them a story about the incident when he was a boy celebrating after a battle and by accident shot off his thumb. He did not recall anything that they had said and did not remember their leaving nor his going back to bed. When he awoke the next morning he found the chairs drawn up just as he had recalled he had placed them.

Samuel M. Forrest

Barry and Fay were the first of the tall man and short man teams of comedians. They were tremendously popular and their plays "Muldoon's Picnic" and "McKenna's Flirtation" both ran for years. Many of the lines of their plays became popular sayings throughout the country. For instance every one quoted one of their opening lines. When they would make their entrance there would be a terrific reception with four or five minutes of applause. During the applause Barry and Fay would walk up and down the stage having a heated argument. The audience thought the argument must be very important, because of their manner, although, because of the applause, no word could be heard. When the applause died down the first words the audience could hear were: "I have always contended and shall continue to maintain that no cigar can be genuine Havana when you get more than three for ten cents."

At the end of the run of "McKenna's Flirtation" Hugh Fay retired and William Barry went out with a play of his own called "The Rising Generation." I went with him. I was part author of the play, the stage manager and I acted a part—in fact I was practically Barry's boy and spent most of my time with him.

During the tour one morning, at breakfast, Barry said that during the night he had the most vivid dream that his old partner Hugh Fay had died. While telling about his dream a bell boy came into the dining room and handed Barry a telegram from Effie Fay (Hugh's daughter) saying that her father had died.

Colonel Theodore Roosevelt

There is a story current in our family that comes from the southern branch. It runs that some one (I believe a relative, anyhow a lady) was dying. The year was approximately 1830. The family were gathered around her bed. Suddenly they heard the great knocker on the door sound three times. The woman straightened herself in the bed and said "There is death knocking." She fell back dead. The family ran down to the door and found no one.

Roy Chapman Andrews

In 1926 there had been no rain in Peking, China and vicinity for five months. The Chinese had paraded the iron Rain God through the streets—in their minds he is the court of last appeal. Still nothing happened!

The Tashi Lama of Tibet, who was then residing in Peking, announced that two weeks later at noon he would publicly pray for rain. The foreign newspapers had a good many amusing articles at the Tashi Lama's expense. How could he save his face if nothing happened?

On the appointed day I went out to Central Park, which is a part of the Forbidden City, where the platform had been erected for the ceremonies. There were perhaps ten thousand people as spectators. The Tashi Lama mounted his platform in company with a retinue of priests, burned incense and solemnly prayed for rain. There was not a cloud in the sky.

I returned to the Peking Club where we all speculated as to what the Tashi Lama was going to say for himself. Believe it or not, at four o'clock great clouds began to roll up and by a quarter to five we had a downpour which lasted for an hour and a half.

The story of this miraculous happening travelled all over Central Asia. Hundreds of thousands of Mongols poured into the city to make their obeisance to the spiritual God of Tibet who had so justified his powers.

I have heard in Mongolia and Central Asia of the many miraculous things which the Lamas are able to do. From personal investigation I know that many of them are nothing but rather transparent tricks. Still I wish I could explain how the Tashi Lama was willing to gamble his reputation on producing rain from a cloudless sky.

(On the subject of rainmaking Ellsworth Jaeger told me: "I have attended at least twenty rain dances in the South West at various Pueblos and invariably rain came seemingly to prove the potency of the ceremonial. The rain came at different times at each dance—sometimes within a few hours and sometimes quite close to the end of the dance. Some of these dances occur on set days; as for instance, the rain dance of the Santo Domingo Pueblo always is given on August fourth."

Mr. Jaeger suggested that I write to Ernest Thompson Seton who had been even to more dances. I received the following answer:

"Your letter of July 14th to Mr. Seton has come to my desk. You may accept this letter as a joint one from both of us.

"I wonder if you know my book *Rhythm of the Redman,* written under the nom de plume of Julia M. Buttree. In that I give a detailed description of the Corn Dance at Santo Domingo. This dance is a prayer for rain and is the expression of the most conservative of the Pueblos.

"Mr. Seton and I have seen 20-odd consecutive years of this dance. We know of reliable parties who have seen enough to constitute almost 30 consecutive years. The evidence is that never has the dance failed to bring rain. It usually comes before the dance is wholly over, but always within 24 hours. And when I say it brings rain, I mean RAIN. It comes not as a gentle shower, but as a deluge. Each year we take our summer school to see this dance, and always advise them to leave the pueblo before the end of the dance if they wish to keep dry and to avoid bogging down in the clay roads.

"On July 14th of this year the corresponding dance was held at the pueblo of Cochiti. Although we had had exceedingly dry weather for weeks before, there was a literal cloudburst before the end of the day. It extended in a straight line for some 20 miles from the pueblo, but all the surrounding country continued dry as before.

"Hoping that this will be of some help to you, I am

Yours sincerely,

Julia M. Seton

Mrs. Ernest Thompson Seton")

Roger B. Whitman

One morning after breakfast I remained at the table reading the paper. Doors of the room were closed and there was no one else of the household on that floor. At my feet were three cats eating from a single dish. As suddenly as if a bomb had burst among them, the three cats jumped, and leaped to a distant part of the room with every show of fear—tails fluffed out and backs ruffled. One tried to get through a closed door; the other two crouched against a far wall. All were looking toward the plate that they had left. I could give no reason for their sudden action. There had been no sound, nor had anything appeared or happened that affected my senses. Their fear lasted for only two minutes or so. They then calmed down, and a little later returned slowly to the plate and resumed eating. Their action had been abrupt, and whatever had caused it affected them all at the same time. Also, the end of it was equally simultaneous.

Two days later my wife was in the kitchen getting the cats' supper out of the icebox. As they began to feed, there was a similar episode. Only two cats were present. Something invisible to her and not apparent to her senses startled the cats to such an extent that one leaped over the back of the other one and dashed under the sink, while the second cat fled under the range. There were the same visible signs of terror. As in the previous instance the effect lasted only a minute or two, when they again calmed down.

Fulton Oursler

Mr. Mulholland has asked me if, during my thirty years of psychic research, I have encountered phenomena which I believed to be genuine.

Yes, emphatically, I have. I have witnessed happenings in séance rooms that could not be explained on the basis of trickery; nor were they the outgivings of psychopathological subjects. However, I have never had any experience which seemed to me to indicate in any way the actuality of spirits or that the phenomena were due to the intervention of ghostly forces.

To me, the most interesting of many such experiences were those commonly called predictions. The riddle of time and space has always seemed to me much more important than the question of personal survival; and I have had actually hundreds of experiences that seemed to indicate the validity of the "slit in time" theory advanced in the last few years by the great Freudian apostate, Jung. There is not space here to develop his theory which, I may say, I came to independently. I do not know if I formulated it before Jung did, but I certainly formulated it before Jung announced it.

Some of my experiences with these phenomena were published in the Proceedings of the American Society for Psychic Research, and in the book by Doctor Walter Franklin Prince called, *Noted Witnesses for Psychic Research*.

I have selected for Mr. Mulholland's purpose one that has not previously been published.

These events happened in the spring and summer of 1916. I was holding a series of "sittings," as they are inelegantly called, with an English medium, Grace Hanes. She practiced that variety of mediumship known as "automatic writing." She would sit at a table, pencil in hand, with sheets of blank note paper before her. She would not look at the paper, but instead, would talk with me on all sorts of subjects. While she conversed, her hand would write rapidly until several sheets of paper would be covered with script.

The odd thing about it was that, often though not always, the writing would be in reverse so that we would have to hold it in front of a mirror in order to read it. The messages were invariably signed, "Leowin," and they were universally dull and uninspired. The general purport was that God was in his heaven and all was right with the world. At no time did Leowin ever write anything that was worth the trouble we went to.

Finally, I forsook Leowin and all his works. For several months I did not see or hear from Miss Hanes.

Then, one afternoon, I packed my bags to go off on a summer holiday. I was in the hallway when the telephone rang; and, as I had little time to catch my train, I was annoyed. The caller was the medium, who said: "Mr. Oursler, I have just had a message for you from Leowin. He says that you are about to go away on a trip."

My annoyance deepened. It seemed to me, in my skepticism, that perhaps the medium had obtained some information about me and was trying to capitalize on it.

"Lots of people know that," I answered. "Leowin ought to know that I am already late for my train, so will you please excuse me?"

"Wait!" entreated Miss Hanes. "That is not all of the message. You don't know it, but while you are away, you are going to be offered a new position."

"That," I said disagreeably, "is unlikely."

"Leowin says it is inevitable. He is very much worried about it. He is afraid you will be greatly tempted to take it. He says you must not do so under any circumstances. It will interfere with all the rest of your life. No matter how wonderful it may seem to you, Leowin warns you— turn it down. You needn't bother to say goodbye; hurry up and catch your train."

I caught the train and it took me to New York. From there I took a train to Whitestone Landing, in Long

Island, where I was a guest at the home of Howard Thurston, the foremost of American magicians, and one of my old friends.

At his pleasant house at Beachhurst, I spent a happy afternoon; and, for hours after Mrs. Thurston had gone to bed, he and I sat over whisky sodas and talked, as only two men who like each other can talk, endlessly and quite aimlessly.

The next day I left for Boston, and, a few hours later, I received a special delivery letter from Thurston.

He said: "All the time that we were talking, a plan was forming in my mind. I believe that you are the ideal manager for my show. The season opens four weeks from now. Why not come back to New York at once and start to work?"

Well, Leowin was right, not only about the offer, but also in his gratuitous advice. It would have greatly changed my life if I had taken that job.

Now, it is easy to say that this can be explained on the theory that Miss Hanes and her familiar spirit made a lucky guess. But I have had too many such experiences to be satisfied with that simple solution.

Lowell Thomas

Back in my school days I had a girl chum, a young lady who vanished from my life when I grew up. I had entirely lost track of her. After the World War, upon returning from ten years of wandering around the globe, I was walking along a street in the Broadway night life district and to my surprise saw the name of my school friend, Beula

Bondi, featured in electric lights in a theater marquee. I went back-stage with the hope that it was the same girl. It was, and there was a reunion, with memories of gay college days.

Said Miss Bondi: "Tommy, although I have not heard from you in years and years, you have not been entirely out of my thoughts. For several summers I have lived in the foothills of the Berkshires, and every time I passed a certain house I had a strange feeling, a feeling that you were there living in that house!"

At that time I had never been in the Berkshires and knew nothing about Dutchess County, and had never heard of lovely Quaker Hill. But, two years after meeting Miss Bondi, who is now a celebrated character actress of the screen, I decided I wanted a place in the country, and it must be within one hundred miles of Manhattan Island. Whereupon I began a systematic search of everything within that distance. My dream was to find a perfect all-year-round climate, plus scenic beauty, plus good neighbors. For one reason or another I eliminated Long Island, Northern New Jersey, and both the West and East shores of the Hudson. Eventually my travels brought me to Dutchess County, and to historic Quaker Hill, a ten-mile-long ridge in the Southeastern corner of the country, which is one of the loveliest spots on earth—not as spectacular as the Vale of Kashmir—but in its own way just as beautiful.

And, there on one spur of Quaker Hill I saw just the Colonial house I wanted. The dowager who owned the estate at that time had not thought of selling. But, at last a deal was made. And that, as you have guessed by now, is the same which Beula Bondi had for many years associated with her college friend, the house in which she, with her prophetic eye, saw me living.

This I discovered later after I had moved into the neighborhood.

* * *

My friends' stories I leave unanswered. Not that I believe that I understand everything—I do not even understand why the raps first came to the Fox Sisters on All Fools' Eve.

INDEX

INDEX

INDEX

INDEX